THE FEDERAL THEATRE PROJECT, 1935–1939

Edinburgh Critical Studies in Modernism, Drama and Performance

Published
The Speech-Gesture Complex: Modernism, Theatre, Cinema
Anthony Paraskeva

Irish Drama and the Other Revolutions: Irish Playwrights, Sexual Politics, and the International Left, 1892-1964
Susan Cannon Harris

Modernism and the Theatre of the Baroque
Kate Armond

Beckett's Breath: Anti-Theatricality and the Visual Arts
Sozita Goudouna

Russian Futurist Theatre: Theory and Practice
Robert Leach

Pina Bausch's Dance Theatre: Tracing the Evolution of Tanztheater
Lucy Weir

The Federal Theatre Project, 1935–1939: Engagement and Experimentation
Rania Karoula

Forthcoming

Modernist Disguise: Masquerade in Modern Performance and Visual Culture
Ron J. Popenhagen

Greek Tragedy and Modernist Performance
Olga Taxidou

www.edinburghuniversitypress.com/series/ecsmdp

THE FEDERAL THEATRE PROJECT, 1935–1939

Engagement and Experimentation

Rania Karoula

EDINBURGH
University Press

Edinburgh University Press is one of the leading university presses in the UK. We publish academic books and journals in our selected subject areas across the humanities and social sciences, combining cutting-edge scholarship with high editorial and production values to produce academic works of lasting importance. For more information visit our website: edinburghuniversitypress.com

© Rania Karoula, 2021, 2022

Edinburgh University Press Ltd
The Tun – Holyrood Road, 12(2f) Jackson's Entry, Edinburgh EH8 8PJ

First published in hardback by Edinburgh University Press 2021

Typeset in Sabon and Gill Sans by
Servis Filmsetting Ltd, Stockport, Cheshire

A CIP record for this book is available from the British Library

ISBN 978 1 4744 4545 0 (hardback)
ISBN 978 1 4744 4549 8 (paperback)
ISBN 978 1 4744 4553 5 (webready PDF)
ISBN 978 1 4744 4557 3 (epub)

The right of Rania Karoula to be identified as the author of this work has been asserted in accordance with the Copyright, Designs and Patents Act 1988, and the Copyright and Related Rights Regulations 2003 (SI No. 2498).

CONTENTS

List of Illustrations	vi
Acknowledgements	viii
Series Editor's Preface	ix
Introduction: What Was the Federal Theatre Project?	1
1. A Theatre is Born	10
2. The Living Newspaper Part 1: 1935–1937 – The Revolution Begins	38
3. The Living Newspaper Part 2: 1937–1939 – How Not to Sing for Your Supper	68
4. The Negro Unit: Electrifying Harlem, Electrifying the Nation	88
5. The Children's Theatre: Playing with Pinocchio and the Beavers	120
6. The Federal Dance Project: Dance, Race, Greek Tragedy and Helen Tamiris	147
7. The Legacies of the Federal Theatre Project	183
Epilogue: Was it All Worth it? The Legacy of the FTP in Contemporary Performance	196
Notes	200
Archival Material	218
Bibliography	220
Index	232

ILLUSTRATIONS

2.1 *Triple-A Plowed Under*. Scene twenty-three. Directed by Joseph Losey. New York, 1936.   51
2.2 *Injunction Granted*. Scene eighteen. Directed by Joseph Losey. New York, 1936.   54
2.3 *Injunction Granted*. Directed by Joseph Losey. New York, 1936.   55
2.4 *Injunction Granted*. New York, 1936. The play's set design. The use of platforms, runways and steps shows the influence of Okhlopkov and Meyerhold.   56
2.5 *Injunction Granted*. Directed by Joseph Losey. New York, 1936. Norman Lloyd as the muted clown.   57
2.6 *The Cradle Will Rock*. New York, 1937. Marc Blitzstein with the cast in rehearshal.   62
3.1 Allan Tower (Electric Company Manager) and Norman Lloyd (Consumer) in *Power*. Ritz Theatre, New York, 1937.   75
3.2 *One-third of a Nation*. Federal Theatre's Summer Theatre School at Vassar Experimental Theatre, 21 June to 31 July 1937. Stage design by Howard Bay.   78
3.3 *One-third of a Nation*. Opening and closing scene. Adelphi Theatre, New York, 1938. Stage design by Howard Bay.   81
4.1 Jack Carter and Edna Thomas as Macbeth and Lady Macbeth. *Macbeth*. New York, 1936.   96
4.2 Nat Carson: designer of the set, costumes and masks for *Macbeth*. New York, 1936.   98
4.3 The 'cauldron' scene, in which the witches can be seen. *Macbeth*. New York, 1936.   100
4.4 Macbeth surrounded by the voodoo men and women. *Macbeth*. New York, 1936.   102
5.1 Paul, Mary and Windy in *The Revolt of the Beavers*. Adelphi Theatre, New York, 1937.   128
5.2 Paul, Mary and the Professor in *The Revolt of the Beavers*. Adelphi Theatre, New York, 1937.   129

5.3	The Chief and his gang confronting the Barkless and working beavers in the woods. *The Revolt of the Beavers*. Adelphi Theatre, New York, 1937.	132
5.4	Pinocchio and the Pretty Puppet dancing. *Pinocchio*. Ritz Theatre, New York, 1938.	140
5.5	Pinocchio, the Cat and the Fox. *Pinocchio*. Ritz Theatre, New York, 1938.	141
5.6	The Circus. *Pinocchio*. Ritz Theatre, New York, 1938.	142
6.1	Helen Tamiris in *Salut au Monde*. New York, 1936.	152
6.2	The circle of women in *Salut au Monde*. New York, 1936.	153
6.3	Tamiris in *How Long Brethren?* New York, 1937.	155
6.4	'Pickin' Off de Cotton' from *How Long, Brethren?* New York, 1937.	157
6.5	'Upon de Mountain' from *How Long, Brethren?* New York, 1937.	158
6.6	'Scottsboro' from *How Long, Brethren?* New York, 1937.	160
6.7	'Sistern an' Brethren' from *How Long, Brethren?* New York, 1937.	161
6.8	'How Long, Brethren?' from *How Long, Brethren?* New York, 1937.	164
6.9	Hecuba speaking to the women of Troy after its sack. *Trojan Incident*. New York, 1938.	171
6.10 and 6.11	Cassandra's dance. Tamiris as Cassandra. *Trojan Incident*. New York, 1938.	172

ACKNOWLEDGEMENTS

This book would not have been written, were it not for the enthusiasm, belief, support and advice of several people. Firstly, I would like to thank Professor Olga Taxidou for the encouragement and guidance she has given me over the last few years regarding the book and my academic path. Thank you also to Anna Vaninskaya, Robert Leach, Nicola McCartney, Claire Kydonaki, Sam Green and the late David MacLennan for their direct and indirect influence and encouragement at various stages of this effort. Finally, I would like to thank all my students for being inquisitive and excited every time I lectured and tutored them about the Federal Theatre Project. I am grateful to Ersev Ersoy of Edinburgh University Press for being patient with my endless questions and for calmly helping me navigate the administrative processes of publishing this book. My thanks also extend to the anonymous readers of the draft chapters, whose comments were very useful and inspiring.

The author and publisher wish to thank the Federal Theatre Project Collection, Special Collections Research Center, George Mason University Libraries for permission to use copyright material. My thanks also extend to the Library of Congress, Music Division, Federal Theatre Collection. Every effort has been made to acknowledge all copyright permissions but if any have been inadvertently missed, the necessary arrangements will be made.

Lastly, this book would not have been written without the support, love and help of my husband George; looking after our wee daughter, taking on more parental and home responsibilities, allowed me time and quiet space to do my writing. Knowing when to make me another great cup of coffee and provide words of encouragement gave me the energy to keep going. And although of a completely different discipline, he kindly read draft after draft, offering constructive and inquisitive feedback. And a massive thank you is reserved for Nefeli; I may not have written the bedtime story she was hoping for, but she still wants to read 'mummy's book'.

SERIES EDITOR'S PREFACE

Edinburgh Critical Studies in Modernism, Drama and Performance addresses the somewhat neglected areas of drama and performance within Modernist Studies, and is in many ways conceived of in response to a number of intellectual and institutional shifts that have taken place over the past ten to fifteen years. On the one hand, Modernist Studies has moved considerably from the strictly literary approaches, to encompass engagements with the everyday, the body, the political, while also extending its geopolitical reach. On the other hand, Performance Studies itself could be seen as acquiring a distinct epistemology and methodology within Modernism. Indeed, the autonomy of Performance as a distinct aesthetic trope is sometimes located at the exciting intersections between genres and media: intersections that this series sets out to explore within the more general modernist concerns about the relationships between textuality, visuality and embodiment. This series locates the theoretical, methodological and pedagogical contours of Performance Studies within the formal, aesthetic and political concerns of Modernism. It claims that the 'linguistic turn' within Modernism is always shadowed and accompanied by an equally formative 'performance/performative turn'. It aims to highlight the significance of performance for the general study of modernism by bringing together two fields of scholarly research which have traditionally remained quite distinct – Performance/Theatre Studies and Modernism. In turn, this emphasis will inflect and help to reconceptualise our understanding of both Performance Studies and Modernist Studies. And in doing so, the series will initiate new conversations between scholars, theatre and performance artists and students.

Olga Taxidou

For George and Nefeli

INTRODUCTION: WHAT WAS THE FEDERAL THEATRE PROJECT?

'To The Men and Women Who Made Federal Theatre.'[1]
Hallie Flanagan's dedication in her autobiography, *Arena*.

The beginning of the Great Depression in the USA was marked by 24 October 1929, or Black Thursday, a devastating event with far-reaching social, political and economic effects and one that shook the USA's position as the greatest proponent of capitalism. Unlike Europe, which had suffered extreme economic and emotional deprivation and alienation after the end of World War I, the USA surfaced from the war to face an economic boom. American industry had expanded by producing mainly war artillery, with the government offering large cash subsidies to boost industrial production. Due to this thriving economy, the prices of mass-produced commodities decreased, and the American people earned higher wages and could afford more luxuries than before, creating a boom in consumerist behaviour. The economic affluence of the 1920s was also visible in the entertainment world, as Broadway theatres and cinema halls were packed with people enjoying vaudeville or jazz acts and the new Hollywood releases. Hollywood became the capital of the popular entertainment industry.

When this era of economic affluence was abruptly interrupted in October 1929, the USA found itself in a desperate economic state; there were four million unemployed in 1930, rising to more than twelve million by 1932. Signs of poverty became visible very soon with shops closing, factories standing idle, soup-kitchens opening up, and breadlines and 'Hoovervilles' appearing on vacant lots across the cities.² In farming communities, which had already suffered during and in the aftermath of the Great War, there was more grief to come. The collapse of commodity prices, a string of bank failures, the lack of political will and absence of legislation to control landlords who were driving farmers off their lands and into the cities, as well as natural disasters, added to the feelings of desperation, fear and hopelessness.

With Franklin D. Roosevelt's election, things began to change. His ideological New Deal plan attempted to stir the USA towards economic recovery, as well as instil renewed faith in capitalism. Not much was achieved during his first term in office, however. In his annual address to Congress on 4 January 1935 Roosevelt was critical of his administration's first-term ventures; at the same time, however, he highlighted the liberal vision behind his New Deal plan.

> We have ... a clear mandate from the people, that Americans must forswear the conception of the acquisition of wealth which, through excessive profits, creates undue private power over private affairs and, to our misfortune, over public affairs as well. In building toward this end we do not destroy ambition, nor do we seek to divide our wealth into equal shares on stated occasions. We continue to recognize the greater ability of some to earn more than others. But we do assert that the ambition of the individual to obtain for him and his family a proper security, a reasonable leisure, and a decent living throughout life is an ambition to be preferred to the appetite for great wealth and great power.³

Roosevelt's New Deal policies inspired the public, as they aimed at stabilising the economy, offering new prospects and jobs to the millions of unemployed and promising to work towards the improvement of social and living conditions. Among the unemployed was a large group of actors, musicians, writers and journalists that were particularly influenced by the Depression. The New Deal involved several cultural programmes to rehabilitate all these professionals, not in the private sector, but in state-funded schemes. During Roosevelt's second term, on 6 May 1935, the Works Progress Administration (WPA), a massive employment relief programme, was established under the direction of Harry Hopkins, one of Roosevelt's closest advisors and a key architect of the New Deal. During its first three months, the project had already dispensed billions in infrastructure undertakings. Now it was time to implement a more daring enterprise.

Under the wing of the WPA the Federal Project Number One was initiated. It was comprised of four art divisions and the Historical Records Survey, the four divisions being the Federal Art Project, the Federal Music Project, the Federal Theatre Project and the Federal Writers Project; each division had its own director. The aim was to employ artists, writers, journalists, musicians, actors/actresses and theatre workers in jobs closer to their expertise. Of all divisions, it was only the Federal Theatre Project (FTP) whose appointed director was a woman: Hallie Flanagan, who was a close friend of Harry Hopkins and a well-established experimental theatrical director and playwright at Vassar College. The project ran from 1935 to 1939, the shortest time compared with the other four, and proved to be the most controversial.

Similarly to the other projects, the FTP's main intention was to employ most of the unemployed theatre artists on relief until the economy recovered. However, from early on, Flanagan clearly outlined that

> It is not a relief project in which artificial jobs are dealt out to people of inferior talent, but rather a plan which begins by saying: in rethinking theatre activity in terms of the art and economics of 1935, we need theatre enterprises which will supplement our already existing splendid New York stage.[4]

Flanagan's comment presents a different interpretation of the project's relief status; the project would employ unemployed actors, writers or technicians (as opposed to already established 'stars') but in this process it would not compromise on quality, innovation or versatility. The FTP's productions would complement the ones already produced by Broadway, but it would attract a different audience. Through its relief status, the FTP would also acquire an almost socially engaged status, as it would strive to represent the so far unrepresented people and stimulate a social and theatrical response through its plays' subject matter. All these would occur under the auspices of the American government. Such a social transformation of the theatre's function represented the first attempt within American cultural life at launching a theatre which united American politics with the theatre of its time. In this way, the American theatre was no longer linked exclusively with the private sector and its prescribed aestheticism, and was instead seen as an aspect of national politics.

It was the first time in history that the United States would initiate direct government funding that would resemble that of its European counterparts. However, Flanagan was careful to point out that

> It was not a national theatre in the European sense of a group of artists chosen to represent the government. It was never referred to by me as a *national* theatre, though critics increasingly spoke of it as such. It was rather a *federation* of theatres. That was the origin and meaning of its name.[5]

It was the use of the key word 'federation' that attempted to differentiate and justify the FTP's existence within the annals of American theatrical history.

The emphasis on regional locality, on the constant awareness of changes and its ability to exchange resources would create a unique, mobile and adaptive theatre, the likes of which could emulate change and experimentation, and be adaptive and relevant to its audience's life and realities. It would be a theatre built out of American life and experiences.

Because of this process and structure, the FTP would be a different project to the European type of national theatre. The aim was for it to be more independent, to be aware of and more in touch with its local audience's needs and respond to them more quickly. It was an ambitious plan aimed at creating branches all over the country and drawing on an audience that had never before experienced a theatrical production. In its attempt to claim a space for itself and become an entity disengaged from Broadway practices, the FTP appropriated new techniques of performance and created sub-groups of theatrical groups (such as the Living Newspaper, the Negro unit, the Children's Theatre and the Dance unit) to be more inclusive and, simultaneously, critically mobilize the different audiences both aesthetically and socially.

Relying on federal funding and attempting to create new theatre proved to be a difficult and politically tricky enterprise. Flanagan's idealism regarding the federation of theatres, although unfaltering, was constantly receiving blows from the project's major enemies in Congress and the government as well. Because of its status as a relief agency, the FTP's majority of funding (ninety per cent) was directed towards salaries of qualified workers. The remaining ten per cent was available for space rentals, publicity, costumes, scenery design, lighting, and everything else necessary for the operational running of a production. Because of such limited funding, the FTP units had to rely on donations and they also charged minimum admission fees only to those able to pay them.

There was vast bureaucracy involved and required by the federal government and every cent spent had to be justified. This attitude put immense pressure on administrative staff, who struggled to keep up with the government's demands for paperwork and with trying to open up theatrical productions. At the same time, not all regional FTP units enjoyed a smooth relationship with their WPA state directors. When the relationship was working, the units were creating exciting productions and the funding was justified. But when the relationship was poor, frictions emerged that led to censored productions, funding cuts and bureaucratic impasses. The FTP's federation of theatres was an ambitious project, but the unit was ill equipped to deal with the challenges of decentralisation, as well as embracing the local FTP units as part of a collective national theatrical identity.

Hallie Flanagan struggled with the unit's failure to achieve this new national theatrical identity. But she also struggled with providing high-quality new productions without completely alienating the already established theatre industry. It was no secret that Flanagan thought that Broadway had become complacent, repetitive and too comfortable in accommodating an indifferent middle-class audience. At the same time, the established theatre did not want to be associated with a relief project, as it felt that out-of-work actors could come up with only low-quality, commercially unsuccessful productions. So, the project, and Flanagan personally, had to defend it on numerous occasions against accusations of amateurism, financial shortcuts and, in some cases, imitation.

Not being able to attract high-calibre, well-trained professional actors meant that the project had to invest time and money in continuous training for its workers. In this way, however, the FTP created professional opportunities for nurturing new actors, directors, playwrights and designers. At the same time, it offered performance opportunities to a number of ethnic and religious minority groups. Among the talent it nurtured were Orson Welles, John Houseman, Marc Blitzstein, Marlon Brando, Burt Lancaster, Elia Kazan and Arthur Miller, and some of the theatre personalities it employed were Elmer Rice, Clifford Odets, Philip Barber, Edith Isaacs, J. Howard Miller and Rosamond Gilder.[6] But its legacy, or its greatest achievement, was in being branded the 'people's theatre'. As Flanagan herself writes,

> the greatest achievement of these public theatres was in their creation of an audience of many millions, a waiting audience. This audience proved that the need for theatre is not an emergency [. . .] It is a necessity because in order to make democracy work the people must increasingly participate; they can't participate unless they understand; and the theatre is one of the great mediums of understanding.[7]

Creating an intrinsic link between the theatre, the people and democracy is reminiscent of the Ancient Greeks. By establishing a historical and theatrical continuity between Ancient Greece and contemporary America, Flanagan furnishes the FTP with a legacy dictated by democracy and the free will of the audience.

The FTP was disbanded by an act of Congress on 30 June 1939 and its employees found themselves without work overnight. Officially, the reasons for this decision were financial but, as Flanagan herself admits, they were political.[8] Her attempt to create a pioneer theatre that would be part of rethinking, rebuilding and redreaming America, a vital force in democracy, was unceremoniously but, ironically, democratically disbanded. Flanagan went back to Vassar College, where she continued her theatrical work, experimenting and inspiring new generations of students, theatrical personnel and colleagues. Some of the people the FTP nurtured went on to become well-established Hollywood and Broadway personas and some even ventured to Europe to continue experimenting with new techniques. The increasing Communist and Cold War paranoia generated a creatively stifling atmosphere within the USA; the outbreak of World War II not only exacerbated this atmosphere but increased the feeling of insecure living in a fragile societal and economic balance. With world peace hanging by a thread and American society faced with such challenges, the need for the Federal Theatre to reflect on the changes, to offer a space for expressing and challenging anxieties, loss but hope as well, was greater than ever. With the federation of theatres abolished, it was up to the individuals who were once part of that collective to fill the void and to offer alternative voices, realities and space to the American audience.

This book will cover all five years of the FTP's existence and life. Unlike past and current bibliographies, it will not attempt to see the project in its entirety or concentrate on its statistics and finances. The overarching objective of this book is to make a considerable contribution to the FTP phenomenon by producing a comparative study of the history, politics and performances of the New York Living Newspaper, Negro, Dance and Children's units. The choice to concentrate on the New York unit, as opposed to other regional ones, is two-fold. Firstly, although there has been considerable attention, literature and research devoted to the subject, I wanted to create a dialogue and critically assess the works produced there in relation to the project's indebtedness to the tradition of the European avant-garde and the modernist theatrical explorations of Bertolt Brecht. By reading the project in tandem with its European counterparts, the book vocalises the direct links between the FTP's array of theatrical and dramatic experimentations and Europe. Although such a link was admitted by some of the key persons involved with the project, there has been considerable effort to establish the FTP's works, particularly the Living Newspapers, as purely 'American'. Secondly, many of their contemporary European counterparts travelled and/or collaborated with American practitioners in New York, as opposed to other parts of the USA. And similarly, many of the Americans travelled to Europe and collaborated with the Europeans either before or after the project's termination. Finally, it was the New York unit's productions that attracted the wrath of Senator Martin Dies, architect of the House Un-American Activities Committee (HUAC), and were blamed for the dissolution of the whole project.

In order to achieve this ambitious plan, the book will combine archival work, theatre history and performance theory while also employing more traditional methods of analysis such as close reading of plays. The majority of the archival material used forms part of the George Mason University Libraries Special Collections on the Federal Theatre Project. In these archives, I found invaluable material that ranged from the actual playscripts, rehearsal and performance photographs, blueprints of scenic designs and costumes, interviews conducted with past members and unpublished articles. Seeing the project under the scope of transatlanticism will allow a broadening of the studies regarding the FTP and propose a consistent comparative study between the American and European theatrical traditions of the time.

Chapter 1 explores the aesthetic, historical, social and political conditions that gave rise to the phenomenon of the FTP. It draws on its connections with the American workers' theatre and the British theatre of the period, as well as the theatrical experimentation of its European counterparts, particularly the Blue Blouse, Vsevolod Meyerhold and Bertolt Brecht. At the heart of it all stands Hallie Flanagan. Her intimate knowledge of theatre, her close relationship with Meyerhold and her overall expertise in the European theatrical developments during the 1930s were instrumental in the development of the FTP. Her job at Vassar College as a theatre/drama teacher illuminates her eagerness to experiment and challenge the theatrical status quo from an early age; her trip to Europe in 1926 during her Guggenheim fellowship and her exposure to British, French, Italian and predominantly Soviet theatre of the time established her desire to modernise the American performance discourse. The trip was also instrumental in helping formulate the American version of the Living Newspaper, in bringing together European and American theatre professionals and generating a dialogue on the new revolutionary potential of theatre among them. The chapter will also briefly examine the influence and theories of Bertolt Brecht, as well as the British Workers' Theatre Movement, and MacColl and Littlewood's Theatre of Action and Theatre Union, before looking into the American workers' drama of the 1930s. Examining the FTP through the spectre of transatlanticism opens up the debate regarding the interconnectedness of the American and European theatrical traditions, challenging and disrupting the 'them versus us' discourse imposed during the Cold War era and exploring a universal approach to exposing social issues on stage that overcomes individual nations.

Chapters 2 and 3 concentrate on the New York Living Newspaper unit. Chapter 2 discusses the first two years of the unit, its structure, internal political and aesthetic struggles. It chronicles the very first Living Newspaper production, entitled *Ethiopia*, which was never performed for the public; it was the first victim of administrative and political red tape. The incident was an early indication of the tumultuous relationship among the FTP, the New Deal administration and conservative Republican and Democrat Congressmen. It then moves on to deal with the controversies surrounding the polemical *Triple-A Plowed Under* and *Injunction Granted*. It provides close readings of the plays, and critically assesses decisions taken as to what material was to be included or not, the stage design and the director's input. At the same time, it highlights their close connection with contemporary European theatre and Meyerhold and Brecht's modernist theatrical experimentations. It concentrates on the aesthetic struggles of the plays' writers and directors (Elmer Rice and Joseph Losey), as well as the political complexities brought about by the FTP administration, the US government and Congress. Lastly, the chapter includes a discussion of *The Cradle Will Rock*; although not a Living Newspaper, the play represents an excellent example of the continuous censorship the FTP faced throughout its existence.

Chapter 3 follows on from where Chapter 2 left off as it considers in detail a shift in the tone, style, content and polemics of the Living Newspaper. It also discusses in depth the shift in its target audience from low-income workers to the middle class. Concentrating on such examples as *Power* and *One-third of a Nation*, it explores the attempt of such plays to disassociate themselves from the influence of their European counterparts, thus trying to establish theatrical aesthetics and politics that could bear the mark of 'made in the USA'. At the same time, this chapter continues to look into the mounting pressure put on the whole of the FTP and on Flanagan herself as they both failed to fall in line with Congressional political attitudes.

Chapters 4 and 5 extend the conversation to the Negro unit and Children's Theatre. One of the most exciting aspects of the whole FTP was the creation of different theatrical units that could express the diverse cultural voices within the USA. Chapter 4 concentrates on and discusses the well-documented production of *Macbeth*, as directed by Orson Welles and John Houseman, and the censored version of *Lysistrata* that played for one performance only in Seattle. Chapter 5 discusses another exciting venture, the establishment of the Children's Theatre, which aimed to create theatrical productions that were both entertaining and educational. Plays produced included original scripts and also adaptations, and were acted out by live actors, marionettes and puppets. Not without its controversies, the Children's Theatre was accused of being too subversive and educating children in Communism. The plays studied in this chapter include *The Revolt of the Beavers* and *Pinocchio*.

Chapter 6 will concentrate on the Dance unit, on Helen Tamiris, a unique modernist dancer and choreographer with a keen eye for, and interest in, dance as social commentary, and on the reimagining of Greek tragedy through dance. Although originally an integral component of the FTP, under the auspices of Helen Tamiris, the Federal Dance Project was formed as an autonomous project in 1936 till it was reabsorbed into the FTP due to politically motivated budget cuts. However, both Flanagan and Tamiris held the same principle and ideal of bringing culture to the American public, exploring social issues and allowing inexpensive access to performances. This chapter will explore two productions, *How Long Brethren?* and *The Trojan Incident*. These productions are manifestations of theatrical and dance experimentation, of contemporary social and political issues, and examples of Tamiris's genius.

The final chapter will try to assess the significance of the FTP. It will look further at the reasons behind its demise, which will have already been discussed throughout the preceding chapters. It will then concentrate on the claim made earlier, relating to the close connection between the FTP and continental modernism/avant-garde that survived even after the project's termination. For that reason, it will study Flanagan's 1948 play *E=mc²: A Living Newspaper About the Atomic Age*. The play, a Living Newspaper and Flanagan's first (and last) play after the termination of the FTP, is an important example of how the legacies of the FTP can be combined with those of European modernist political theatre. Conceived and produced almost simultaneously with Ewan MacColl's 1946 *Uranium 235* and Bertolt Brecht's 1947 *Life of Galileo*, Flanagan's play serves as an afterword for both traditions, hints at the legacies they have left behind and materialises the dialogue between European and American modernism.

A short epilogue will situate the FTP and its plays and experimentations within modernist cultural conditions. It will question whether its influence is valid nowadays within a transatlantic environment and whether new performance art can claim it as inspiration.

I

A THEATRE IS BORN

Hallie Flanagan: American Theatre Reborn

The FTP, and its history, legacy and theatrical tradition, are intrinsically linked with its national director, Hallie Flanagan. She was there at the beginning of the project and stayed faithful to it till the very end, trying to save it from being disbanded, even at the very last minute. Flanagan presents an interesting figure within American theatrical history. Starting from an academic position at Vassar College, she was hand-picked by Harry Hopkins to run a national federation of regional theatres that proposed relevant art, experimented with new theatrical modes of representation and created a new space for previously unrepresented groups to voice their existence. Flanagan's life, up to the moment she became director, was preparing her for that role and for all the difficulties and challenges that came with it.

Hallie Flanagan was born in Redfield, South Dakota, and was raised in Iowa. She attended Grinnell College, where she majored in Philosophy and German. But it was the drama club that captured her imagination and captivated her for the rest of her life. While in college she met her first husband, Murray Flanagan, and also Harry Hopkins, with whom she formed a strong friendship. Flanagan married Murray after graduation in 1912 and had two children, Jack and Frederic, but Murray became ill with tuberculosis and passed away in 1919. On her own and with two children to look after, she decided to work. She returned to Grinnell and started teaching freshman English at the college in the autumn of 1920, the year the college introduced courses in playwriting and dramatic production, led by William Bridge. Flanagan began attending the weekly meetings of the local chapter of the Drama League of America and started writing plays. She soon became Bridge's assistant and started helping with the plays' performances.

Just as her first play, entitled *The Garden of Wishes*, was due to open in the Colonial Theatre in 1922, Flanagan was faced with a second personal tragedy. Her son Jack was diagnosed with spinal meningitis and died three weeks after diagnosis. Trying to move on, she and Frederic relocated to Chicago for the summer, where she worked under Irving Pichel and Alexander Dean (known for their experimentation with new staging methods) in their theatre productions at the Three Arts Club. Her experience there reaffirmed her love for theatre, playwriting and directing, and when she returned to Grinnell she put what she learned into practice. At the same time, she learned that her one-act play, *The Curtain*, had won first prize in the Iowa State Playwriting Contest; it would be published in *The Drama* magazine and be produced at the local Des Moines playhouse.

One of Flanagan's ambitions was to study under George Pierce Baker, who was teaching playwriting to graduate students at nearby Harvard. The success of *The Curtain* attracted Baker's interest, gaining her admission to the 47 Workshop for playwriting, and she became Baker's production assistant midterm. Baker was an important figure in the 'new' theatre movement that was under way during the years that preceded World War I. During his extensive travels in Europe, Baker witnessed the evolution of dramatic traditions in the works of Shaw, Ibsen, Maeterlinck and Synge. He also noted the respect and importance that were afforded to drama (similar to literature, poetry and painting), its centrality in people's life and its importance as a medium for unravelling social and political dilemmas. By contrast, the American theatre of the time was still dominated by Puritan notions of what could and could not be shown on stage, and the American audience was trained to request light, easy and inoffensive entertainment.

During her year at Harvard, Flanagan often travelled to New York to see plays and to provide critical assessments of the performances that Baker required of his students. One of the performances that captured her imagination was the Moscow Art Theatre's production of Gorky's *The Lower Depths*.[1] She was particularly intrigued by the director's use of colour in order to underline a character, an idea that she would later use in her directorial efforts at Vassar College. Flanagan finished her year at Harvard by completing the full-length satirical play required by Baker, entitled *Incense*. Just before she left in the spring of 1924, Baker proposed that she should spend a year in Europe seeing plays and observing the theatrical traditions in the UK, Ireland, France, Germany and the Scandinavian countries. She should spend considerable time in Russia, observing the experimentations of Stanislavsky, Meyerhold and others.[2] And she should also visit Italy, meeting with Gordon Craig, whose theatre designs were revolutionising European theatre. As such a trip would require significant finances, Flanagan started making relevant enquiries, having secured Baker's endorsement. These enquiries led to the 1926 Guggenheim Fellowship, the first awarded to a female playwright, and to Flanagan's year-long trip to Europe, where she met all of the above and more.

She spent an extraordinary year in Europe watching new plays and observing new modes of representation. Her book *Shifting Scenes of the Modern European Theatre* (published in 1928) offers a very detailed account of her trip, the playwrights, directors, designers and actors she met, and her opinions on the new theatrical developments. Her visit begins in London, where she is particularly surprised at the formality surrounding English theatre and the fact that performances take place only at night. Flanagan is not impressed by the variety of plays and comments how 'the theatres are alike, the settings are alike, the plays are alike, the audiences are alike'.[3] With the exception of watching John Galsworthy's play, *Escape*, and meeting him, she found most of the plays uninteresting and the likes of Noël Coward – the theatrical idol of the moment in England – and his sophisticated drawing-room comedies disagreeable. She went as far as to comment that 'the theatre in London is dead. Curious to see rows and rows of people politely applauding a dead thing. The theatre is dead because there is no wonder in it and no belief.'[4] Watching Shakespeare in Stratford-on-Avon left Flanagan with a lasting disappointment. Walking along the Avon, she remembered how deeply Shakespeare's words originally affected her, but the 1926 productions of *The Merchant of Venice*, *Midsummer Night's Dream*, *The Tempest* and *Henry IV* left her unimpressed and with a strong sense that the English theatre was totally dissociated from life. Interestingly, Flanagan did not mention anywhere in her book anything about the flourishing and influential British Workers' Theatre Movement (discussed later in this chapter), its agit-prop performances or its knowledge of the Blue Blouse techniques.

London did not provide the inspirational beginning to the trip that she had hoped for, but things improved considerably when she moved to Ireland. Having seen the Abbey Players on their regular tours of America, Flanagan was impressed by their direct appeal to modern audiences and was looking forward to seeing them again in their own theatrical space. She spent ten days watching several productions and meeting actors, directors and designers, but she felt that their best days had passed. She had a memorable evening in the company of Yeats, Sean O'Casey and Augustus John at the home of Æ (George William Russell), during which she heard them criticise a recent art exhibition in Paris and denounce the cultural backwardness of America, and Frank Fay (actor and co-founder of the Abbey Theatre) talking in detail about theatre in Ireland, acting and playwriting. She was to meet Yeats again; in that meeting he talked very formally about the future of Irish drama, expressing the view that its future no longer resided in the mystic approach to beauty but would be born 'of the passion for reality'.[5] Flanagan was puzzled at the diversity of opinions among the people working together for the national theatre in Ireland, but it was that diversity that deepened her curiosity and led her to meet Lady Augusta Gregory.

During that meeting, she spent hours listening to Lady Gregory's recollections of how the Abbey Theatre was formed, how Yeats influenced it and how Synge and O'Casey were nourished by it. She was fortunate enough to examine original portfolios from the early days of the Abbey, their theatre magazine, old programmes, costume and design sketches, as well as press clippings from the 1911 American tour. She heard many anecdotes, particularly about Bernard Shaw, who was a favourite guest. But what stayed with her was Lady Gregory's desire to create a new theatrical space for Irish theatre and drama to experiment with finding its voice and its place among Irish life and society. Flanagan decided that she would bring that desire back to the USA with her.

Next stop on her trip was Oslo, where she visited Ibsen's house and had long conversations with Bjørn Bjørson regarding the National Theatre of Oslo. In the productions there she noticed how the audience was cordial but aloof; how the acting was in the manner of realism; and how the adherence to the traditional methods of acting and presentation might account for the lack of younger actors, actresses and stage personnel.[6] Her observation stood in contrast to Ibsen's revered position as the person who led the fight in Europe against dramatic conservatism. It seemed that, by 1926, Norway had returned to more traditional theatrical standards and even Ibsen's plays could not escape them.

Sweden made a better impression on Flanagan. She noticed how the tranquillity and vigour of Swedish life were reflected in the theatre, ranging from the demographic and behaviour of the audience, to the acting style and to the repertoire of plays ranging from Wagner and Shakespeare to Strindberg and Pirandello. She noticed how two trends were developing simultaneously: on the one hand, an attempt to establish a more traditional style of acting, and on the other, a more experimental approach, stemming from a renewed attempt to interpret Strindberg. In Uppsala she met Strindberg's widow, Harriet Bosse, who dedicated herself to the interpretation of her husband's plays, abandoning the realistic type of acting and production. Flanagan saw her perform in a theatrical space that was 'Greek in conception, a lofty pillared temple'.[7] Bosse stayed true to her husband's spirit and was eager to communicate to Flanagan the need to study, present and represent Strindberg's plays together, 'in a cycle'; she felt that only Eugene O'Neill was writing plays similar to her husband's.[8] As much as she was fascinated by her encounter with Bosse, Flanagan could not but feel that, similarly to Norway, Strindberg was being enshrined rather than approached in such a way as to give him a new lease of life.

Up to that point, her tour of Europe and its national theatres was not as exciting as she might have hoped. However, all that changed as soon as she arrived in Denmark, where she met Gordon Craig, whom Flanagan had greatly admired from way before her trip but she was unaware that he would be in Copenhagen while she was visiting. She ended up spending most of her time in the Royal Theatre, for which Craig had been invited to design the scenery and costumes for Ibsen's *The Pretenders*, directed by Johannes Poulsen. Craig's work on this production came after a break of almost fifteen years, during which he had not worked inside a theatre. Craig, although brilliantly smart, knowledgeable, energetic and imaginative, had a fiery temperament that caused him difficulties when collaborating with other people. His dream of having a theatre of his own, especially in the UK, did not materialise, and Craig resorted to travelling in Europe and writing *The Art of the Theatre*, *The Theatre Advancing* and his theatrical journal, *The Mask*, which established him as a reformer of scenic design. Craig advocated more abstract, architectural theatrical scenery. He quickly told Flanagan, 'I hate "theatrical" scenery [. . .] Three dimensions are needed, a background for the actor, simple but capable of infinite variety through light. Play, actor and scene should be one.'[9]

His ideas and theories had a profound effect on Flanagan, especially his emphasis on the connection between stage design and acting. Craig was adamant that designs on their own are flat; unless joined with the acting, they can never really be seen and appreciated, or their function revealed to the audience. When design and acting are brought together, the synergy they create impacts on the audience in a very powerfully imaginative way. For these reasons, Craig was an enthusiastic admirer of Ancient Greek theatre. He strongly advocated to Flanagan that

> the theatre of today is based on pretence [. . .] The Greeks never pretended. They believed fiercely in what they performed. What they performed revealed their inner life and its values [. . .] unless actors and spectators collaborate there can be no great drama [. . .] Art, I repeat, is not a pick-me-up, it is a communion.[10]

Her meeting with Craig offered her new perspectives on the relationship between theatre design and acting, actors and directors, actors and audience. At the same time, their encounter reinforced her preliminary ideas about the importance of experimenting with new forms of theatrical representation, in terms of both design and directing. With her head and notebooks full of ideas and experiences, Flanagan was ready to continue her trip to Russia, where she spent the majority of her time.

Flanagan's visit coincided with the ninth anniversary of the October Revolution. The revolution had forced an apocalyptic vision of the world on the artistic community and rendered necessary the renegotiation of the practices and ideologies it had employed up to that moment. With the establishment of the Bolshevik government, there was a growing need to create 'a vast apparatus of information, news, education and propaganda'.[11] It was the theatre that responded quickly to the revolutionary call to combat illiteracy and to propagate collectivisation and regional politics. The new ways of performing included the living newspaper, mass spectacles re-enacting recent historical events (such as Mayakovsky's re-enactment of the storming of the Winter Palace), theatrical trials and literary montage combining slogans, poetry, speeches and other texts. In this way the audience became as much a part of the performance as the actors were, since the issues represented were dealing directly with their daily livelihood.

While there, she was surprised to find how enthusiastic the people were about theatrical performances and how 'alive' they seemed within the theatrical space.[12] Flanagan originally approached Russia with an idealistically literary, almost mythologised, outlook. As she herself claimed, during the first few days,

> I am under a spell. I can not eat nor sleep. I do not want to go to the theatres, to talk to anyone. I want only to walk in this ugly, beautiful, baffling city [Moscow], to be lost in the tumult of voices, to become a part of the splendour of old Russia, and a part of the strangeness of new Russia pouring irresistibly through the streets of Moscow.[13]

She acknowledged how it is a city full of contradictions, the most puzzling and yet consistent of which is the use of the city's space for public rather than private good. Although the housing problem is unsolved (with living quarters extremely congested), there is a vast amount of space devoted to libraries, museums, theatres, laboratories, schools, maternity clinics, academies and universities. These contradictions further fuelled Flanagan's imagination about Russia, about its culture, literature and societal context. Standing next to a Russian of the 'new order', Flanagan would be reminded of the urgency to visit theatre; 'if you can enter them without prejudice you may see more. You may, perhaps, see what Russia once was, what she now is, and is to be.'[14]

Theatre in Russia at the time was of two kinds: Stanislavsky's Moscow Art Theatre with its studio branches – the Second Art Theatre and the Kamerny – and the experimental and revolutionary theatre of Meyerhold and the Blue Blouse. When Flanagan interviewed Zalka, director of the Revolutionary Theatre, she was told that the new revolutionary theatre and drama in Russia was not a museum – it was life.[15] The main prerequisite was that it had something to do with everyday life. And it was not written by one person but rather constructed by the dramatist, actor and designer, with the active participation of the audience. Without the latter, Russian theatre of the time would be ineffective and empty of meaning.

Flanagan was impressed and inspired by the broad reach of the theatre in terms of its audience, and saw theatre employed as an educational tool everywhere she looked. And behind it all was Vsevolod Meyerhold. It was in Meyerhold that the new theatre in Russia found an archetypal leader, whose exciting and experimental theatrical ideas helped it find a way of expressing its angst, hopes and daily life. One of the productions that Flanagan saw was *The Death and Destruction of Europe*. Taking place to the accompaniment of jazz, 'insolent rhythms mercilessly underscore the theme, that the nations of the earth are dancing on a mine which is presently to explode capitalism and the bourgeoisie'.[16] Watching America being satirised by other nations, Flanagan was captivated by the crudity and youthfulness of the production and half-expecting the audience to take over the stage and become part of the action.

Flanagan was fascinated by Meyerhold, by the depth of his theatrical experience and his affecting energy. She noticed how his revolutionary theatre made use of everything he had studied and been part of, from his four years of acting under Stanislavksi at the Moscow Art Theatre and his dabbling with *Commedia dell'Arte* in Italy, to his study of the function of the chorus and the use of the mask during his visit to Greece. And at the heart of it all was his desire to create a theatre of its time, one that would experiment with new modes of presentation and acting techniques, and would create a new relationship between actor and audience. Invited to watch a rehearsal of *The Inspector General*, Flanagan experienced first-hand Meyerhold's brilliance, as well as his directing style. But it was watching his production of Sergei Tretyakov's *Roar, China!* that Flanagan finally found what she came to Russia to see.

In it, she noticed the role of the actor within Meyerhold's imagining of the theatre, as well as his use of biomechanics. As she comments,

> he is an actor using the play as a ball to be tossed now to another actor, now to the audience; he is a super-machine, his movements attaining a rhythmical beat of power and precision; he is a worker, a part of the social order he illustrates on the stage.[17]

Regarding the construction of the scenery and use of props, she observed how Meyerhold never uses the wharf, river and boat realistically (the boat does not pretend to be an actual boat) but as a means of helping the audience best visualise the play. The acting of the Chinese coolies is exaggerated, and their speech is at a different tempo and rhythm to that of the English passengers and American officer. Lighting is suddenly reversed throughout the play to highlight the different predicament of the Chinese coolies as opposed to that of the British colonisers and American capitalists. The figure of the Boy, resembling the tragi-clown of *Commedia dell'Arte* with his painted white face under black, tumbled hair, and being mistreated in perfect jazz time, further accentuates the play's themes and message to the audience. Witnessing the synergy of all these elements, Flanagan could not but deeply admire and praise Meyerhold's theatrical experimentations.

Although deeply absorbed by the revolutionary theatre of Meyerhold and the Blue Blouse, Flanagan could not resist visiting the sixty-three-year-old Konstantin Stanislavsky. Stanislavsky and his Moscow Art Theatre had been a source of inspiration for many European and American theatre professionals and critics. As mentioned above, Meyerhold studied under him before departing and developing his own method of acting and directing. Flanagan met Stanislavsky and watched a revived performance of *Tsar Fyodor Ivanovich*. In it, she observed the maturity of his acting system and its close connection with the theatre of the past. As opposed to Meyerhold's, she noticed how one enters Stanislavsky's theatre only as a spectator; there is no invitation to merge with the action on stage or to witness present life, but to escape it.

During their interview, Stanislavsky mentioned how he wanted to do a revolutionary play but on his own terms. It would have to be a play that met a 'standard of excellence', not simply because it was revolutionary and of its time; he also observed how, because of the chronological proximity to the Revolution, artists had not had enough time to reflect. The play should 'grow out of experience, but one must first live the experience, then go back and approve it in the light of later experiences'.[18] Stanislavsky also appeared aware of his inability to comprehend what makes young people enthusiastic: 'what am I, and what do I represent in the new and nascent life of the theatre?'[19] He acknowledged the differing societal and economic circumstances between the time when he and his generation were growing up and that of the children of the Russian Revolution. But he hoped that his acquired knowledge and experience could be of benefit to generations of theatrical artists to come.

Flanagan was respectful of Stanislavsky's views, but she seemed to side with Zarka and Meyerhold's views on the function of the theatre as being of its time, not a museum. These views were further reinforced when she visited the Second Moscow Art Theatre (known as MAT 2) and the Kamerny under the direction of Alexander Yakovlevich Tairov. Both theatres were predominantly interested in style, the first in impressionism and the second in expressionism. Of all the productions that she saw and discusses in the book, she favoured *Bloxa, The Flea*; the play was conceived as a toy, to be wound up and performed by children. MAT 2 was run by its actors and led by Michael Chekhov. Serafima Birmain, describing how the theatre worked, reiterated to Flanagan the company's collective nature: 'sometimes one directs or designs, sometimes another, sometimes several [. . .] Each play must be different and no director must ever be felt in the finished performance.'[20]

Unlike the MAT 2, Kamerny was run by Tairov and was a one-man theatre. Its plays and theatrical direction were invested in logic and abstraction rather than emotions and feelings. As Flanagan commented, Tairov was interested in creating a theatre that would be based on the 'actor-idea'; 'actors are not the instruments through which life, propaganda, or spirit is expressed. The play is, instead, the vehicle through which the actor-concept is expressed.'[21] Unlike with Chekhov and Meyerhold, in Tairov's theatre the actor becomes an abstract idea. The materialistic outlook of the body of the actor allows Tairov the means for the creative act that is the essence of art, according to his system. Tairov wants to train his actors in such a way that their body, muscles, voice, feelings and expressions can respond to their governing mind. Similarly to that of Meyerhold, Tairov's training involved acrobatics, gymnastics, dancing and eurythmics but was also invested in what he called 'finding the image'; 'the image is the inner essence, not of the part, but of the actor, which, when released, will best express the idea'.[22] Flanagan also noticed that in the Kamerny the stage setting was based not on the needs of the play but rather on the needs of the actor; as she observed, 'the stage is never conceived as a setting, but as a playing space for the actors'.[23] Flanagan found Tairov's system exciting but also demanding for the actor; she rightly observed that the expressionism and abstraction he aimed for are quite often clouded by the emotions inherent within the same human medium of the actor from which he wants to extract it. She acknowledged, however, that when it worked, Tairov's system extended the boundaries of theatre to include what she called a geometry of the soul.

From Moscow, Flanagan travelled to Leningrad (St Petersburg), where she continued to visit Russian theatres and join the Russian artists in engaging conversations about the role of theatre within the new revolutionary reality. As she was to re-emphasise a few years later, 'the Russian drama is not literary, not aesthetic or even pictorial: it is a drama in which the actors appear in their own clothes. It is a drama of reality, not one of pretence. It presents life itself.'[24] Flanagan immersed herself so deep in Russian theatre that the rest of her tour was overshadowed by the abundance and exuberance of Russian theatre. Her next stop was Riga, and after that she visited Berlin. There is no mention in her book of ever crossing paths with Brecht or his plays; instead, much of her focus lies on Max Reinhardt's theatre and his influence. Reinhardt was in America while Flanagan was touring Europe, so it was left to his disciples to introduce her to his ideas. What she took from this introduction was Reinhardt's desire to experiment with all types of theatre. As she claims, 'unlike Tairov, unlike Meyerhold, [Max] is not consumed by any single idea'.[25] However, she did not spend much time in Berlin or in its theatres. As she departed from Germany, the person who left a lasting impression on Flanagan was the dancer Mary Wigman, whose experimental new dancing made Flanagan enthusiastically assert that she was a dancing genius.

The last countries that Flanagan visited included the Czech Republic, Austria, Hungary, Italy and finally France. In each of these countries she watched performances and engaged in conversations with leading directors, actors and critics. In the Czech Republic she noticed how most plays were simple in plot and direct in appeal to the spectators; she felt that it was the latter's desire to see on stage a dramatic intensification of their own experiences, leading to a psychological analysis of human motive, that determined dramatic production. Austria was still under Max Reinhardt's spell, while Hungarian drama was conventional in terms of themes, direction and stage design. In Italy, Flanagan finally saw her favourite characters from *Commedia Dell'Arte* and experienced Craig's work and ideas more directly. She saw multiple performances in Florence and visited the Teatro Goldoni in Venice. In Rome, she met and discussed Italian Futuristic theatre with Anton Bragaglia in his Teatro degli Indipendenti, and later had a further conversation on Italian drama with Luigi Pirandello. Pirandello's views on drama gave Flanagan a better understanding of his plays. Flanagan's last destination was Paris. There she met Georges Pitoëff and discussed his way of directing more traditional plays by Shaw and Shakespeare. Through William Lèon Smyser, she attained an awareness of the chaotic state of Parisian theatre; French theatre was in a state of transition, not having a clear direction of where it was heading. French dramatists were still looking to Jacques Copeau for direction, innovation and revolt. Flanagan left France with a distinct sense that it was a country full of plays yet unwritten.

Flanagan's year-long trip through Europe furnished her with many ideas, images and visions of what modernist European theatre was. Upon her return to the United States, she put all this information in her book, *Shifting Scenes*; it was through this book that many American academics and theatre artists were informed of the new techniques, the more active social function of the theatre and the necessity of the people 'for legitimate representation as protagonist on the political stage'.[26] As soon as she returned to Vassar, she implemented many of these ideas in the theatrical productions of the Vassar Experimental Theatre, which became renowned for their quality, originality, controversial themes and content, and experimental modes of representation.

She took a break from her academic career in Vassar in 1935 when she was invited to serve as director of the FTP. This was a great opportunity for Flanagan not only to help in the restructuring of the American nation after the Great Depression but also to influence the structure of American theatre through the introduction of new forms of drama, new modes of representation, and the experimental use of scenery and lighting. This new form of American drama would be accompanied by new content infused with societal, economic and historical themes. At the epicentre of this new American theatre was the audience. Flanagan wanted the American audience to be part of the theatrical experience just as she witnessed in Russia, where 'it was impossible to tell where audience leaves off and drama begins'.[27] The interrelation between the creative process and the audience was reminiscent of Meyerhold's theatre, which she so much admired and studied closely.

But it was not only Meyerhold and the European theatrical traditions that influenced Flanagan's vision of the FTP. It is imperative to introduce and critically assess the project's problematic inheritance of both the American and Soviet workers' theatre, and at the same time examine the influence of Bertolt Brecht's theory of epic theatre and the strongly working-class audience-based productions of the British workers' theatre in the 1930s. In this way, one forges a transatlantic link between specific performative practices that transcended physical boundaries and ideologies; at the same time, such a reading highlights the FTP's desire to incorporate the above traditions and practices within the context of liberalism in an attempt to legitimise itself as an independent, innovative and critical theatrical agent.

Connecting the Dots:
The Theatre of the Blue Blouse and Meyerhold

Flanagan's European trip and book acted as a bridge between the two continents and their respective dramatists, and can be seen as a predecessor of the FTP's theatrical experimentations and vision for American cultural life. As discussed above, the main emphasis of the book was on the revolutionary theatre in Russia and predominantly on Vsevolod Meyerhold, his constructivist experimentations and his theory of biomechanics. Meyerhold was Stanislavsky's student and an actor in the Moscow Art Theatre but very soon became disillusioned by Stanislavsky's method, which precluded the interactive relationship between the actor and the audience. For Meyerhold, the theatre was a place 'where author, actor and spectator are magically fused'.[28] He wanted to break down the barrier created by illusionist pre-revolutionary theatre, which left the spectator a passive agent, trapped in the human emotion of the performance, and constantly reminded that s/he was not in a theatre and that what s/he was watching was irrelevant to his/her daily life.

Meyerhold was attracted to antirealism, symbolism, experimentation and the revolutionary politics that gave emphasis to a social and popular discourse. In constructivism, Meyerhold foresaw a new means of exposing his audience to his notion of theatre. He redefined the usage of the stage by abolishing the front curtain and cyclorama, and minimising the distance between the stage and the auditorium. Therefore, as soon as it stepped in the theatre, the audience was exposed to all the lights and machinery that made a production feasible and was extremely close to the actors. His stage dispensed with any unnecessary decorations and props; instead, it was filled with steel girders, steps, swings, bars and bridges across its width. As designer Nikolai Asimov had commented, constructivism 'considers the stage as a known quantity of space, the dimensions of which are in no way hidden from the audience'.[29] One of Meyerhold's most famous productions, in which his notion of the stage was manifested, was Crommelynck's *The Magnificent Cuckold*. As Slomin reported, 'the stage was completely denuded, no curtains, no rafters, no backdrops. It was occupied by a mill-like construction with platforms, stairs, wheels, rolling discs, windmill sails, a trapeze, a viaduct, and inclined surfaces.'[30]

In accordance with the new development of the stage, Meyerhold proposed a new theory of acting called biomechanics. For Meyerhold, the actor was no longer an imagined character with psychological depth or an abstract idea. S/he had a purely functional value that would communicate organically with the other elements of the performance. The emphasis was on the body, since he believed that the essence of humanity is expressed not by words but by bodily gestures and attitudes. Meyerhold had remarked that 'the mute eloquence of the body [can do miracles], word is but an embroidery on the canvas of movement'; for him, the ideal actor would display acrobatic and athletic qualities and be a mime, acrobat, dancer, juggler and comedian.[31] Meyerhold's biomechanics freed acting from exerting an emotional impact on the audience; instead, the actor was seen as a machine, part of the revolution, and 'he [was] a worker, a part of the social order he illustrate[d] on the stage'.[32]

Meyerhold's theatrical experimentations placed emphasis on the political function of the theatre. By 'the merging of cinema, radio, circus, music hall, sport, and comedy', by fusing modern design with political content, by redefining the relationship between actors and audience (having his actors enter through the audience and placing the theatrical action in any part of the auditorium), Meyerhold created a theatre that challenged already established stage theories, serving the needs of a new audience and of a new ideology.[33] In this committed theatre, Flanagan saw the effectual conditioning of a mass audience to a new social order, the accommodation of the desires of a long-forgotten public, the fusion of the dramatist, actor and audience, and the development of new exciting techniques that could be appropriated by the American stage.

Meyerhold's constructivist approach towards the theatrical space, his assault on traditional conventions of representation and his emphasis on the more active participation of the audience found allies among not only American practitioners but also Europeans, including Bertolt Brecht, whose formal experimentations, use of montage, desire to create a dialectical open-ended relationship between the performance and its audience, and emphasis on the possibility of political praxis echoed Meyerhold's ambitions. At the same time, though, the aesthetics of the avant-garde were under attack. Lukács's furious assault on expressionism and his bitter feud with Bloch and Brecht over realism could have easily been directed towards Meyerhold's stylised theatre. According to Lukács's views, Meyerhold's theatre could be charged as antirealistic and formalistic. Similarly, his theories and experimentations stand in direct opposition to the apolitical experimentation advocated by Greenberg in his reinvention of an American avant-garde just one year before the FTP ceased operations. Meyerhold, who provided a working formula for Flanagan's vision of an experimental and socially conscious theatre, was deemed a formalist by the Soviet regime for not complying with the aesthetics of Socialist Realism, and lost his life as a result of such an accusation.

Another major influence for the FTP was the Soviet Blue Blouse movement. Bigsby writes that in 1923 Mayakovsky and others announced, through their magazine *The Left Front of the Arts*, 'that art should be functional, that it should aim at reportage, that it should model itself to some degree on journalism, that truth lay in a vitalised documentary'.[34] In the same year, the first Blue Blouse group was formed in Moscow by a group of students at the Institute of Journalism. The group was influenced by the tradition of the spoken newspaper: during the revolution and because of large-scale illiteracy, the newspaper was read out aloud in front of the public.[35] By acknowledging this past oral tradition, the influence of Constructivism and the close relationship between theatre and journalism, the Blue Blouse was set up as a 'living newspaper' group that would present the news but, at the same time, employ both popular and new avant-garde techniques. When asked what the Blue Blouse was, its official magazine (*The Blue Blouse*) replied that

> it was a living newspaper, a presentation in 'agit-form' of reality, a 'montage of political facts'; it was adaptable to widely different conditions of performance; it was created by the working class; it used all the means of theatrical expression, especially those derived from the work of Vsevolod Meyerhold and Nikolai Foregger; and its texts aimed for the qualities exemplified in the work of Vladimir Mayakovsky, Nikolai Aseev and Sergei Tretyakov – brief, precise, and compelling; it was derived from 'popular forms'; and it sought out its working-class audiences in their own locations.[36]

The main aim of a Blue Blouse performance was to inform the illiterate public about actual social and political events reported in newspapers and magazines. Thus their performances were direct and agitational, and their political content was accompanied by a montage of satirical songs, acrobatics and posters. The importance of all these elements was stressed in their 'Simple Advice to Participants', in which they claimed that 'words in BB are everything, movement, music, acting add to them, make them more expressive, more meaningful, able quickly to organise the feelings and will of the audience – content and form are equally necessary'.[37] This statement reveals that, for the Blue Blouse group, both content and form were integral elements of their performance. The group, being directly involved with the creative process and performative aspects of the production, felt that by striking a balance between the formal experimentation of the avant-garde and the popular means of presentation, and then relating those to the political content of their work, they would achieve a more powerful performance.

A Blue Blouse performance would not last longer than an hour. The presentation would usually take place in a local theatre and would start with the actors' parade through the public, thus instantly involving the audience in its performative process. The parade would be followed by the dramatisation of international and national news, usually presented in a satirical manner, and enveloped by folk and jazz music, acrobatics, dancing and biomechanical gestures. Hallie Flanagan, who, while in Russia, had observed some Blue Blouse performances, commented that

> These actor/acrobats take possession of Russia's free, high stage, they leap upon the bare boards or upon the machines. They need no curtain to separate them from the audience for they have no illusion to maintain. They never pretend to be imagined characters, they remain members of the society which they illustrate on the stage.[38]

Flanagan's comments emphasised that the Blue Blouse's staging of the Living Newspaper was stripped of all those elements that could create an illusionist effect for the public and avoided the conventions of naturalist presentation. The combination of popular and avant-garde techniques aimed at assaulting realism in the theatre, but also at offering a continuity between popular performing traditions and new experimentations. By bringing the actor and the feeling of the theatrical stage closer to the destitute and illiterate people, the group succeeded in entertaining, satirising but also informing them about the changes that affected their lives.

The Blue Blouse movement thus succeeded in proposing a revolutionary dramaturgy in both form and content that could reach large audiences. The theatre became a kind of social expressionism and problematisation. Although it was a form of agit-prop theatre, its aims were to create a Soviet type of play with actuality as its subject, one that would express the benefits of Socialism/Communism but, at the same time, expose the defects of the system (or of the people around the system).[39] The Moscow correspondent for *The Christian Science Monitor* had commented that

> The theme of one of their satirical pieces is the unfortunate plight of a poor Soviet Citizen whose existence the bureaucrats in various institutions refuse to recognize, because he has somewhere mislaid his indispensable 'document' or passport. The familiar types in state institutions with preoccupied faces and the inevitable bulging portfolios are hit off neatly,

while a huge red pencil in the hands of the 'bureaucrat' adds a further element of the grotesque and the ludicrous.[40]

Through this example one can see how the Blue Blouse's living newspaper attempted to theatricalise society and its own methods of presentation, and to expose its audience to the absurdity of the bureaucratic system. In the theatre of the Blue Blouse, the combination of avant-garde aestheticism, satire and socio-political concerns contributed to political debates. It challenged the new order that was in the process of being established and offered a fresh, accessible view of the complexity of the social, economic and political engagements to an audience with no formal education.

Meyerhold and the Blue Blouse's collective expression of the performative action provided a new model for the configuration of the aesthetic and the political in theatre. This model was further disseminated in the autumn of 1927, when the Moscow Blue Blouse started a performance tour of Germany. Many German theatrical groups were influenced significantly by this new form of theatre and, subsequently, many Blue Blouse-type groups were set up there. Through the spread of the workers' theatre, the Living Newspaper became an international mode of politically involved theatre that aimed at mobilising its audience and at presenting it with new and experimental forms of production.

The Influence of Bertolt Brecht

The experimentation in the Soviet and German workers' theatre happened almost simultaneously with Piscator and Brecht's work on the epic theatre. Both Piscator and Brecht emphasised the importance of the theatre as a medium that not only represented life but could situate itself as a model of life. They also stressed the architecture of a class struggle-based theatre, of the anti-illusionism and anti-expressionism of a play's performance, the factual representation of themes, the use of musical scores, film projections and the constant interaction of the actors with the audience. The aim of the play was to present a theme in such a way that the audience would not become totally absorbed by the action but rather would be invited to witness all the unfolding events both critically and dialectically. As Brecht commented,

> The epic theatre is chiefly interested in the attitudes which people adopt towards one another, wherever they are socio-historically significant (typical) [. . .] The idea is that the spectator should be put in a position where he can make comparisons about everything that influences the way in which human beings behave. This means . . . that the actors' social gest becomes particularly important.[41]

The prominence given to the dialectical aspect of the performance discloses a continuity between the work of the Russian avant-garde and that of Piscator and Brecht. By directing and educating the audience to act and change the world and by allowing new techniques of performance to re-address the relationship between the actor and his/her role, the epic theatre complemented the new aesthetic of political theatre.

Although this book will not deal in detail with Brecht's theory of the epic theatre, it is imperative to discuss it briefly. Brecht has remained a controversial and polarised figure, in both Europe and the USA, because of his proclaimed Marxism and the way his epic theatre of political commitment and engagement weaved social, political, ideological and economic matters together. Brecht's theatrical experimentation and rebellion against traditional theatrical conventions and the necessity for change came as a result of both personal experience and theoretical reflection during the early 1920s. However, it was during the late 1920s and early to mid-1930s that his position on the dialectical, political and historical significance of the theatre was fully materialised.

Brecht's Marxist political convictions led him to propose the theory of the epic theatre as an alternative to the old dramatic theories and styles of performance. The emphasis of this new theatre was on the problem of the aesthetic reception of the play and its relation to its audience. Brecht commented that

> *A theatre which makes no contact with the public is a nonsense.* Our theatre is accordingly a nonsense. The reason why the theatre has at present no contact with the public is that it has no idea what is wanted of it. It can no longer do what it once could, and if it could do it it would no longer wish to. But it stubbornly goes on doing what it no longer can do and what is no longer wanted.[42]

Brecht's comment introduced the issue of whether the theatre considered the conditions of its time. For him, the old bourgeois traditional theatre was merely repeating a formula that might have served its public for many years, but did not recognise the new economic, social and political order. By refusing to adapt itself to the new challenges, the old theatre was obstructing the revolutionary social and political consciousness of the people. For Brecht, it was time to make theatre new.

The new theatre aimed at appealing to the intellect of the spectators and demanded their full concentration and attention; thus, the emphasis was both on the content and on the formal elements of the play. The debate concerning the status and function of form and content within the theatre formed part of Brecht's theory of the epic theatre. Brecht believed in the social change and action that theatre could accomplish and was committed to the challenge of giving 'a social perspective on private experience', of confronting and criticising social establishment and perceptions.[43] His plays' political and social agenda would be expressed through the process of historicisation and accompanied by a commitment to theatrical experimentation.

Brecht's main reaction was against the bourgeois establishment that had created and enforced a specific and unchallenged world view. Bourgeois political economy and theory dealt with the forms of bourgeois society as if they were universal, eternal and unchanging relationships, rather than historical forms of a system that was full of contradictions and subject to radical transformation. Through his writings, Brecht ventured to encourage the audience to be more critical and questioning 'by adopting the cool, investigative attitude appropriate to the scientific age'.[44] His 'scientific age' opposed the bourgeois cultural phenomenon and notion of morality that underpinned their views of the unchanging nature of humanity. By depicting the social and emotional deprivation caused by the bourgeois social order and capitalism, he revealed to his audience a world view hidden beneath a palimpsest of constructed social narratives and realities. He regarded his art as political, as it did not ally itself with the ruling group and, using Marx's eleventh theorem on Feuerbach, stressed the fact that, whereas the philosophers aimed at interpreting the world, the main point was to change it.[45] It was the latter that he wanted to apply to his new 'scientific' theatre.

Brecht's 'scientific', documentary and epic style of writing emphasised the 'crude' development of the scene rather than the fixed style of performance that was rooted in the emotional response of the audience. He commented that 'changes are to be provoked and to be made perceptible; sporadic and anarchic acts of creation are to be replaced by creative processes whose changes progress by steps or leaps'.[46] Brecht's notion of 'crude thinking' involved a deliberate gestic action on the part of the dramatist or artist; by thinking dialectically about the social praxis of a work of art in relation to its audience, s/he revealed to their audience the fundamental political relations behind the characters' actions and how the latter influenced its daily reality and life. This, in turn, instigated a new cognitive process on the part of the audience as it began also to think crudely, actively and dialectically about what it witnessed on stage. Combining coarseness with boldness, 'crude thinking' empowers the audience to challenge established perceptions and representations, thus resulting in social awareness and praxis. Brecht's theatrical theory liberated theatrical writing, performance and presentation; by acknowledging the relationship between power and knowledge, and creating a theatrical language and style that could provoke both reaction and change, Brecht proposed a new form of intellectual and artistic dialectics that would be open-ended and full of contradictions, with the ability to transform or challenge reality. Brecht's theatre was instrumental in revealing to the audience that their daily actions were the result not simply of autonomous desires or needs, but rather of complex networks of social relations.

Unlike Meyerhold and the Blue Blouse, Brecht was, from very early on in his career, fascinated by the notion of 'America' and 'Americana' as the space for reinscription, reinvention and resignification. He was enthralled by some of America's cultural exports (such as jazz and boxing), and the American city of Chicago became the epicentre of such plays as *In the Jungle of Cities* and *Saint Joan of the Stockyards*. Writing for *The New York Times* in 1935, Brecht commented how the purpose of the modern stage was to introduce new experimental forms (such as film projections and moving platforms), and how these new facilities allowed the further use of music and graphic elements to complement the written text. At the same time, though, he emphasised a new attitude towards dramaturgy. According to Brecht, this new dramaturgy

> has as a purpose the 'teaching' of the spectator a certain practical attitude; we have to make it possible for him to take a critical attitude while he is in the theatre (as opposed to a subjective attitude of becoming completely 'entangled' in what is going on).[47]

This article, addressed to the American public during his first visit to the USA, reiterates clearly Brecht's vision of the modern theatre: not only would it employ new forms that would enhance the presentation of themes previously excluded from stage, but, more importantly, it would enable and promote the audience's critical outlook on what is presented on stage. Therefore, theatre is no longer interested in simply presenting a series of events; by instigating the audience's critical attitude, it creates a dialectical dialogue between stage and audience, whose end product should be the audience's wish 'to change [the world]'.[48]

Brecht's opportunity to visit his imaginary *topos* of 'Americana' came in 1935 with an invitation to participate in the production of his play *The Mother* (freely adapted from Maxim Gorky's similarly entitled novel) by the Theatre Union. His disappointing experience and his problematic collaboration with the Theatre Union have been documented at length. Although it did not bring him many collaborators, there were a few American practitioners that were attracted to his epic theory and his effort to change prevailing theatre practices. Interestingly, most of them would soon find themselves involved with the FTP in different capacities. Among them were Joseph Losey (whom Brecht had met a year earlier while both men were visiting Moscow), Mordecai Gorelik, Eric Bentley (who translated many of his works and furthered a better understanding of Brecht within America), and Marc Blitzstein and his wife, Eva Goldbeck. Brecht deeply admired Gorelik, and during his collaboration with the Theatre Union Gorelik remained the only person open to Brecht's ideas on the epic theatre. Losey and Blitzstein were also creatively influenced by Brecht and introduced him to the work of the FTP's Living Newspaper unit. Although there are no records of any attempts by the FTP to perform any of Brecht's plays, according to Losey, Brecht was impressed by his production of *Injunction Granted*.[49] For Losey, Brecht's theatrical importance was immense, as he was 'expounding his enthusiasms, articulating his "eye" which was our eye too'.[50] At the same time, it was during an FTP gathering that Blitzstein performed his song, 'The Nickel Under Your Foot', about prostitution, and on Brecht's suggestion decided to write a whole play about all forms of prostitution; the play produced by the FTP was *The Cradle Will Rock* and it was dedicated to Brecht.

His discussions with Losey, Blitzstein and other American theatre people, and his attendance at performances such as Odets's *Waiting for Lefty* and those of the Living Newspaper unit revealed to Brecht the existence of technological and dramaturgical innovations within the American theatre. However, after his experience with the Theatre Union, he felt that, within the American theatrical scene, the tradition of the bourgeois aesthetic still persisted, and its left counterpart did not attempt to challenge it on a large scale. By still relying on middle-class patrons and aiming to please their parochial taste, the American left theatre (including the FTP) seemed unwilling to challenge fundamentally the theatrical status quo. At the same time, by failing to cultivate in workers a distinct sense of class consciousness (separated from the values of the middle class), it could not produce any revolutionary portrayals of the workers' social awareness. Resisting the developments of the theatre of the new age, the American left theatre remained closely associated with the more naturalistic style of performance, thus emphasising the representation of a character's emotions, which resulted in the audience's empathetic response. Brecht's notions of dialectical thinking and critical distance were rejected as either too difficult or not attractive enough for the American audience, and, as the fate of the FTP suggests, the American theatrical scene soon resorted to the old bourgeois aesthetic to which it was accustomed.

Dreaming of the Left: The British Workers' Theatre Movement, Ewan MacColl and Joan Littlewood

The 1920s and early 1930s constituted a particularly prolific period in theatrical movements in Britain, particularly in relation to the Socialist imagination. For many artists of that period, Socialism finally presented a viable aesthetic and political means through which to represent on stage the realisation of the workers' conditions of existence, as well as their power. Embracing an agit-prop/avant-garde form of expression, the workers' movement in Britain was not afraid to experiment, taking its cues from its Soviet counterparts, mentioned previously.

Raphael Samuel took great care in presenting in much detail the history of the Socialist theatre in Britain between 1880 and 1935. In his historical approach, he commented that, in the years after the end of the World War I, a 'considerable expansion in politically minded drama groups' took place.[51] The Independent Labour Party (ILP) was particularly supportive of Socialist drama across the country and staged Ernst Toller's *Masses and Man*, Upton

Sinclair's *Singing Jailbirds*, Elmer Rice's *The Adding Machine* and Georg Kaiser's German expressionist play, *Gas*. There was even mention of a Living Newspaper being staged by Holborn Constituency Labour Party in 1926, based on the Russian model.[52]

The Workers Theatre Movement (WTM, 1926–35) was an important aspect of British drama. It placed more emphasis on an agit-prop style of performance and saw itself as a theatre of action, dealing with contemporary issues. Theatrically, WTM broke away completely from realistic and naturalistic dramaturgical traditions and concentrated primarily on agit-prop and modernist forms. Responding to actual events, happening in real time, a WTM performance would include sketches, cabaret and vaudeville, and would, preferably, take place outdoors. Ewan MacColl recalls how, on their way to a locality, they would write the sketch, come up with satirical songs, rehearse it for thirty minutes, and then put it on in a market place or a factory before the police would show up.[53] One of the biggest influences on the WTM was the revolutionary theatre in Russia: Eisenstein's montage techniques and Meyerhold's biomechanics. As Füllöp-Miller commented, the abolishment of the curtain – 'that symbol of mystery which had hitherto separated the world of the stage from that of the auditorium' – and the fascination with machinery, once representing the worker's slavery but now 'a symbol of his deliverance and a sign of power', came from the Russian stage.[54] Meyerhold's acting method and use of the body in a performance was mimicked by the WTM in their development of an acting style that incorporated mechanical movement with acrobatics and athletics, thus exploring the plasticity of the actor's body. Lastly, it also adopted the idea of making the audience a lively, participatory 'actor' in and commentator on the drama unfolding on stage.

Their performances reflected the social, political and economic changes occurring at the time and responded to specific events happening locally all over the country. From 1931 onwards, most of the performances were street-based; they did not use costumes (apart from dungarees) or make-up and the actors used megaphones to project their lines. The stage was laid bare (thus facilitating the street performance) and was filled visually by the 'rhythm, gesture, and pace' of the actors' bodies.[55] That was mostly true of the provincial WTM groups (such as the Salford 'Red Megaphones' or the Bowhill Players), whereas the more central groups' performances took place indoors. For example, the West Ham United Front troupe announced in 1935 the possession of their own hall, equipped with a stage and electricity; Theatre Action in Manchester set up a permanent home; and the Rebel Players in London, after changing their name to Unity Theatre, established a permanent base in a converted music hall.

The WTM promoted agit-prop techniques to British theatre, exposed the British audience to new modernist performances, and gave voice to workers' concerns, demands and living conditions. The regional structure, allowing local groups to set up and produce new plays with no financial backing from government, made agit-prop theatre available to striking workers, but also to any audience that wanted to be exposed to a new theatrical experience. Unlike the FTP, the WTM aimed to reach the working masses and voice their regional concerns. Like the FTP, the WTM wanted to expose on stage the more dynamic, fluid, rich and flexible societal structures. Theatre was not simply a thing of leisure or a medium through which personal or romantic matters were explored. Society was not made up of just the aristocrats, the rich or the upper middle classes. The anxieties and lives of the lower classes were of equal importance and the no-nonsense approach of the WTM made sure that they found a place on British stage.

By 1936, the WTM, after seven or eight intense years of theatrical activity, ceased operation. Its end reflects the different paths that the groups decided to take. As its name suggests, it was a movement that aimed at motivating workers to participate creatively (acting, directing or writing) and actively by attending performances. However, ultimately, it could not control the ways in which groups wanted to engage with the theatrical space and material. The Rebel Players' breakaway, their renaming as the Unity Theatre in 1936, the controversy regarding the latter's production of Odets's *Waiting for Lefty* and its huge success revealed the tensions and divergent attitudes. The Unity Theatre, which received a great deal of assistance from the professional producer André van Gyseghem, was advocating for plays that required a more conventional curtained stage (as opposed to the agit-prop, outdoor performances that the WTM preferred).[56] It did not abandon agit-prop altogether but was eager to develop new dramatic forms and modes of performance that would extend the presentation and consideration of workers' issues. And it wanted to promote new writing; of its 250 performances, at least half of them were new plays, some written especially for Unity. The plays included *Where's That Bomb?*, written by two taxi drivers, Robert Buckland and Herbert Hodge, a comedy about a sacked aero-engine fitter, offered a job writing patriotic stories on toilet paper; *Cannibal Carnival*, also written by Hodge, which satirised colonial imperialism; a Living Newspaper, *Busmen*, about the bus strike in 1937 during the coronation of King George IV, which led to the court-martial of seven of the leaders; Jack Lindsay's *On Guard for Spain*, which supported the International Brigade; the panto *Babes in the Wood*, an attack on Chamberlain's policy of appeasement, which broke new ground by not only satirising Hitler and Mussolini, but also impersonating Chamberlain on stage; *Plant in the Sun*, an ensemble piece of drama based on a strike in the shipping department of a New York sweet factory, starring Paul Robeson along with Alfie Bass; and lastly, plays by Sean O'Casey, Arthur Adamov, Jean-Paul Sartre, Maxim Gorky, and the British premiere of Brecht's *Mother Courage and Her Children*.[57]

Another movement that came out of the WTM was the Theatre of Action in Manchester, driven by Ewan MacColl and Joan Littlewood. By 1933, MacColl was dissatisfied with the work in the Red Megaphones; he was tired of the constant police harassment, resulting from performing outdoors, as well as ashamed of the quality of the works performed. Littlewood, having recently arrived in Manchester from France, also realised the limitations of her training at the Royal Academy of Dramatic Art (RADA). Together, they discovered their desire for a flexible theatre, one that would correspond to the ever-changing facets of political and social life and the needs of actor training. In 1934, the Theatre of Action was formed; as MacColl stated, they wanted to 'create a theatre of synthesis in which the actors will be able to sing, dance and act with equal facility'.[58] They were immediately drawn to Meyerhold's biomechanics and Piscator's decision to have some of his actors trained in dance, as well as Stanislavsky's theory of acting. Trying to bring all these different elements together, MacColl recalled how they found that synthesis in Yevgeny Vakhtangov's theatre. Vakhtangov was greatly influenced by the acting techniques of both of his teachers, Stanislavsky and Nemirovich-Danchenko, as well as Meyerhold's theatrical experiments. His productions incorporated music, masks, abstract costumes and experimental setting designs, as well as a more analytical set that encompassed a psychological examination of the characters' motivation and actions. MacColl could not recall how they knew of Vakhtangov's approach, but one possible source could have been Brecht. Writing in the 1930s, Brecht was aware of Vakhtangov and acknowledged a commonality with his own acting style, but found Vakhtangov's style lacking the social insight and didactic function of his own gestic form.

Lastly, the Theatre of Action was influenced by the Workers' Laboratory Theatre in New York; through two workers, Lazar Copeland and Benny, the group was in communication with the Laboratory Theatre, who sent it scripts. Among them was a two-page one called *Newsboy*; the play lasted around fifteen minutes and involved a newsboy, 'who did a kind of stylistic dance on the stage while he constantly shouted the headlines of the world's news'.[59] MacColl and Littlewood produced the play by having small groups of two or three actors acting out the news; there was no special podium on stage, no curtain, no attempt to discontinue the action happening on other parts of the stage. Any changes were reflected by using basic lighting.

Theatre of Action lasted till the end of 1934; by 1935, MacColl and Littlewood were contacting many of their old colleagues again in the hope of creating a new theatre company. That company was the Theatre Union – announcing itself as the theatre of the people – and its creation coincided with the Spanish Civil War. All people involved with the Theatre Union would be involved in studying theatre. Whether an actor or technician, everybody was expected to study a different period or aspect of theatre and would then report their findings to the rest of the company. MacColl and Littlewood took it upon themselves to collate the syllabus. They both hoped that, through this process, everyone involved in their company would be educated in the different forms and modes of theatre, the different ideas and themes, and the different performative theories and tools. Through this process, a sense of theatrical community would be instilled in all involved, as well as a sense of continuity regarding theatrical knowledge.

Among the plays performed by the company were Lope de Vega's *Fuente Ovejuna* (*The Sheep-well*), a classical sixteenth-century Spanish play about the revolt of a village community against their ruthless commander. The villagers band together and kill him; when pressured and tortured by the king's magistrate (who was sent there to investigate the events), all the villagers respond in solidarity 'Fuenteovejuna did it.' The play was performed during the Spanish Civil War and the correlations between the play's narrative action and the actual war could not have been more astute. This production was followed by *The Good Soldier Schweik*, based on Jaroslav Hašek's unfinished satirical dark comedy about World War I. Aware of the stage play adaptation by Erwin Piscator and Bertolt Brecht (for the 1927–8 season of Piscator's theatre Piscatorbühne), the Theatre Union employed the back-projection techniques used in Piscator's production, rejected the life-sized marionettes and relied on its past expertise of staging episodic agit-prop performances with dance elements incorporated.[60] They also produced Aristophanes' *Lysistrata* (MacColl's first contact with Ancient Greek drama) before presenting their first Living Newspaper.

The Last Edition, produced in 1939, was the company's response to the outbreak of World War II. The play dealt with the events that led to the war – with the theme of unemployment running like a thread throughout it – as well as mounting a strong, satirical response to Chamberlain's decisions and war narrative. Unlike the early American Living Newspapers (1935–7), which did not have a single author, this one was written by MacColl. MacColl claimed that the company had not seen an actual performance of an American Living Newspaper but had heard of the one produced by the Proletkult and of the FTP's *One-third of a Nation*.[61] At the same time, one must not forget that MacColl had been informed of the Blue Blouse's performances in the late 1920s.[62] All this knowledge enveloped *The Last Edition*'s performative and scenic structures.

The play opened at the Lesser Free Trade Hall and its staging greatly resembled that of many of the American Living Newspapers in its choice of multiple platforms on stage. As MacColl recollected, there were two further platforms, in addition to the central one, running the full length of the auditorium so that the audience was enclosed on all sides. As such, the audience became an extra actor, participating by being situated in the middle of all the action happening on stage. This use of multiple platforms allowed for choices when it came to directing and staging; a continuous action could happen simultaneously on all three stages, other scenes could use only one or two of the stages or the conflict could be presented 'in terms of the two side-stages versus the top stage'.[63] To that, they added songs and dances, and the production resembled a fast-moving variety show with which the company felt very familiar.

The production was stopped by the police after five performances; both MacColl and Littlewood were arrested and fined for behaviour that could lead to a breach of peace. The company managed to survive for a few months after the event but was disbanded a few weeks after the beginning of World War II. It remained inactive for the duration of the war, but after its end it reassembled; instigated by Littlewood, the Theatre Workshop was set up as both a production theatre and a training school, where new acting techniques would be tried and experimented on. Carrying on the Theatre Union's manifesto, the Theatre Workshop would continue developing its unique theatrical voice to reach new working-class audiences that had not experienced theatre before, it would combine Stanislavsky's method with agit-prop and improvisation techniques in terms of acting, and it would create new scripts and plays, tailor-made for the company, in line with its aims and its social and political agenda. An example of such a play is *Uranium 235*, first performed at the Newcastle People's Theatre on 18 February 1946, which will be discussed in some detail in Chapter 7.

From this brief discussion of the British Workers' Theatre and MacColl and Littlewood's work at the Theatre of Action and Theatre Union, one can appreciate the parallel development of political theatre in the UK and the USA. But, more importantly, a direct connection is established between theatrical practitioners and theorists in both countries regarding the role of theatre in the 1930s. It is quite ironic that Flanagan did not mention the British Workers' Movement and did not watch any of its performances during her stay in London in 1929. Her disappointment regarding British theatre might have been transformed to excitement, had she experienced any of their performances or studied the regional structure of the theatrical troupes. For both Flanagan and the Theatre Union, the emphasis of the theatre they were creating was for the people and of its time. Adding further to this connection is the influence of the European and avant-garde theatre. Stanislavsky, Meyerhold, Brecht, Piscator and the Blue Blouse had become household names for any socially and politically aspiring actors, playwrights, directors and designers in Europe and America. Their influence and importance, highlighted in the above reading of British theatre, was also evident in the development of the FTP, thus reinforcing the transatlantic link and reading performed in this book. The last influential ingredient in harbouring a continuity between these developing theatres was the American workers' theatre of the 1930s, examined below.

Coming Home: American Workers' Drama of the 1930s

Closer to home, the American workers' theatre of the 1920s and early 1930s also exerted its influence on the FTP. After the collapse of the national economy, many writers became preoccupied with Marxist philosophy and proletarian literature. The concept of political commitment and the artist's conscious involvement in social issues informed the new theatre and the intelligentsia. W. H. Auden reflected this attitude when he wrote

> Yesterday, the belief in the absolute value of Greek;
> The fall of all curtain upon the death of a hero;
> Yesterday the prayer to the sunset,
> And the adoration of madmen. But today the struggle.[64]

During the 1920s, groups of worker–players were formed and performances were staged at labour meetings, at strike rallies and in parks to entertain but also inform their public. The Proletbühne (a German workers' group founded in 1925), Artef (Yiddish Workers Theatre, 1926) and the Workers Laboratory Theatre (1928) modelled themselves on the agit-prop Blue Blouse and their performances had 'a hard-hitting directness of statement [. . .] Satirical rhymed verse and powerful rhythmic refrains characterised most of their work.'[65] They also employed vaudeville acts, circus techniques, minimal lighting, choruses to dramatise the conflict between two opposing groups (one usually being the workers and the other the capitalists), and direct addresses to the public. Because of the lack of funding and time to train themselves professionally, these groups also employed Meyerhold's biomechanic technique and the documentary themes from Piscator's theatre. The equal importance given to the form and content of their performances appealed to the workers' theatre. As John Bonn commented,

> it is not enough to bring our message to the masses ... A production with the best political content is worthless if this content is not presented in a form which is interesting for a worker audience. Propaganda and entertainment must be interwoven in a worker theatre performance.[66]

Bonn's comment, reminiscent of the Blue Blouse's manifesto and Brecht's didactic plays, manifested the extent of the European theatre's influence on the development of its American counterpart. Because of the speed and dexterity of their performances and the clarity of their political message, the American workers' theatre captured its audience's attention and imagination.

Their target audience was the masses of workers and their aim was to propagate the idea of the theatre as the space where class struggle could take place and thus agitate the workers into social action.[67] Their performances were very polemical, directly reflecting Marxist ideology and Communist ideals. Goldstein has quoted the ending of one such play, entitled *Unemployed*, which presented one individual (attempting to fuse himself with the mass of workers) proclaiming in front of an audience of workers that

> Yes, I am an agitator – an agitator for the fight against exploitation and oppression, an agitator for the freeing of the working class, an agitator against all misleaders who under the mask of friends of labor betray us to our exploiters. Yes, I agitate for the defence of the Soviet Union, the only country in the world where there are no more exploiters, the only country in the world where the workers are free, the only country in the world where the worker rules.[68]

The militant discourse of this excerpt reflects how the American workers' agitprop groups accommodated the mythical dimension of the Soviet worker as an all-powerful individual, who is part of the all-powerful class of workers, to represent the American worker's struggle for social justice. It is no coincidence that their attempt to represent the American worker's struggle did not take place within the legitimate and capital-supported space of Broadway, which was inimical to their political values. These groups partly funded themselves and also received some financial support from local organisations, thus creating a new public *topos* where their struggle for political, cultural and social representation could take place.

Hallie Flanagan was aware of the developments in the American theatre. She acknowledged that it was 'a theatre of workers', whose object was to create 'a national culture by and for the working class of America'.[69] She recognised this theatre as a weapon in the class struggle and as a means of reorganising society. In Flanagan's article, the fusion of the aesthetic and political function of theatre was evident. She insisted that the new theatre should be detached from the elaborate stylistics of Broadway and that their style of acting should escape the illusionism of realist theatre, as the workers needed to represent themselves and their cultural background. She insisted that

> The workers' theatres intend to shape the life of this country, socially, politically and industrially. They intend to remake a social structure without the help of money – and this ambition alone invests their undertaking with a certain Marlowesque madness.[70]

Her anticapitalist observation (later referred to during her hearing in front of HUAC) reiterated the policy of the workers' theatre. Unlike Broadway, Hollywood and the radio, which had accommodated themselves within capitalism and thus rendered their critical appropriation problematic, the workers' theatre had an economic autonomy that offered a new space where both formal experimentation and social commentary could occur.

For Flanagan, the new theatre's ability to survive outside the capitalist economic system and Broadway's established aesthetic modes of representation offered a key to its revolutionary potential. Through this act, the theatre would be free 'from the non-essentials which have become synonymous with it – divorced from expensive buildings, stage equipment, painted sets, elaborate costumes and properties, made up plays' – and would become instead 'a place where an idea is so ardently enacted that it becomes the belief of actors and audience alike'.[71] Flanagan thus believed that the economic autonomy of the workers' theatre could ensure its aesthetic autonomy too, and serve as both an educational and a propaganda agent. By appropriating the theatrical art of Gordon Craig and Adolphe Appia on the workers' terms, the new theatre could produce a form of theatre that would engage critically and dialectically with its audience. Her emphasis on the theatre as a *topos* of social struggle and formal experimentation would later materialise in the Living Newspapers' fascination with the relationship between art and politics and the different approaches to this relationship.

As the Depression intensified in the early 1930s, theatrical groups such as the Theatre Union, the Group Theater and the Theater Guild were established. These groups were influenced by the experimental performances and themes of the workers' theatre but chose to abandon the overtly agitational character of the plays' content. These new groups aimed at creating a new theatre with multiple origins that would be represented as fundamentally American. As they no longer aimed at explicitly gaining support for the Soviet Union and the Communist cause, their target audience expanded to include the middle class. The works of major playwrights of this decade – such as Clifford Odets, Elmer Rice and Malcolm Cowley – manifested an active concern for social and political issues, centred, however, on the main issue of the livelihood of the American people. The best-known play was Odets's *Waiting for Lefty*, which gave an intimate insight into the life of taxi drivers. The play was not totally free of a militant discourse, but it was free enough for Broadway to allow it to run for seventy-eight performances.[72] *Waiting for Lefty* did present the conflict between the agents of political and economic power and the rights and needs of the deprived class of taxi drivers but, unlike previous plays, it did not entail an agitational call for a general public strike. As Kruger has commented, the play offered instead 'an exemplary *imitation* of agitation (complete with plants in the house) for an essentially disengaged audience'.[73] With this new theatre, the previously agitational workers' theatre was exorcised; this new theatre could equally accommodate itself within the space that Broadway offered in an attempt to entice the support and participation of the middle class.

This new attitude in theatre was followed by the rebranding of the League of Workers' Theatres as the New Theatre League and its magazine, the *Workers' Theatre*, as *New Theatre*.[74] The new theatrical dogma dictated that 'a theatre greater than the labor movement but drawing its inspiration from the latter and continuing the new social outlook on a broader social scale' should exist.⁷⁵ Through the establishment of a theatre that aimed at creating a broader socially based theatre, the workers' theatre was ostracised once again from any legitimate space of representation. The working class, which had attempted the creation of a new experimental and socially–politically involved theatre, not only failed to be decentralised, as Bonn suggested, but also was at the heart of the theatrical metropolis and had suffered a serious facelift. The shift in the new theatre's target audience and its approach to social and political issues signalled a slight but steady rejection of its radical programme in favour of a more liberal, 'naturally American' one.

2

THE LIVING NEWSPAPER PART 1: 1935–1937 – THE REVOLUTION BEGINS

> Although it has occasional reference to the Volksbühne and Blue Blouses, to Bragaglia and Meyerhold and Eisenstein, the Living Newspaper is as American as Walt Disney, the *March of Time*, and the *Congressional Record*.[1]
> Flanagan, 'Introduction' to *Federal Theatre Plays: Prologue to Glory, One-third of a Nation, Haiti.*

> I see, together with the re-making of American citizens, the making of a theatre which bears unmistakably the mark 'Made in America'.[2]
> Flanagan, 'Opening Statement', House Un-American Activities Committee.

In the Beginning There Was *Ethiopia*

For Flanagan, the Federal Theatre represented American theatre's chance to 'wake up and grow – wake up to an age of expanding social consciousness'.[3] She abandoned the notion of the stage as a place 'where sophisticated secrets are whispered in a blasé initiate' and instead wanted playwrights to produce plays that would

> include such economic facts as unemployment, taxation, the obligation of government to the unemployed and to art, the values and dangers of organization to the theatre worker, the effect of trade unionism on art,

the spending of federal funds in relation to censorship, the value of the theatre to recreation, education and therapeutics.[4]

Within an environment of economic and social unrest, it is noteworthy that it was up to a government-sponsored institution with a nationwide scope to mobilise the public and awaken their awareness to issues that influenced their daily routine.

Up until the establishment of the FTP, Broadway monopolised the theatrical world. The plays offered by Broadway were restricted in themes and in access to the public. There was also a belief that the arts and theatre had become an expensive enterprise and the property of the few. Thus, the FTP became an agency representative of the people's needs, frustrations and demands. For the FTP to perform its task, it needed theatres 'experimental in nature, specializing in new plays of unknown dramatists, with an emphasis on regional and local material'.[5] Its repertoire would include the works of canonical playwrights such as Shakespeare, Ibsen and Shaw, but these texts alone could not stimulate the awakening of the American people's social consciousness. For this reason, Hallie Flanagan and Elmer Rice (the director of the New York FTP branch) proposed the creation of the Living Newspaper unit, after securing the sponsorship of the Newspaper Guild. Morris Watson was placed in charge of the staff of journalists and playwrights on relief rolls. So, instead of simply standing in line every day to receive a free meal, all these artists would be given jobs and receive a wage. In this way, not only would they still be employed, doing jobs they both loved and were trained for, but they could also contribute towards the production of some of the most exciting American theatre of the mid-twentieth century. Within the project, actors, playwrights and journalists would work together to produce plays that would dramatise the social, political and economic conditioning of the American people. As Flanagan had commented:

> The staff of the living newspaper, set up like a city daily with editor-in-chief, a managing editor, city editor, reporters and copyreaders, began as Brooks Atkinson later remarked 'to shake the living daylights out of a thousand books, reports, newspapers and magazine articles' in an attempt to create an authoritative dramatic treatment, at once historic and contemporary of current problems.[6]

The Living Newspaper unit was attributed a collective status in which all the members involved were responsible for the dramatic outcome. 'Official' authorship of the text was not bestowed on a single person, although this changed by 1937.

Both Flanagan and Rice believed that the Living Newspaper should present new experimental plays, both in subject matter and in technique, in order to create a socially and theatrically conscious public. At the same time, the new plays would be free from the commercial consideration that dominated Broadway; it was commercialism, according to Rice – himself a successful Broadway playwright and producer – that was the enemy of experiment, innovation and everything artistically worthwhile. This desire for experimentation was a direct result of Flanagan's awareness of the American workers' socially provocative theatre and her first-hand experience of the Blue Blouse group and Meyerhold's productions. Moreover, many members of the Living Newspaper unit and the FTP (such as Joseph Losey, Morris Watson, Marc Blitzstein, Elmer Rice, John Bonn and Jules Dassin) were familiar with these groups, and their experimentations and views on the political expression of the theatre; some had travelled individually both to the Soviet Union and to Germany, and had attended many performances and seminars that greatly affected their views on American theatre.

With the Depression troubling American society and the WPA established to assist in the employment of artists, Flanagan's belief that 'it is time that the theatre is brought face to face with the great economic problems of the day' became a reality.[7] As the already established theatrical canon could not offer plays dealing with the new social reality, a need for new and socially involved plays was generated. Partly to employ as many artists and journalists as possible, but also to attempt to fill the gap for new plays, the Living Newspaper unit was set up. Echoing the Blue Blouse's belief that 'the repertoire of the Living Newspaper cannot be prewritten and laid down from any central agency . . . On the contrary it must be the collective work of the local group', and so emphasising the need for a decentralised theatre that would be accessible to all the public, the Living Newspaper established units all over America.[8] However, it was the New York productions that caused an immediate sensation among their audience; at the same time, they caused such controversy that it resulted in both censorship and suspension of the whole project.

By the time the Living Newspaper was incorporated into the FTP, its dramatic form and theatrical modes of representation were already developed. The Voice of the Living Newspaper introduced the time, place and location of the dramatic action, interrupted and commented further on the events staged, addressed the public directly, presented different perspectives on the issues discussed and often sided with the disadvantaged. The stage was deprived of all the ornaments that could disrupt the audience's attention from the action and the use of ordinary objects in ways different from their customary significance defined a more symbolic and simple approach to the new audience. The use of a series of different devices (such as puppetry, visual projections, shadow acting and crowd scenes) offered a more dramatic momentum to the presentation of facts. Lastly, the experimentation with lighting (by isolating characters on single spots) proposed a new appropriation of the theatrical space that was complemented by the new style of acting. As Mike Gold commented, it was the American Living Newspaper's responsibility to inherit this tradition and employ it within the socially awakened theatre 'in a new way and [to] do it well'.[9]

The Living Newspaper unit resembled its European antecedents in structure: that is, there was a proper editorial staff with reporters, sub-editors and editors who researched each topic in depth and were not permitted to invent anything. They were also committed to using new and political forms of stagecraft. They commented that

> it is the job of modern theatre to break through the technological barriers of decadent stagecraft as well as the ideological barriers of decadent thought. Modern theatre has already broken through many of these barriers – both in the technical and ideological sense, but . . . the theatre is still dominated by characters pitting 'one psychological trait against another psychological trait,' with each conflict taking place inside a more or less traditional atmospheric shell of wood, canvas and paint. The Living Newspaper, on the other hand, can confidently say that it has attempted – and more often than not succeeded – in transcending these limits. It has peopled its stage with interesting characters but they are the physical, human manifestation of forces that are longer and more important than individual psychology. They are individuals whose psychology is, in fact, the product of these forces.[10]

By acknowledging its past tradition, the American Living Newspaper aligned itself with the modern theatre's practice of agitation, experimentation and engagement with social issues. But unlike its antecedents, the American Living Newspaper soon abandoned theatrical eclecticism in favour of a more detailed form of investigating theatre, centralised over one issue. As Arthur Arent stated,

> the Living Newspaper is the dramatization of a *problem* – composed in greater or lesser extent of many news events, all bearing on the one subject and interlarded with typical but non-factual representations of the effect of these news events on the people to whom the problem is of great importance.[11]

The Living Newspaper staff decided that an emphasis on one subject and its multiple representations would enable them to communicate multiple solutions to the immediate problems and thus allow the audience to rethink a specific issue in a variety of circumstances. Thus, almost every Living Newspaper followed the same pattern: the play would begin with a recent, shocking event that would expose the problem and, through its representations, the protagonist would be forced to recognise the need for a solution. They also reached that decision after one of the first Living Newspapers produced, called simply *1935*, was not received as successfully as they had hoped. The play presented many events that had occurred during that year in a highly satirical manner, directed not simply at the representatives of capital but at the public itself. It was very close in structure to its European predecessors, but the Living Newspaper staff felt that it was impossible to research the news effectively every day so as to revise the script. At the same time, because of the large number of events and since only one scene could be devoted to each of them, they deemed that this style of play was exposing the problems but never fully engaged the audience in critical reflective thinking.

The Federal Theatre's desire to offer free, uncensored and adult theatre was faced from the start with bureaucracy and political intrigues consequent on it being a government-sponsored theatre. The Living Newspaper production entitled *Ethiopia* concentrated on one issue and aimed at presenting the conflict that had arisen in the African state after its Italian conquest (under Mussolini's orders) by quoting speeches made by both Haile Selassie and Mussolini himself, as well as including a broadcast by President Roosevelt. The play condemned the invasion, and by extension the American government for failing to prevent it. Flanagan enticed Elmer Rice with the prospect of producing and experimenting with this new theatrical form. Rice was a prominent playwright and Pulitzer Prize-winner. Prior to his collaboration with the FTP, he had travelled to the Soviet Union in both 1932 and 1936; during his trips he saw a variety of performances, witnessed the theatre's popularity and commented on the perception of the theatre as a 'transcendent medium for cultural communication'.[12] Rice was invited to participate in the creation of the FTP by Harry Hopkins and shared with Flanagan a vision of theatre that was of high quality, offered low admission prices, secured permanent employment for the workers, was decentralised and afforded the audience a functional, creative and participatory role.

Rice was excited to be working with the Living Newspaper format within the American context and saw in the project both a way of finding employment for jobless journalists and an original type of drama that would revive and electrify the American theatrical scene. Along with Rice, Arthur Arent was employed to work on the script; it was his first exposure to the Living Newspaper format, one that he would go on to develop further within the FTP with *Power* and *One-third of a Nation*. *Ethiopia* was scheduled to open at the Biltmore Theatre in late January 1936, four months after Mussolini's invasion of the country, with the admission price of 25 cents. The play's subject matter was chosen both because it was big news at the time but also because one of the first groups of actors sent by the relief office was an operatic company of African Americans who had been stranded in New York. According to Flanagan, originally, they were unsure how to use the company but decided they were to play the drums and act as native Ethiopians. She stressed that 'there was no caricature; the characterizations and quotations were as literal as we could make them'.[13] The play was dramatically exciting and instructive as it incorporated rhetoric, ritual and new forms of presentations. Its opening scene struck a chord with the audience; no actual speech from any of the main characters took place. Instead, they witnessed a group of Ethiopian soldiers going about their daily lives during the conflict.

> Teletype: WALWAL, ETHIOPIA, DEC. 5, 1934 ... ITALIANS, ETHIOPIANS. CLASH NEAR SOMALILAND FRONTIER: Ethiopian encampment at Walwal, flat terrain. It is the mid-day rest, soldiers in their white shammas are sprawled on the ground, eating, drinking, etc. A few musical instruments are seen on the ground. Soon the first few notes of a native song are heard, vague at first, then growing clearer as one instrument after another takes it up. It is a sad, keening sort air. The song mounts and soon a single plaintive voice is heard. The harmony picked up by all, pianissimo. Sharply the song ends, and without pause the players start a livelier tune. A soldier starts to dance. The song rises, the tumult increases. At its very apex a sudden shot is heard. All stop. The music dies. More shots, nearer and then the sharp rat-a-tat-tat of a machine gun. Pandemonium. The machine gun dies and in its place is heard the regular beat of rifle.[14]

The protagonist of the play becomes the common man, the Ethiopian. The audience witnesses the natives, listens to their voices, their songs, their music and their dance. It is presented in a new ritual that is foreign and has an almost mystical quality but at the same time speaks the universal language of music. The soldiers' ritual is abruptly interrupted by a shot, machine guns and then rifles. It is as if their song and dance are now substituted with the rhythmical beating of guns; the musicality of life and song is substituted with the musicality of death and weapons. The audience would have been keenly aware of the rise of Fascism in Europe and its expansionist plans for Africa; the opening scene of the play with this rhythmical juxtaposition would have heightened the sense of urgency in acknowledging and most likely acting against the new totalitarian ideology.

The following scenes quote the different views expressed in the League of Nations in Geneva, intercepted by Selassie and Mussolini's speeches in their corresponding parliaments. It also quotes the different economic sanctions taken against Italy, intercepting with scenes of killings of Ethiopian women and children. Lastly, they comment on the deal that Samuel Hoare and Pierre Laval achieved to end the war that caused uproar in Europe, particularly in Britain, as it satisfied Mussolini's goals, and led to the dissolution of the League of Nations and to Hoare's resignation. The play ends in a similar fashion to the first scene as the rhythmic beat of the war drums are heard over Europe (predicting the coming of World War II). The different figures, wearing uniforms of the countries they represent, are lit up by pin spots and blacked out once they finish. There is also a projection of marching feet and the tramp-sound they make is amplified on the sound system. The audience then, in quick succession, listens to the following:

> ENGLAND: Home Fleet in the Mediterranean!
> ITALY: 300,000 troops in Africa!
> ETHIOPIA: A rifle for every man!
> FRANCE: Half a million under arms!
> RUMANIA: More planes! Poland: More soldiers!
> JAPAN: More troops to China!
> GERMANY: More money for guns!
> RUSSIA: One million men in uniform!
> ENGLAND: Oil sanctions!
> ITALY: Sanctions mean war!
> ETHIOPIA: 200 killed today!
> FRANCE: France fights beside Britain!
> RUMANIA: Rumania backs France!
> POLAND: Re-arm!
> JAPAN: Naval Parity!
> GERMANY: Heil Hitler!
> RUSSIA: Down with Fascism!
> ENGLAND: Watch Italy!
> ITALY: Watch Britain!
> ETHIOPIA: Fight to the death!
> FRANCE: Watch Germany!
> RUMANIA: Be ready!
> POLAND: More bullets!
> JAPAN: Watch Russia!
> RUSSIA: Watch Japan!
> GERMANY: Der Tag!
> *The single word 'war' is passed right down the line, from England to Germany, the music blares out in a mounting climax, the feet tramp. Blackout.*[15]

The dramatic ending of the play alerted the audience to the complexities of the Italo-Ethiopian War and also to the worldwide implications that could affect their everyday life. The combination of factual material with new dramatic forms of presentation excited the audience and provided it with a clearer sense of understanding and realisation regarding its societal and political responsibilities. New paths of action were suddenly revealed and new opportunities of participation were granted through the new medium of the Living Newspaper.

Jacob Baker, one of Harry Hopkins's assistants, had major misgivings about the play, as expressed in a letter to Flanagan on 18 January 1936; in his amended reply on 23 January, he emphasised that 'no one impersonating a ruler or cabinet officer shall actually appear on the stage'.[16] Although Watson and Flanagan assured the government that the play contained carefully documented and factual material, did not caricature anyone and was politically unbiased, its material was deemed dangerous and its representation of any foreign politician was forbidden. Rice threatened to resign, should the project be cancelled, and in a final meeting with Baker he repeated his position. Baker, undeterred, presented Rice with his resignation statement that he had already prepared. Flanagan recalled how 'it was one of several occasions on the project when homicide would not have surprised me'.[17] The play never reached its audience and it was only performed once in front of employees, critics and reporters. Rice, having accused the previous day the government of playing 'the shabby game of partisan politics at the expense of freedom and the principles of democracy', commented at the end of the performance how 'to try to present a play called *Ethiopia* without presenting any of the chief officers, ministers to members of foreign governments is a lot like trying to put on a performance of *Hamlet* with the Melancholy Dane left out'.[18] The press was quick to pick up on the controversy surrounding the play and reacted widely the next day to the first censorship incident by the Democratic government. The most disturbing comment came from Brooks Atkinson, an American theatre critic for *The New York Times*, who commented that the cancellation of *Ethiopia* proved 'how utterly futile it is to expect the theatre to be anything more than a "sideshow" under government supervision'.[19] The *Ethiopia* incident revealed the uncomfortable and dubious relationship between the Living Newspaper unit, the government and WPA officials.

Rice's resignation shocked all involved with the Living Newspaper, as it signified that the unit was not free from governmental criticism and censorship when presenting controversial issues. At the same time, it offered some breathing space for Flanagan, who did not want the Federal Theatre to become a spokesperson for any political or ideological party. It was also welcomed by the WPA, since it occurred in connection with a production dealing with international politics rather than a more contentious one of domestic social and radical politics. For Flanagan, the *Ethiopia* incident also signified a shift as 'this now doubly cautious lady [speaking of herself] believed she must achieve a balance between "safe" plays and socially relevant plays if the project were to survive'.[20] However, with Rice's resignation, the attempt to produce another Living Newspaper called *South* was abandoned, as its theme was regarded as 'too hot'.[21] Flanagan had also previously condemned the script for

Money and disapproved of the script for another production entitled *Russia*, documenting Lenin's role within the Russian Revolution.[22] Rice's reaction to these rejections was fierce and he claimed that 'we are confronted here not only with an evidence of the growth of fascism which always uses censorship as one of its most effective weapons, but with the resolute determination of the Democratic Party to be re-elected at all costs'.[23] This first evidence of censorship by a democratically elected government, occurring simultaneously with the rise of Fascism in Germany, challenged the Federal Theatre's status as an autonomous and politically engaged theatre. It was not long before many artists shared Watson's views that the FTP should be divorced from the WPA, since

> so long as it is part of the WPA, it will be subject to petty and unfair attacks from those who see red in every letter of relief. Is it too much to ask that the Government grant a straight subsidy for something for which the community is hungry?[24]

Watson's concerns would later be fully realised, but for that moment and after the *Ethiopia* incident, it seemed that every Living Newspaper would be criticised for its proclamation of politics, whether domestic or international.

TRIPLE-A PLOWED UNDER AND INJUNCTION GRANTED

Philip Barber replaced Elmer Rice as the New York director (with Bill Farnsworth as his assistant) and the Living Newspaper unit, although shaken, continued its plans for new productions. The next two projects, *Triple-A Plowed Under* and *Injunction Granted*, established the FTP's international reputation for experimental theatre but, at the same time, were reminiscent of its capacity for controversy. Both productions were directed by Joseph Losey and Arthur Arent was their chief editor. Losey is an interesting case, as he was an important figure in 1930s New York political theatre, travelled to the Soviet Union in 1935, was instrumental as a theatre director in the first two years of the Living Newspaper's life, collaborated closely with Bertolt Brecht in 1946–7 on the staging of the American version of 'Galileo', and built a successful directing career in Hollywood before being blacklisted in the 1950s and spending the remainder of his career directing some commercially successful films in Europe. While in the Soviet Union, he met Meyerhold, went to his classes, saw *The Inspector General* and attended his rehearsals of *Camille*; he also met the people running the Vakhtangov Theatre, attended a cinema seminar with Eisenstein, and met Brecht and Hans Eisler. Losey also staged and directed an English version of Odets's *Waiting for Lefty* for a Moscow audience. But more importantly, he met and developed a close relationship with Nikolai Okhlopkov, whose experimentation with central stage – mingling stage with auditorium, creating runways and stairs adjustable for each production – produced a flexible, innovative theatre that influenced Losey and other contemporary directors and stage designers. Okhlopkov's influence can be observed on the staging of *Triple-A* but more predominantly in *Injunction Granted*, which can be construed as Losey's homage to Okhlopkov.

Triple-A Plowed Under (1936) presented, in twenty-six stylised scenes, the history of the agricultural depression up until the then recent invalidation of the New Deal's Agricultural Adjustment Act (AAA) by the Supreme Court. However, the curtain did not go up on this production without difficulties. Many veteran actors reacted to the documentary style of the production, as they felt it minimised their roles as performers. Furthermore, they disagreed with its theme, as they felt nobody in New York would be interested in farmers' lives. Rumours that the Federal Theatre Veteran League, a self-proclaimed group combating any Communist tendencies in the theatre, considered the play unpatriotic and planned to storm the performance and have it closed, reinforced the feeling that the play was too dangerous to be allowed on stage. Only after the intervention of both Flanagan and Barber, who gave reassurances of its success, did the play finally open on 14 March 1936.

The play's portrayal of the simplicity and honesty of the farmer–worker and the problems s/he went through during the 1920s and early 1930s was deeply effective. The audience witnessed the farmers' contribution during World War I, their unfair treatment after the end of the war when their mortgages were foreclosed and farms auctioned, the deliberate destruction of crops to keep prices up (while the unemployed were starving), the devastating effects of the 1934 drought, their organisation into cooperatives and the creation of the AAA. They also witnessed how the Supreme Court deemed the creation of the AAA unconstitutional and how the farmers, workers and unemployed decided that only by being united and organised could they contest the power of the middle man. In the opening scene, the Voice of the Living Newspaper (William Randolph Jr) announces the key historical cause of the farmers' contemporary problem; through the loudspeaker he calls '1917 – Inflation'.[25] The entire scene is played behind scrim; and the audience is faced with a crowd of soldiers marching up and down the ramps (their march creating a rhythmical beat similar to the one in *Ethiopia*) while a red spotlight highlights their action. As their marching grows louder, another spotlight flashes to reveal three speakers standing on a platform above the soldiers. A crowd of farmers, standing in shadow at stage level, is prodded by the speakers to increase production, 'Your country needs you', 'FARMER, SAVE THE WORLD'.[26] This first scene, reminiscent of Lord Kitchener's slogan, and its staging dramatises an already stratified class system in which the farmers (representing labour) stand at the lowest level of the social hierarchy; the speakers, on the other hand, representing the government, stand at the highest level, controlling the economics and shaping society. Scene two begins with the Voice of the Living Newspaper once again informing the audience of the facts: 'The 1920's. Deflation'. The farmer is left on his own to deal with the issue of over-production in peacetime and is forced to face foreclosure.[27]

Whereas the theme and dialogue of the play were quite simplistic, its stylistic theatrical representation caused a sensation. The stylised characters (representing classes rather than individuals as such), the use of projections, lighting and shadows, the visual documentation of events, the episodic treatment, the unforced didacticism and the agit-prop ending were unified organically and offered the audience a new theatrical experience. As the director Joseph Losey commented, in the play 'there were a lot of little vignettes. It was approaching a movie technique: parts on the stage on different levels were picked up by spots – like film cuts'.[28] Scene three is such an example; it begins again with the Voice of the Living Newspaper presenting in a factual manner the economic statistics relating to the years between 1920 and 1935. During these fifteen years, farm income falls by 5.5 billion dollars and unemployment rises to 7,578,000. To represent this economic snowball effect, Losey presents the impoverished farmer informing the car dealer that he is unable to buy the car ('I can't buy that auto'); he, in turn, informs the manufacturer that he cannot collect the new shipment ('I can't take that shipment'); and the latter informs his worker that he has to lay him off ('I can't use you any more'). He, in turn, declares that he cannot eat ('I can't eat'), signifying that he can no longer support the farmer.[29] It is not only the staccato repetition of the word 'can't' and the shortness of the exchanges that make the point more poignant. The stage directions very clearly instruct that all four spotlights are on all the actors at the beginning; each actor turns his head sharply to the left to deliver his line to the next one, and as soon as he finishes – on the count of one – the light goes out. It is only the worker, the last one standing, that speaks directly to the audience. And once he is done, lights out. In an almost didactic manner, reminiscent of Brecht's ending of *The Threepenny Opera*, Losey exposes the problems set out in the play and what follows is a further exposition of the farmers' plight.[30]

Scene sixteen, subtitled 'Drought', represents a climactic moment in the play. According to Losey, it is presented as a tableau scene, which begins with the Voice of the Living Newspaper announcing over the loudspeaker:

> Summer, 1934: Drought sears the Midwest, West, Southwest. (*Lights up center, upon a tableau of a FARMER examining the soil; a sun-baked plain, stretching away to a burning horizon. From the loudspeaker two voices are heard, one crisp, sharp, staccato; – the other sinister and foreboding. The VOICES are accompanied by a rhythmic musical procession that grows in intensity and leaps to a climax of shrill despair.*)
> FIRST VOICE (over loudspeaker): May first, Midwest weather report.

SECOND VOICE (over loudspeaker): Fair and warmer.
FIRST VOICE: May second, Midwest weather report.
SECOND VOICE: Fair and warmer.
FIRST VOICE: May third, Midwest weather report.
SECOND VOICE: Fair and warmer.
FIRST VOICE: May fourth, Midwest weather report.
SECOND VOICE: Fair and warmer. Fair and warmer. Fair and warmer. Fair and warmer.
(*The FARMER who is examining the soil straightens up, and slowly lets a handful of dry dust sift through his fingers*).
FARMER: Dust!³¹

Once the lights are up, the audience is faced with the lonely figure of a single farmer, representing his whole class, examining the soil on a sun-baked plain stretching to a burning horizon. Unlike in previous scenes, two voices are heard over the loudspeaker, one speaking in a staccato manner and the other in a foreboding manner. The repetition of their phrases regarding the weather and its immutability is accompanied by a musical procession that intensifies as the scene is acted out. These two voices, which dominate the scene, are juxtaposed by the arched figure of the farmer, whose first, only and final word in the scene merges his desperation with uncontrollable, unpredictable Nature. By using agit-prop techniques such as direct address and short dialogues to represent a specific reality, the scene offered a powerful representation of a reality that, up to that moment, the audience was uninformed of and paved the way for the solutions the play advocated.

With the AAA deemed unconstitutional by the Supreme Court (scene twenty-two) the play concludes in scene twenty-five that the solution needs to be two-fold: the first strategy is legislative, with the creation of a Soil Conservation Act that would offer similar benefits to the AAA but would be written within the Constitution and thus not exposed to the whims of any court. In this way, the crisis in American democracy that, for the past twenty-four scenes, the play has been arguing exists can be averted or at least rectified. The amoral political and economic tendencies and the 'middle man' would be eradicated. The second, and more partisan or politically explicit, strategy is the creation of a Farmer–Labor party that would protect the rights of farmers and workers. The play ends with a direct address to the audience and the repetition of the phrase 'We <u>need</u> you', first by a farmer and then by a chorus of farmers, and 'We need <u>you</u>' by an unemployed person and then a chorus of unemployed.³² The emphasis first on 'need' and then 'you' is purely agitational, and the inclusion of a tableau of farmers, women and unemployed on stage with their arms extended communicated very clearly the play's sociopolitical message, emphasising solidarity between the classes and reinforcing their belief in the democratic process. In this way, the play, for all its documentary and experimental techniques, incorporated an emotional component that generated a more empathetic response to the farmers' plight on the audience's part and a more sympathetic stance towards the New Deal policies.

Five weeks after the censorship of *Ethiopia*, *Triple-A* marked the official debut of the Living Newspaper in New York at the Biltmore Theatre on 14 March 1936. The stylistic representation of events and the play's montage staging encouraged André van Gyseghem to describe the play as 'typically Russian in creative imagery'.[33] The play was received well by the public; Norman Lloyd, who acted various roles in it, recalled that 'a lot of people who saw that show had never been to the theatre before . . . They would talk back to the Supreme Court justices . . . People felt very partisan about things in those days, they really participated.'[34] Richard Lockbridge commented how 'it is an engaging audience. Its face is not frozen, it is not sitting on its hands; when it hisses, it is not self-conscious, and when it cheers, it means it. It is young, lively and I suspect, hard up.'[35] And as *The New York Times* reviewer noticed, 'the fact that it [Washington] has given sanction to the showing of *Triple-A Plowed Under* must refute all arguments for the present that it is bent on stifling free speech'.[36] At the same time, though, it caused much controversy among politicians and some theatre critics. It was characterised as 'bearing a propaganda message' for the AAA, as being a representative of 'the flower of American Brain Trust Communism' and 'the most outrageous misuse of the taxpayers' money that the Roosevelt administration has yet been guilty of'.[37] None the less, the staging of *Triple-A* – which closed on 2 May 1936 – represented the acknowledgement of a new theatre technique that invigorated American theatre and put the Federal Theatre at the heart of American life.

These critics and politicians were not the least impressed by the Living Newspaper that followed *Triple-A Plowed Under*. *Injunction Granted*, written by the Living Newspaper staff under the guidance of Arthur Arent, supervised by Morris Watson and directed once more by Joseph Losey, was closer in both dramaturgy and tone to the American workers' theatre and the experimentations of Brecht, Meyerhold and the Blue Blouse. In *Triple-A Plowed Under*, the staging presentation of events carried a symbolic tone, as exemplified in the projection of the Preamble to the Declaration of Independence on a screen against coinciding shadows of the Founding Fathers, judges, politicians and nameless farmers (scene twenty-three, Figure 2.1). *Injunction Granted* is more editorially selective in the information used, while its twenty-eight scenes are longer and follow a historically progressive line. The stage is not simply seen as a space for presentation, as it allows – with its 'system of runways, platforms and hatches [. . .] [and] complicated lights' – each scene to converge in the finale's thematic intent.[38] At the same

Figure 2.1 *Triple-A Plowed Under*. Scene twenty-three. Directed by Joseph Losey. New York, 1936.

time, its use of farce and satire, and particularly its introduction of the figure of the Clown, are reminiscent of elements found both in a Blue Blouse performance and in Brecht's plays.

The play was a chronological presentation of labour history, from its negligible establishment to its biased treatment by the American courts (quoting actual cases) and to the final formation of the Congress of Industrial Organizations (CIO). The title derives from the phrase that American judges used countlessly when ruling against any group of workers trying to form labour unions. For Arent, who supervised its writing, this particular play represented 'a militantly pro-labor account of the working man's fight for liberation through unionization'.[39] Although Arent's comment was not totally amiss, he seems to have completely disregarded the progressive political awareness and growing class consciousness that the audience experienced through the progression of the play. In scene twelve, the audience observes the discussion two workers have during their lunch break, as they try to understand what constitutes an injunction, and how it happens and why. In Brechtian didactic style, the dialogue is comprised mostly of a series of questions and answers. From this short scene, the audience learns that an injunction can prevent a worker from striking, complaining, publishing or even praying. To one of the workers' amusement that praying is not against the law, the other replies:

> FIRST WORKER: But a court order must be obeyed.
> SECOND WORKER: And if it isn't?
> FIRST WORKER: You go to jail.
> SECOND WORKER: What if the judge is wrong?
> FIRST WORKER: He can't be wrong.
> SECOND WORKER: Where is the jury?
> FIRST WORKER: There is no jury.
> SECOND WORKER: The bill of rights says – (*Second worker rises*)
> FIRST WORKER: . . . that nothing shall deprive a man of life, liberty or property without due process of law.
> SECOND WORKER: But if there is no trial by jury –
> FIRST WORKER: *shrugs*) The courts consider an injunction due process.
> SECOND WORKER: How does one get an injunction? (*Sits down again, and continues to eat his lunch*).
> FIRST WORKER: He asks for it, and the court issues it.
> SECOND WORKER: Without a hearing?
> FIRST WORKER: Most times, yes. The court issues a temporary injunction and orders the hearing before considering a permanent injunction.
> SECOND WORKER: (*rises and closes lunch box*). Then, there is a hearing.
> FIRST WORKER: If it's a strike, it's been broken.
> SECOND WORKER: You mean to tell me that an employer can get a court to issue an injunction without notice and without a hearing.
> FIRST WORKER: Without notice, and without a hearing. (FIRST WORKER *rises*)
> SECOND WORKER: And, if the injunction is disobeyed, the violator goes to jail for contempt?
> FIRST WORKER: Yes.
> SECOND WORKER: Without trial by jury?
> FIRST WORKER: Without trial by jury.
> *Blackout*[40]

The dialogue between the two workers is fast; the sentences are short and repetitive. When acted out, they follow a specific tempo, a specific rhythm that invites the audience to pay attention to the information provided. By having two workers analysing what an injunction is and how it works, the audience has access to legal knowledge provided in simpler terms. At the same time, it can perceive more clearly the discrepancies between the liberties that the American Constitution and Bill of Rights have afforded it for years and the way courts can manipulate, bypass or reinterpret the law to befit certain business interests. The absurdity of this situation is continued in scene thirteen, in which different employers, with their respective lawyers, queue up in front of a judge and take up injunctions against their workers. The judge's smack of the gavel every time he grants one is picked up by the orchestra, which repeats it with a drumbeat. Similar, then, to *Triple-A*, the repetition of the beat reinforces the judge's compliance with business interests and his indifference towards the working class. As the figure of the Clown very satirically comments with a sign at the end of the scene, '*The Interests of the Workingman are not affected . . . Grimm's Fairy Tales.*'[41]

One very interesting addition to the structure of *Injunction Granted* was the use of the muted clown figure (on top of the Voice of the Living Newspaper) as a mediator and visual commentator on the action. The clown figure was improvised during rehearsals and was acted by Norman Lloyd. The muted clown was based on the character of Harpo Marx; he was wearing tennis shoes, a long, wide-sleeved jacket and patched trousers.[42] The Clown hit himself over his head with a diploma at the end of the Principals' speeches that glorify industrialisation, progress, education and American expansion (scenes twelve and eighteen). He wore placards commenting on the event taking place (scene fourteen) and mocked real characters (scene fifteen and scene twenty-three, in which he entered with a blue eagle mounted on a stand, covered with a hood; when he unveiled it, he revealed a caricature of General Hugh Johnson mounted on the blue eagle). He blew horns and balloons in disapproval of what a character proclaimed (scene eighteen), orchestrated the applause in the battle between capital and labour like a conductor (scene eighteen, Figure 2.2), stroked them with a slapstick (scene twenty-four) or presented them with questionable gifts (scene eighteen, in which he gives John Rockefeller Jr with a large dime and Howard Heinz a large pickle). The figure of the clown reinforced the satirical and farcical elements of *Injunction Granted* (for example, at the end of scene nineteen, after their speeches, Heinz and Rockefeller lock arms, turn their backs to the audience and bow; at the sound of music they dance cheerfully off the stage) and, as Goldman commented, it approached 'the caricature aspects of certain agitprop and satirical cabaret sketches'.[43]

The reverberation of the phrase 'Injunction granted!' in every court openly ridiculed the judicial process. The solutions offered were again two-fold. Firstly, there ought to be proper social legislation; it was initially the Guffey Act, to regulate the price of coal and provide for collective bargaining, that was immediately dismissed as unconstitutional. And then there was the Wagner Act or the National Labor Relations Act, which obliged employers to bargain with representatives of their employees to guarantee a free flow of interstate commerce; once again, this was deemed unconstitutional.[44] The second solution was, similarly to *Triple-A*, the creation of a union. Twelve unions of the

Figure 2.2 *Injunction Granted*. Scene eighteen. Directed by Joseph Losey. New York, 1936.

American Federation of Labor formed the CIO, headed by John L. Lewis. The play ends with his speech, a call to arms:

> My voice is the voice of millions of men and women employed in America's industries, heretofore unorganized, economically exploited and inarticulate. These unions, comprising the Congress of Industrial Organizations, adequately reflect the sentiment, hopes and aspiration of thirty million additional Americans who heretofore have been denied by industry and finance the privilege of collective organization. This statement issued by the Iron and Steel Institute is designed to be terrifying to the minds of those who fail to accept the theory and the financial interests behind the steel corporations shall be regarded as the overlords of industrial America. That statement amounts to a declaration of industrial and civil war. It contravenes the law. It pledges the vast resources of the industry against the right of its workers to engage in self-organization of modern collective bargaining. Organized labor in America accepts the challenge of the overlords of steel (*At the word 'challenge' all signs are lifted up*).[45]

The stage is filled with workers, women and unemployed, who hold placards celebrating or pledging allegiance to the CIO (Figure 2.3); Lewis presents

Figure 2.3 *Injunction Granted*. Directed by Joseph Losey. New York, 1936.

himself and his voice as the representative unified voice of the millions of men and women working in American industries. His strongly worded statement sounds like a call to arms and places the workers in direct opposition to the capital controlling their lives and the economy. For a committed Marxist such as Losey, though, what sits uncomfortably is his (and Arent's) interpretation of the class struggle issue. They do not advocate a revolution per se. Instead, the solution to the problem, it is suggested, can come only through the constitutional voice of the law and the New Deal reforms; as one of the characters in the play cries out, 'I tell you, what we need is a law!'[46] Nowhere is the word 'revolution', understood in Marxist terms, ever uttered. And the dialectics of class struggle are rewritten within the liberal discourse of the New Deal. As Losey himself admitted many years later, he and others (probably Arent and Watson) 'were very far from making total ideological commitments, but we did make humanitarian and idealistic ones'.[47]

What Losey compromised politically, he tried to make up artistically. For him, this play represented an ideal opportunity to materialise stylistically what he had learned and witnessed during his trip to Moscow in 1935. While there, he had met Meyerhold, had long discussions with Brecht and witnessed

Figure 2.4 *Injunction Granted*. New York, 1936. The play's set design. The use of platforms, runways and steps shows the influence of Okhlopkov and Meyerhold.

Okhlopkov's experimentation with the use of space. Losey commented on how Okhlopkov 'had a completely flexible theatre which was something I had always dreamt of', and claimed that although it was a collective effort, the development of the performance's style was designed primarily by him and Arent.[48] Losey's staging brought together elements used in European theatre and American folklore. The stage had an element of plasticity to it, reminiscent of Okhlopkov's experimentation, in an attempt to create a fluid stage area. There were runways and platforms that created ten areas where action could take place and which would be selected by lighting (Figure 2.4). For Losey, it was important to create a continuity among all the scenes; thus, while a scene was being acted and highlighted by spotlights, the rest of the stage remained dark with the actors still on stage. This flow of scenes created some extraordinary tableau moments that the audience would have found unusually fresh and exciting, and, by the end of the performance, it would have been able to link all the events it witnessed.[49]

Losey also employed projected headlines and placards either held by the characters or worn by them (Figure 2.5). In this way, techniques associated with a written newspaper were used in a new way to clarify or exemplify events and people related to the action. Losey cleverly brought together all these new experimental forms and used them in such a way that the audience

Figure 2.5 *Injunction Granted*. Directed by Joseph Losey. New York, 1936. Norman Lloyd as the mute clown.

did not merely feel that they were spectators but became active players in the happenings on stage. This unity of design, of amalgamating formal elements with the content of the play, was very important and reminiscent of European avant-garde drama; it was soon lost, however, especially after Losey's departure from the FTP, as content and techniques became separate entities, exemplified by the *One-third of a Nation* Living Newspaper discussed in the next chapter.

Losey and Watson's conscious decision to use comedy and satire to deal with the contentious issue of labour unionisation and uncover the fallacies of the New Deal patronage and the more open endorsement of the CIO did not go down well with the WPA, or with politicians, critics and Flanagan herself. Barber and Farnsworth, after attending a rehearsal, objected strongly to the tone of the play and advised Flanagan to consider cancelling it, despite its highly experimental theatrical scenes and the quality of the acting. Flanagan initially wrote to Losey and Watson, and asked them to 'clean up the script and make it more objective', but both of them disregarded her.[50] After the play's opening night performance, on 24 July 1936, though, Flanagan was so enraged by the production that she wrote a lengthy and angry letter to both men. In it she commented how

1) The production seems to me special pleading, biased, an editorial, not a news issue. (Witness the one-sided treatment of the C.I.O. rally; the voice reading Hoover; the scene showing judges asleep, etc., etc.) Whatever my personal sympathies are I cannot, as custodian of federal funds, have such funds used as a party tool. That goes for the communist party as well as the Democratic Party. To show the history of labor in the courts is appropriate; to load that document at every turn with insinuation is not appropriate.
2) The production, in my opinion, lacks a proper climax, falling back on the old cliché of calling labor to unite in the approved agit-prop manner [...]
3) ... [The] production uses too many devices, too much hysteria in acting ...
4) The production is historical drama and hence, by reason of comprehension, is open to the charge of superficiality. I think we should consider whether history should not rather be used, as it is in *Triple-A*, to illuminate the present, not lead up to it in the chronological manner.[51]

Flanagan's reservations and fierce reaction were primarily a result of her role as director of the whole FTP, and secondly, of her own aesthetics of politically engaged theatre. Flanagan had already experienced the power of censorship and, at the same time, was aware of her responsibilities towards all the artists the project employed. She was made aware, from early on, that many conservative senators did not approve of Roosevelt's plans and the FTP would be among the first projects to be scrutinised for both its finances and its performances. The fact that *Injunction Granted* attacked politicians in such a personalised and satirical way met with Flanagan's opposition. At the same time, her previous status as a director enabled her to express some criticism of the aesthetics of the play. She had already claimed that 'this consciousness that we are part of the economic life of America, that we are one with the worker on the stage and in the audience is the very core of the Federal Theatre'.[52] For Flanagan, each worker needed to be made aware of the labour movement but the play failed to present the struggle of the working class and instead resorted to an anachronistic historical approach and presentation of its subject. Whereas *Triple-A Plowed Under* ended with repetition of the phrase 'We need you', asking the audience to support the new Farmer–Labor Party and thus initiate a process of solidarity, *Injunction Granted* ended with an invitation to the audience to endorse the CIO, engage in self-organisation and stand up to the existing plutocrats. The challenge that this performance presented, in terms of formal experimentations, presentation and social mobility, was one that Flanagan did not want to take up.

Her fears concerning the production were not unfounded, as very soon it was unfavourably reviewed by critics of the daily newspapers, especially since the play included a direct quotation from Earl Browder, leader of the Communist Party in the United States. One of the first to comment on the play was Brooks Atkinson, who suggested that 'the Moscow stylisation ... has been adopted', thus supporting Flanagan's view of Losey and Watson as both aesthetically and politically biased.[53] Losey's past association with the Communist Party theatre groups, his influential trip to the Soviet Union and his appropriation of modern revolutionary techniques made him an easy target for political criticism. Watson, on the other hand, was a well-known union activist and his close collaboration with Losey seemed to portray the Living Newspaper unit as a political sympathiser with Communism. As both rejected Flanagan's pleas for a revision of the play's content, more negative criticism sprang up. Granville Vernon denounced the play, since 'as propaganda it has no place in the taxpayers' theatre, and as art it has no place in the theatre at all'.[54]

Unlike *Triple-A Plowed Under*, which was dismissed as a 'pink play', *Injunction Granted* was portrayed as a 'red play'. Flanagan, aware that the negative criticism was intensifying and the controversy over *Ethiopia* was still fresh in people's mind, was eager to suppress any immediate association of the Living Newspaper with revolutionary Communism, especially since her appointment as national director of the whole project was not unanimous. She was openly criticised during a hearing in the Senate, when Senator James J. Davis voiced his disapproval of the WPA's decision to allow 'money meant for relief to be spent by a woman infatuated by the Russian Theatre and the U.S.S.R'.[55] Faced with such hostility, and in a last attempt to salvage the reputation of the Living Newspaper, Flanagan wrote another letter to Watson and Losey, denouncing the production as 'old-fashioned Union Square shouting' and emphasising that 'I will not have the Federal Theatre Project used politically. I will not have it used to further the ends of the Democratic Party, the Republican Party or the Communist Party.'[56] Pressured by both internal and external criticism and despite the support received from audiences and unions, *Injunction Granted* was closed prematurely in October 1936. The Living Newspaper suffered another blow as Losey resigned in protest against this decision and the unit lost a director with theatrical vision. As Losey commented,

> I broke with the Living Newspaper over the withdrawal of *Injunction Granted*. I was not fired and at no time was I under any pressure from Morris Watson. I was under considerable pressure from Flanagan and Barber which was disagreeable . . . Flanagan found my political militancy increasingly inconvenient.[57]

Years later, he still maintained that the play was arbitrarily stopped because of political reasons (in opposition to what Flanagan has argued in *Arena*). The freedom to develop the form, content and style of the Living Newspaper as they had been in *Injunction Granted* was taken away, unless one was willing to stay firmly within the New Deal cultural politics.

The four months between the closing of this production and the opening of the next Living Newspaper, *Power*, proved difficult for the unit, since it was faced with cuts in its budget, failed to attract paying customers and had to reject bookings from trade unions wanting to see *Injunction Granted*. The first two years of the Living Newspaper's existence were also marked by constant controversy between the creative staff and the administration of the FTP and WPA. Flanagan had repeatedly requested that playwrights produce plays that would encompass the changing society and any social, political and economically unresolved issues, and thus give a voice to unrepresented social groups. She also believed in Hopkins's claim that the FTP would be free and uncensored, hoping that, under those conditions, a new theatre would be created on its own terms, which would address not only the professionally trained spectators, but a 'vast new audience'.[58] However, her reaction to the productions of *Triple-A Plowed Under* and *Injunction Granted* voiced the awkward relationship between a politically engaged theatre and its federal patronage. This awkward relationship was not simply the result of the 'inherent' discrepancy between the FTP's relief status and its theatrical evolution, as Mathews has suggested.[59] It was also the result of the administration's unwillingness to acknowledge and tolerate a narrative discourse that did not comply with that of the liberal New Deal. As a result, the Living Newspaper and the FTP were faced with censorship, the very thing that Hopkins had pledged would never occur in the democratic American arena.

More Troubles for the FTP: *The Cradle Will Rock*

Triple-A Plowed Under and *Injunction Granted* were not the only cases that caused trouble for the FTP, and for Hopkins and Flanagan. To the relief of the WPA, two further Living Newspapers, one with the working title *War and Taxes* and the other concerning the socialisation of medicine (which reached the stage in 1940 in an altered form and with the title *Medicine*), were never performed. The main issue, however, arose in 1937 with the production of Marc Blitzstein's opera *The Cradle Will Rock*. The original idea for the play, named *Sketch No. 1*, was conceived in 1935; it involved Jane (a prostitute), her Pimp, a Gent and a Cop. Dealing with the issue of prostitution, the sketch was also a parable about capitalism, with Jane unable to negotiate a proper wage and falling victim to the predatory conditions. The music was a ground-breaking synthesis of different styles, ranging from blues, to jazz, to Stravinsky, Eisler and Kurt Weill, whom Blitzstein deeply admired.[60] Blitzstein was a huge fan of Brecht and Weill's *The Threepenny Opera* and wanted to produce something similar for the American stage. When, in late 1935, he was given the opportunity to perform *Sketch No. 1* in front of Brecht, he did not hesitate. According to his recollection, Brecht asked him,

> Why don't you expand this? In our society, prostitution can involve many more things than just our lily white bodies. There is prostitution for gain in so many walks of life: the artist, the preacher, the doctor, the lawyer, the newspaper editor. Why don't you pit them against this scene of literal selling?

Blitzstein soon after told Minna Lederman, 'I've taken up his [Brecht's] idea and am making an opera of it,' and ultimately dedicated the resultant work, *The Cradle Will Rock* (Figure 2.6) to Brecht, 'since it was his ideas which impressed and influenced me so deeply'.[61]

The opera was revised several times before its final script and score, consisting of ten scenes (Blitzstein called them sketches), was ready in 1937. Blitzstein had discussed his play with Orson Welles and John Houseman, the two accomplished directors and producers of Project 891, an independent unit funded by the FTP, which presented new and experimental productions of classical drama and canonical plays at the elegant 934–seat Maxine Elliott's Theatre at 39th and Broadway. The play was set in the fictitious city of Steel Town USA, dealing with the real political confrontation between the CIO and Bethlehem Steel Corporation, and employing a very sarcastic and witty tone. Its caricature of capitalists (like the character of Mr Mister), policemen, the clergy, doctors and even university professors, and its sympathetic depiction of heroic union agitators, workers and the prostitute with a heart of gold, now called Moll, emerged as a critical representation of

Figure 2.6 *The Cradle Will Rock*. New York, 1937.
Marc Blitzstein with the cast in rehearsal.

American society. Welles and Houseman wanted the play for the FTP, and when Flanagan heard the opera's score, dramatised by Blitzstein himself, she agreed unconditionally. She commented that 'it took no wizardry to see that this was not a play set to music, nor music illustrated by actors, but music + play equalling something new and better than either.'[62] Although Blitzstein intended the play to be an allegory, its main issues became more topical as rehearsals progressed. The Steel Workers Organizing Committee was successfully persuading the labour force of U.S. Steel to join the CIO and strikes sprang up around the country, resulting in the injury and death of many strikers in clashes with the police.

Blitzstein, in a similar way to Brecht and Weill's opera, used his play to focus on the plight of the lower middle class, to try to awaken them to their status within the confines of liberal capitalism. As he claimed,

> What I really wanted to talk about was the middleclass. Unions, unionism as a subject, are used as a symbol of something in the way of a solution for the plight of that middleclass. I mean the intellectuals, professional, small shop-keepers, 'little businessmen' in the America of today. What can they do? Where does their allegiance lie? With big

business, which is ready to engulf them, buy and sell them out exactly as it does labor, exploit and discard them at will, as a sort of useful but inferior commodity? The play shows various degradations suffered by the middleclass – some of them funny, some of them less funny – and offers a possible solution: which seems to me to be the only chance for dignity, for survival in fact. The middleclass must sooner or later see that there can be allegiance only to the future, not the past; that the only sound loyalty is the concept of work, and to a principle which makes honest work at least true, good and beautiful.[63]

The play was able to achieve its goals because of the ingenious way in which Blitzstein combined his new take on music within an operatic environment with a formal means of presentation that complemented the compelling content. The play's overall structure is indebted to the Blue Blouse agit-prop theatre and previous Living Newspapers, and to the musical theatre of Brecht and Weill. It employed the use of flashbacks (reinforcing the Brechtian principle of estrangement), while its integration of dramatic narrative with music pointed at the Brecht–Weill notion of Gestus in music.[64] But it was its combination of traditional techniques, such as operatic narrative, song, chorus, dialogue and instrumental music, with novel ones, such as speech-song and accented rhythmic recitation (accompanied and unaccompanied), including harsh dissonances and chords, that represented a unique accomplishment and offered a new way of performing opera that was more accessible to a larger audience and defied expectations. As Blitzstein himself argued, 'The use of music is casual; I have tried to make it almost impossible for an audience to be conscious of exactly when music has entered the proceedings, and when it has departed.'[65]

A formidable example of this is provided by the song entitled 'Honolulu', which is included in sketch four. The action takes place on the lawn of Mr Mister's home, where his children – Junior and Sister Mister – lounge on their hammocks. Junior is described as 'sluggish, collegiate and vacant; SISTER is smartly gotten-up and peevish'.[66] The audience listens to the two siblings ridiculing their vacuous middle-class values without realising it in the 'Croon Spoon' song; this is followed by 'The Freedom of the Press', in which their dad, Mr Mister, and Editor Daily comment on the receptiveness of the press to 'fit to print' for whichever side will pay the best.[67] At the end of the song, the music stops and in spoken dialogue Editor Daily agrees with his new boss that Junior 'doesn't go so well with union trouble', at which point Junior and Sister Mister enter the stage, singing a jazzy tune, 'Let's Do Something', and dancing in a frenzied manner.[68] The 'something' that Junior can do is go to Honolulu; the island is depicted as a paradise, in which Junior will be required to do minimal work and thus conquer his boredom. The exchange that follows further exposes the absurdity witnessed so far as Junior questions whether the women there are nice – 'I don't care if they're high born/Just as long as they are high breasted' – to which Mr Mister rhymes, 'Junior, please don't get arrested!' Unable to spell 'Honolulu' (till all remaining characters whisper it to him) but just like that, Junior becomes a journalist.[69] Blitzstein is able to elicit laughter from the dialogue but also highlight a deeper social message because of the way he transforms a popular song form by disrupting the pervasive eight-measure phrase (he used seven) to acknowledge the convention but at the same time criticise and defy it. As he himself commented, 'sometimes the music cooperates with the action, as when Junior's proposed trip to Honolulu is underpinned by some of the tritest Hula Hula music ever heard. Sometimes the music exposes a meaning which the words don't touch at all.'[70]

Having produced *Dr Faustus* so successfully, Welles and Houseman hoped to follow it with an equally successful production of *The Cradle Will Rock*. The FTP had already been singled out by conservative members of Congress as epitomising a waste of government resources and being a representative of the liberal bias of the whole WPA. As mentioned earlier, Flanagan was very excited about the play but was equally aware of the negative views of the FTP coming out of Washington. As John Houseman reflected in his memoirs, '[she] realised, better than her more timid colleagues, that in the storm into which the Arts Projects were headed, there was no safety in prudence and no virtue in caution'.[71] Rehearsals began on 29 March and the opera was due to open on 15 May. Members of the cast, picked out by Welles and Houseman in person, included Will Geer as Mr Mister, Howard Da Silva as Larry Foreman, Olive Stanton as Moll, Guido Alexander as Dick and Bert Weston as Editor Daily, to name but a few. An interracial chorus of thirty-two was also employed, as well as the all-important orchestra. Houseman and Welles ultimately decided not to hold a preview until 16 June, with a dress rehearsal the day before and an official premiere at the end of the month. Against Flanagan's advice, Welles, in collaboration with Edwin Schruers, designed an elaborate stage which involved 'narrow, glass-bottomed florescent platforms, loaded with scenery and props [that] slid smoothly past each other as the scene shifted [. . .] [It was] somewhere between realism, vaudeville and oratory.'[72]

The rehearsals occurred simultaneously with rumours of cuts to the FTP personnel, which were realised on 10 June, when Flanagan received instructions to reduce the New York project's staff by 30 per cent. She was also instructed to delay the opening night of any new productions until after the beginning of the new financial year on 1 July 1937. Such a decision clearly affected the scheduled June preview of *The Cradle Will Rock*, especially since the WPA viewed the play as politically explosive and biased. Some 14,000 tickets had already been sold for nineteen preview performances. Flanagan, with the help of Archibald MacLeish and Virgil Thompson, attempted to persuade the WPA to allow the production to go ahead, but was unable to reverse the decision; as Flanagan later commented, the restriction imposed on new productions was 'obviously censorship under a different guise'.[73] Welles and Houseman found the Maxine Elliott Theatre locked and guarded by the police, and were unable to access the production's costumes, scenery and props. They started looking for another venue in which to perform and Welles proposed that the cast could speak and sing their lines from the audience, thus not risking losing their WPA jobs. While all these events were taking place, much of the night's audience had already gathered outside the Maxine Elliott theatre in anticipation of the premiere.

Defying the orders of the WPA, Welles instructed the crowd to proceed to the old Venice Theatre, which had been rented after some frantic phone calls. This single performance of *The Cradle Will Rock* remains memorable, not simply for its defiance of censorship, but for its enthusiastic reception by the audience.[74] The only prop on stage was a piano, along with Blitzstein playing and performing. The original cast was scattered in the audience and was prohibited from participating in an unauthorised production following orders from Equity. However, as Blitzstein started playing the prostitute's song, Olive Stanton stood up and started singing; many other actors who had decided to defy Equity's order also joined her on stage. Houseman, years later, commented on how

> it must have taken almost superhuman courage for an inexperienced performer ... to stand up before two thousand people, all in ill-placed and terribly exposed location, and start a show with a difficult song to the accompaniment of a piano that was more than fifty feet away.[75]

This 'forced' method of presentation, with the actors progressing to the stage through the audience and the audience's active participation (cheering or mocking the characters), bore a close resemblance to the more agit-prop presentation of a Blue Blouse performance. However, the play's emphatic working-class politics appalled both the WPA and the middle-class Americans, who could not accept the function of the theatrical space as a *topos* where the legitimisation of the working-class struggle could materialise.

Early reviews of the play were mostly positive. Brooks Atkinson, in his rave review, suggested that it was the best 'thing militant labor has put into a theatre yet', with Blitzstein transmuting the industry versus union story 'into a remarkably stirring marching song by the bitterness of his satire, the savagery of his music and the ingenuity of his craftmanship', the finale rocking a great many things, including the audience.[76] Not pulling any punches, Atkinson exposed the embarrassment of the FTP as the incident surrounding the play provided proof 'that a theatre supported by government funds cannot be a free agent when art has an insurgent political motive'.[77] Although criticising its end as 'hokum' and a 'fairy tale', Virgil Thomson agreed that '*The Cradle* was still a good show and its musical quality hasn't worn thin [. . .] it was the most appealing operatic socialism since *Louise*.'[78] Edith Isaacs argued that 'the work introduces a persuasive new theatre form' but George Jane Nathan savagely commented that it 'was little more than the kind of thing Cole Porter might have written if, God Forbid, he had gone to Columbia instead of Yale'.[79]

What started as an exciting new project for the FTP, and for Flanagan personally, turned into a private enterprise and a personal defeat. With Washington still adamant that it would not stage the play, Welles threatened to continue its performance privately. He met up with David Niles, who, when faced with Welles's threat, replied that the government would no longer be interested in it as a property. Flanagan was saddened by such a development, as not only would she lose her most imaginative director and producer, but also this felt like a repeat of the *Ethiopia* incident all over again. The play she had championed and was so looking forward to seeing on stage was a successful venture, but not for her or the FTP as a whole. Instead, the events around *The Cradle* marked a turning point for government-sponsored theatre; in John Houseman's words, 'the honeymoon of the New Deal and the Theatre was over'.[80]

The events surrounding the productions of *Triple-A Plowed Under*, *Injunction Granted* and *The Cradle Will Rock* indicated that the American Democratic administration, its middle-class voters and the established Broadway stage could not tolerate the form of the Living Newspaper as a socially and politically agitational drama. The aforementioned productions offended the political sensibilities of the WPA and politicians from both ends of the spectrum but, as Flanagan anticipated, they offered pleasure to audiences that could appreciate their political satire and whose social struggle was represented on stage. None the less, two further Living Newspapers, *Power* and *One-third of a Nation*, discussed in the following chapter, represented a change in the Living Newspaper's dramatic form, as its agit-prop influence diminished and its discourse became more ideologically associated with the politics of the New Deal. In terms of formal experimentation, this change did not signify a rejection of its progressive objectives, as it still proposed social change and justice. But as Cosgrove argues, 'it had forsaken its revolutionary heritage in favour of the political expediency of social reformism'.[81] What this shift represented was not only Flanagan's desire to produce 'safer' plays that would not rely so exclusively on political agitation and 'leftist' political ideology, but also the fact that liberalism (both politically and culturally) was ultimately embedded within the theatrical aesthetics of American artists.

Liberalism occupies a very complex position within political theory and this book's purpose is not to examine it in relation to the FTP or the overall political situation in the USA at the time. But a few words are necessary to explain how the term will be used and should be read within the premises of this study. I approach the term liberalism as part of the American liberal democracy's cultural discourse to counteract the influence and prevalence of the Communist/Socialist one proposed by the American left. Identified more closely with middle-class values (as opposed to working-class sensibilities), liberalism fosters a sensibility acquitted of any ideological and cultural constraints identified with leftist inklings. At the same time, it forms part of the idea of American exceptionalism, as it promotes a uniquely American approach to social, economic and cultural matters. Seen in this way, liberalism greatly influenced the future theatrical productions of the Living Newspaper unit and it certainly had an impact on how certain members of the audience – as well as politicians – approached the FTP in general.

3

THE LIVING NEWSPAPER PART 2: 1937–1939 – HOW NOT TO SING FOR YOUR SUPPER

> The audience was fresh. It was eager. To anyone who saw it night after night as we did, it was not the Broadway crowd ... one had the feeling every night, that here were people on a voyage of discovery in the theatre.[1]
>
> Orson Welles, as quoted in John O'Connor, 'The Federal Theatre Project's Search for an Audience'.

'A People's Theatre': The Creation of a New Audience

Brooks Atkinson had commented that, culturally, American society had never moved beyond the nineteenth-century view of art as a respectable activity that rich people can enjoy and sponsor; because of the persistence of such views 'art has not yet been absorbed into the democratic way of life'.[2] Atkinson's comment revealed an aspect of American culture that Flanagan, Hopkins and Arent aspired to challenge. Inherent in the American dream's faith in the nation's economic and social betterment was the idea of the cultural enrichment of the people. This cultural enrichment would not be restricted to the affluent classes but would encompass the most deprived masses. By fusing together elements associated with 'high' art and folklore tradition, the Federal Theatre proclaimed its adoption of the politics and aesthetics of the New Deal's cultural democracy. Its desire to create a theatre 'national in scope, regional in emphasis and American in democratic attitudes' reflected this faith.[3] Adopting the term the 'People's Theatre' and both the public and the government as its new patrons, the FTP challenged the presence of a hegemonic literary elite (subsidising Broadway and Hollywood) and acknowledged that its strength rested with the problems caused by the social and economic distress of the Depression era and experienced by the majority of people.

As discussed in Chapter 2, the first two years of the Living Newspaper's existence revealed a conscious exploration of socially and politically sensitive subjects, experimentation with performative elements and the inclusion of the under-represented classes that, although enthusiastically received by the public, caused much distress to both the FTP and the WPA administrations and to their governmental patron. Near the end of 1937, and after having suffered a cut of 30 per cent of their New York personnel, Flanagan, Barber, Hopkins and Arent realised that two things had to change. Firstly, they needed to re-address the issue of the audience; up to that moment, it was the lower classes that were aptly represented in the Living Newspaper's productions and filled the theatres. It was time to make theatre relevant to the middle class, by awakening it to the social conditioning of the working class, especially since the middle class could form part of its public patronage. Secondly, they had to reject the more militant and agitational character of the previous performances and endorse the aspirations of the New Deal programme, which served as its second and financially most important patron. These two changes influenced the dramatic form of the Living Newspaper, its autonomous status as a politically uncensored genre and the ways in which it could engage with current social problems. Seldes's observation that the theatre's new patrons (the public and the government) would eventually make demands that the artist had to meet was very soon realised and the FTP's adjustment to those demands denied the Living Newspaper its exciting avant-garde character.[4]

By referring to itself as a people's theatre, without, however, clearly defining who the people were, the FTP seemed to include all the groups excluded by Broadway, such as people from rural communities, workers, children, blacks and foreign-language speakers. All these groups then served as important constituents in its attempt to establish itself as the new national theatre. Labour organisations constituted the largest percentage of the FTP's audience, since their struggle was so vividly represented on stage. However, after the first two years, the FTP consciously reduced the tickets available to such organisations, especially after being criticised for promoting Communism and revolution.

In trying to address the middle class, the FTP was influence by Kenneth Burke. In his address to the first American Writers' Congress in 1935, Burke confronted his audience with the structure of an American society that was engulfed by a desire for commodity consumption by 'our economic mercenaries' and questioned whether 'the symbol of the worker [is] accurately attuned to us'.[5] Burke found the symbol of the worker inadequate and negative, and proposed the more positive one of 'the people'.

> In suggesting that 'the people' rather than the worker, rate higher in our hierarchy of symbols, I suppose I am suggesting fundamentally that one cannot extend the doctrine of revolutionary thought among the lower middle class without using middle-class values [. . .] I think the term 'the people' is closer to our folkways than is the corresponding term, 'the masses', both in spontaneous popular usage and as stimulated by our political demagogues.[6]

Burke's proposal signified a change in the American intellectuals' approach to the class struggle. Burke alleged that the term 'people' was more inclusive and embraced plurality, as it contained the *'ideal*, the ultimate *classless* feature', offered a unity that the already politically defined class of workers could not and served as a more powerful symbol of commitment.[7] Through the appropriation of middle-class values within the symbol of the 'people', Burke seemed to advocate the obliteration of class boundaries, especially since this obliteration would allow the intellectual's political alignment to be infused with broader cultural elements, thus giving access to a broader audience. Burke went on to comment that

> In the last analysis, art strains towards *universalization*. It tends to overleap imaginatively the class divisions of the moment and go after modes of thought that would apply to a society freed of class divisions. It seeks to consider the problems of *man*, not of *classes of men*.[8]

He acknowledged that the emphasis on the universal symbol of man instead of classes of men was resonant with his class ('the petty bourgeois'), but strongly believed that only through this process could the American intellectual and writer approach the complex structure of propagandistic writing; by employing the symbol of the 'people' he could conduct 'propaganda by inclusion' (unlike the symbol of the proletarian, which suggested propaganda by exclusion) and thus 'propagandize his cause with as full a cultural texture as he [could] manage'.[9]

By appropriating the term 'people' Burke hoped to enrich the debates concerning the working class and to generate awareness of its social and economic struggle with the middle class. That process would awaken the middle class (a potential proletarian ally) from its lethargic state of self-consumption and it would join the anticapitalist struggle. Cultural democracy in the American artistic arena would be all-encompassing, since the symbol of the 'people' could incorporate not only the economic classes but also the literary ones; in this way, the class of the writers, whose work was regarded as effortlessly distinguishable from industrial labour and direct revolutionary action, would not be considered as too divergent. However, his use of symbolism appeared problematic (and still does), especially when seen in relation to the set of complex forces (including McCarthyism) that developed in the 1950s and 1960s. The appropriation of the term 'people' blurred the implied anticapitalist dialectic of the symbol of the 'worker', especially at a time when labour was still fighting for its right to organise, and marked a rejection of a more militant and agitational discourse. At the same time, this new classification presented the class struggle or the working class as a myth and Michael Gold feared that it proposed that proletarian literature should become a petty bourgeois movement.[10] The term's classless feature, unity and inclusiveness proposed a more homogenised and universal category that placed the individual and the all-embracing 'we' at its core, regardless of one's political, economic or social conditioning. More poignantly, however, Burke's thesis created an antagonism between the worker and the people that represented the worker as antipathetic to the 'good of the people'. It has been observed how this antagonism had been used in both the USA and the UK during the general strikes to represent the class of workers as 'holding up the people', thus separating the interests of the workers from those of all the remaining classes and creating a resentful antagonism between them.[11]

The use of the people was also reminiscent of Hitler's use of the myth of *das Volk*, and its symbolism rendered 'a picture of society that [was] not merely un-Marxian but one which history has proven to be necessary for the continuation of power of the exploiting class'.[12] Joseph Freeman emphasised the need for the existence of the symbol of the 'worker', not because it could become a political myth but because, unlike the ambiguous and vague symbol of the people, the worker had an active and visible role within the American reality.[13] The idea that the worker could be seen physically and ideologically working would help uncover the social reality and thus allow change. Burke's utopian belief in the American writer's ability to write for the people, who enlist 'our *ambitions*' (instead of the worker, who enlists 'our *sympathies*'), created an oxymoron, as it stripped the proletarian artist and worker of his/her dialectic struggle with the middle class, thus obliterating their economic and ideological differences and placing them, instead, side by side as allies.[14] The symbolism of the people and its implied identification permeated the American political and cultural arena and became quite visible in the Living Newspapers produced by the FTP in the last two years of its existence, most notably *Power* and *One-third of a Nation*.

Changing the Living Newspaper: *Power* and *One-third of a Nation*

Both of these productions remained the most popular with the administration of the FTP and critics, as they still engaged with socially pertinent issues but had abandoned the sharper social edge of *Injunction Granted*. The dramatic form of the Living Newspaper had undergone many significant changes in the four months that separated the closing of *Injunction Granted* and the opening of *Power*. The first noticeable change was the abandonment of the policy of attributing authorship to the entire unit. Instead, Arthur Arent was credited as the author of both plays. The shift from collaboration to individual authorship signified the Living Newspaper's attempt to disassociate itself from its avant-garde European predecessors and its appropriation of their radical discourse, especially in light of the recent cases of censorship. At the same time, however, it represented the Living Newspaper's adaptability to the Broadway model of play that associated the word 'play' with a dramatic text written by an individual playwright. Up to that moment, the Living Newspaper incorporated both the theatrical and the journalistic modes of productions. The inclusion of journalism was what helped the Living Newspaper transform its methods of dramatic production and allowed it to engage in depth with political issues. By assuming the individual imprint of the playwright instead of that of a group of people, in both its textual and its performative realisation, the new dramatic form of the Living Newspaper renounced the importance of the collaborative system of script writing. In doing so, it negated the reflection of the politically articulated consciousness and problematisations of a group of creators and thus emphasised the more traditional notion of individual creativity.

The introduction of the ideological authority of individual authorship influenced the structure and exposition of theme in *Power* and *One-third of a Nation*. Arent considered there to be two techniques of presentation, the montage and the episodic. He rightly believed that *Injunction Granted* employed montage almost exclusively, but found it 'dull and repetitious' and felt that, through this kind of presentation, the performance was asking too much of the audience.[15] Instead, he preferred the episodic structure, as it could employ fewer scenes that were self-contained and had three primary functions: '1. to say what has to be said; 2. to build to the scene's own natural climax; 3. to build to the climax of the act curtain and the resolution of the play'.[16] Through the episodic structure Arent wanted to create scenes that would each individually dramatise completely one aspect of the problem (unlike *Triple-A Plowed Under* and *Injunction Granted*, where one idea could unfold in two or three scenes). He hoped that this kind of structure would facilitate a clearer understanding of the problem and the possible solutions on the part of the audience.

Burke's discussion of the symbol of the people ideologically framed Arent's symbolic use of a character in both productions. Whereas the juxtaposition of scenes in *Triple-A* and *Injunction Granted* established the development of a common problem experienced by different classes, the scenes of *Power* and *One-third* discussed the problem in relation to the symbolic character of the consumer, the 'little man'. The creation of a representative individual character, which substituted for the classes of workers and farmers of previous productions, 'whose personal questions [were] addressed by the almost paternal Voice [of the Living Newspaper,] now drove the action and motivate[d] particular scenes'.[17] Kruger's remark manifests how the change in dramatic form affected the level of social analysis available to the audience. If the Voice of the Living Newspaper, instead of interrupting the action, commenting and criticising, tended towards a more patronising and instructive approach, then the level of social analysis was not simply minimised; rather, the audience's response was transformed from a more active consideration and understanding to a passive, receptive comprehension of the events dramatised.

Power's subject was the growth of the electricity industry in America and the conflict between private and public ownership. In Flanagan's words, the play represented 'the struggle of the average citizen [the Consumer] to understand the natural, social and economic forces around him, and to achieve through these forces, a better life for more people'.[18] The play began in a very theatrical manner. Following the interlude and the projection announcing the play, the curtain rose; suddenly, there was a power cut and the audience was faced with the stage manager and two electricians carrying switches. Then the voice of the loudspeaker was heard, commenting on the importance of electric power: 'this is the switchboard of the Ritz Theatre. Through this board flows the electric power that amplifies my voice, the power that ventilates the theatre, and the power that lights this show.'[19] What followed this introduction was a series of small tableau moments (the characters' faces lit up by flashes, put out immediately after the characters spoke) based on an actual power cut on 28 December 1936 in Newark, New Jersey, that exemplified for and to the audience how electricity had become a daily necessity and how any supply disruption affected all aspects of life for all classes. These sketches included an operation being performed using torches, a bakery owner's frantic call to the operator assessing a loss of 4,000 dollars' worth of bread, a mother pleading for the heat to come on as her baby is sick, a theatre manager commenting that his theatre is dark, an airport radio operator assessing the difficulty of landing the planes safely and a driver who has just killed a woman crying 'My God, I didn't see her, I tell you it was dark ... I didn't see her.'[20] The scene ends with multiple repetitions of the words 'operator' and 'light(s)', reminiscent of expressionist theatre. *Power*'s opening scene forced the audience to respond quite emotionally, as almost everyone could identify with a mother's agony, a patient's dependency or a driver's accident. The repetition of the words 'operator' and 'light(s)', representing the characters' anguish, delivered in a rhythmically monotonous manner, created an almost hypnotic atmosphere. Although the scene did highlight the importance of electricity, it requested from the very beginning an emotional response on the audience's part.

The second scene examined historically the development of electricity by presenting on stage the personas of William Gilbert, Michael Faraday, Georg Simon Ohm, Zenobe Gramme and Thomas Edison, all commenting on how their scientific developments would make life easier for people. This humanitarian discourse was then juxtaposed with that of businessmen and the stage was filled with the echoing sound of the words 'corporation', 'money', 'profits', 'investment' and 'thousands, millions, BILLIONS!'.[21] At the end of the scene, the audience's attention was focused on the enigmatic figure of the financier declaring that the establishment of one big corporation would economically benefit all businessmen and would dissolve any competition. Arent chose at this stage to explore the monopolising status of electricity that affected the audience economically through the new figure of the consumer. He saw the figures of the consumer and the Voice of the Living Newspaper as 'complementary, the former "creative", and the latter "technical" – the subjective response and the "collective consciousness" of inquiry'.[22] The consumer was initially represented as confused, naïve and ignorant but was meant to appear sympathetic to an audience that could easily identify with his plight. He, under the constant watchful eye and assistance of the Voice, which had assumed an educational role, began to understand what a kilowatt-hour was, realised the absence of different competitive companies offering electricity and reached a level of awareness that required resistance to the existent monopoly.

Burke's positive symbol of the people, the unity and definition of a new 'we', was realised in the play when the consumer acquired a name, Mr Angus K. Buttonkooper. Although the name was reminiscent of a vaudevillian or *Commedia dell'Arte* character, the character of Mr Buttonkooper was not developed psychologically, but rather remained a generic type of consumer, an identifiable representative of the audience present in the performance. He became 'one of us', someone who could belong equally to the middle class or the working class, and it was his compatibility with the 'us–we' that made his character accessible, believable and agreeable when he decided to act (I, xi). Through this character, Arent wanted the audience to approach life within their social roles, awaken their identity as citizens within a democracy and encourage their commitment to the social and economic issues confronting American society. However, unlike *Triple-A*, in which the dramatisation of the exploitation of the farmers took the form of juxtaposing 'a series of confrontations between farmers (or urban workers) and middlemen', *Power* emphasised a series of duologues between the naïve consumer and the authorities (Figure 3.1).[23] *Triple-A*'s exposition of the problem not only involved one individual worker, but also raised awareness of a series of affiliated local groups, thus requiring an active response from all and attempting to create an alternative public *topos* where social struggle and debates could materialise.

In *Power*, public agency was present. However, the emphasis was not so much on the action taken by social groups but on the endorsement of New Deal policies, which faced resistance from hegemonic institutions such as the

Figure 3.1 Allan Tower (Electric Company Manager) and Norman Lloyd (Consumer) in *Power*. Ritz Theatre, New York, 1937.

Supreme Court. The first act ended with 'The TVA Song', sung ironically by the workers, who championed the government effort.

> All up and down the valley
>   They heard the glad alarm;
> The government means business
>   It's working like a charm
> Oh, see them boys a-comin',
>   Their government they trust,
> Just hear their hammer ringin',
>   They'll build that dam or bust.[24]

The shift from socially motivated action to action proposed by the Democratic government's principles reinforced the presence of an already identifiable public sphere and prohibited its evolution as more polemical and class-based. This was further emphasised by the fact that, although the consumer became socially aware of the importance of electricity and took action (thus exemplifying the double sense of the play's title), the play ended with the government fighting the people's battle. Unlike *Injunction Granted*, which portrayed the government as a capitalist institution, little better than industry or the courts, *Power* 'present[ed] the Roosevelt administration as the friend and champion of the people'.[25] The play does contain a social agenda but, by ending with government representatives arguing the case and the unanswered question 'WHAT WILL THE SUPREME COURT DO?', it seemed to rely on the government to deliver it and the court to legitimise it. A take on political action as something available to every citizen, such as that proposed by *Injunction Granted*, was still present in *Power*, but the degree of that participation was minimised and, crucially, affiliated with the elected government.

This notable change in the Living Newspaper's narrative was attuned to the disillusionment of public and intellectuals alike regarding the Socialist discourse and Communism, especially after the Moscow Trials and the rise of Stalinism. Recognising the continual need for representation of social issues, the American intellectual world realised that such a representation had to be conducted through a different narrative. The emphasis placed by Flanagan on the FTP's character as American in its democratic attitudes signified the importance of a more liberal discourse, easily accessible to the consciousness of the American people and able to translate the social angst of European political theatre into a more democratic one. Within this revised discourse, propaganda acquired a more acceptable status. Speaking to the cast, just after the opening night of *Power*, Harry Hopkins declared:

> I want to tell you this is a great show. It's fast and funny, it makes you laugh and it makes you cry and it makes you think – I don't know what more anyone can ask of a show. *I want this play and plays like it done from one end of the country to the other* . . . People will say it's propaganda. Well, I say what of it? It's propaganda to educate the consumer who's paying for power. It's about time someone had some propaganda for him. The big power companies have spent millions on propaganda for the utilities. It's about time the consumer had a mouthpiece. I say more plays like *Power* and more power to you.[26]

As commented, the play had abandoned the more militant narrative of the previous Living Newspapers. However, by adopting a more pro-New Deal attitude, its propagandistic discourse became more acceptable from the WPA administration's point of view, since it served an educational purpose. The play's social edge was still present, but it could not be accused of adopting a narrative associated with a suppressive regime. If the play was propaganda, as Hopkins suggested, it was a kind of propaganda that could spring from a democratic country that allowed freedom of expression and had its people's best interests at heart. Unlike the negative criticism of *Triple-A* and *Injunction Granted*, the critics were less resilient to the democratic propaganda of *Power*.

Atkinson praised it as 'the most indignant and militant proletarian drama of the season . . . staged with government funds', *Life* as 'WPA public ownership propaganda . . . exciting and unique', and *The Nation* as 'a unique piece of art'.[27] The emphasis placed on the plight of the everyman that anyone could identify with, the endorsement of government policies that aimed to improve people's lives and the experimentally scenic presentation of its theme made *Power* the first successfully accepted Living Newspaper, both for its theatrical experimentation and for its social agenda.[28] Arent's new liberal narrative discourse was more compatible with Flanagan's aspirations for a dynamic and democratic American theatre and was further exploited in the production of *One-third of a Nation*.

According to Flanagan, the idea of a new Living Newspaper dealing with the housing problem in New York started after the opening night of *Power* and was further developed during the Federal Theatre's Summer Theatre School (21 June to 31 July 1937) at the Vassar Experimental Theatre. Forty authors, actors, dancers, designers and directors from Federal Theatre units in seventeen states gathered there and formed one collective group; they attended seminars, made costumes, built sets, performed all the roles and critiqued the production or direction of the plays. The main function of the Summer Theatre was experimentation, especially since many people felt that the Federal Theatre had become complacent about its achievements and was reluctant to go beyond the techniques of *Triple-A* and *Injunction Granted*. Within that environment and after six weeks of collaboration, discussion and rehearsals, the group was ready to produce a play. Arent had completed only the first act of a Living Newspaper called *Housing* and the second was still in synopsis. He and Harold Bolton (director) decided to stage it as a one-act play. There are conflicting views as to who proposed the new title, but the Living Newspaper was renamed *One-third of a Nation*, taking its title from Roosevelt's second inaugural speech.[29]

> I see one-third of a nation ill-housed, ill-clad, ill-nourished. It is not in despair that I paint you that picture. I paint it for you in hope – because the Nation seeing and understanding the injustice in it, proposes to paint it out. We are determined to make every American citizen the subject of his country's interest and concern; and we will never regard any faithful law-abiding group within our borders as superfluous. The test of our progress is not whether we add more to the abundance of those who have much; it is whether we provide enough for those who have too little.[30]

By appropriating a phrase from Roosevelt's speech, the Living Newspaper grew closer to the policies of the elected government in its representation of the slum housing conditions. In the New York production of the play this became more evident. The Federal Theatre Summer production, however, differed considerably in its scenic and directorial presentation.

Figure 3.2 *One-third of a Nation*. Federal Theatre's Summer Theatre School at Vassar Experimental Theatre, 21 June to 31 July 1937. Stage design by Howard Bay.

Although dealing with a real issue, Harold Bolton produced a plan of the production, after discussing it with Arent and Howard Bay (stage designer), that was closer to the experimental strategies of the Living Newspaper, and used visual projections, episodic scenes and fragmented quotations from actual speeches and documents. He rejected the idea of a realistic set that would reproduce a tenement on stage and instead used a series of objects, such as pipes, rubbish bins, fire escape ladders, broken toilets and old beds, which were suspended from the ceiling, above the actors' heads (Figure 3.2). The use of these suspended objects signified how they dominated people's daily lives and underlined the fact that they did not really have a home of their own. Bolton commented that, by not employing a conventional setting, the group would

> attempt instead to stimulate the imaginations of our audience so that they can accept the play's premises and complete the syllogism in their own minds. The first step in this direction is to discard conventional scenery and props and substitute an 'objective background' equivalent to the subjective psychological material used by a surrealist painter. Each object in this background has a direct bearing on some phase of the play, and as each in turn is spotlighted, mental connotation will be established in the consciousness of the people.[31]

Bolton viewed the whole production as an organic unit and wanted acting, lighting, stage movement, music and costume design to be simple, explicit and direct, and to approach the play from the same perspective.[32] He also placed emphasis on the function of the Loudspeaker, whom he wanted to be more versatile (as a member of the cast, as the voice of the audience or by playing the role of an ominous Greek chorus, unlike the 'wise-cracking prompter of *Power*') without, however, overshadowing the actors' performance.[33] The play contained both naturalistic and stylised scenes, and the absence of the properties of a realistic set proved challenging for the actors, who had to produce convincing performances. In the stylised scenes, Bolton advised them to 'register a complete scene with a few gestures, an intonation, a posture or a pause'.[34] Lastly, he emphasised how the production needed to be a product of collective effort rather than individuality.

The antirealistic and more expressionist staging of *One-third of a Nation* at Vassar achieved its end result, which, according to Howard Bay, was 'through the logical process of audience analysis, a compilation of inevitable objects that further the content of the play'.[35] The pilot Vassar production was not reviewed by the press, with the exception of *Variety* magazine. *Variety* approved of the 'frankly non-realistic and tremendously effective style of production', and thus ranked the play as equally effective as, if not slightly better than, *Injunction Granted* and *Power*.[36] The stylised production also impressed Langdon Post, the chairman of the Municipal Housing Authority of New York, who, according to Hallie Flanagan,

> had often been impressed by the fact that when he talked about tenements and threw pictures on the screen, no one was impressed. 'The houses look large, and in America size means comfort'. Consequently he said that the sight of people moving as '1/3 of the Nation' actually does move, under the pressure of garbage cans and filthy walls and broken fire escapes gave a truer sense of reality than any number of tenements erected on the stage [. . .] Langdon Post said last night, 'This play performed as it was tonight, can do more to convert people to proper housing than all the shouting I have done in the past three years'.[37]

The effectiveness of Bolton's abstract staging of the play was particularly welcomed by members of regional theatres that could not afford the luxury of a complex realistic production; it also highlighted the ability of the audience to appreciate new theatrical modes of production and the importance to the events staged of the absence of total emotional immersion on the audience's part. The organic unity of all the elements of the play and the emotional distancing it proposed was reminiscent of Brecht's theory of the epic theatre. By staging the very essence of the slums, Bolton succeeded in rejuvenating the desire for formal experimentation that the Living Newspaper seemed to have lost. However, that success was short-lived; by the time *One-third of a Nation* opened in New York, most of these areas of experimentation were replaced by a more realistic stage and style of acting.

By the time the play reached the New York stage, Arent had completed both acts. The opening night took place in the Adelphi Theatre on 17 January 1938, and as the curtains rose 'a set that was virtually a masterpiece of stage illusionism' was revealed.[38] Howard Bay again designed the set, but this time opted for a more realistic design. He reproduced a four-storey dwelling from actual demolished tenements, with narrow hallways, tiny rooms, exposed pipes and dangerous vertical fire escapes, that was almost 40 feet high, and the cubicles functioned as parallel acting areas. The presence of these parallel acting areas created a montage effect, as the action – highlighted by spotlights – could move from one area to the other. This technique became particularly effective in I, iv, where a scenic representation of the devastation caused by cholera took place. Successively, they briefly lighted and then blacked out one cubicle after the other as each scene exposed people's desolation. The scene ended with the voice of the Loudspeaker announcing a factual account of the victims: 'Twenty-five hundred men, women and children lost their lives before that cholera epidemic ended. Five thousand died in the previous one. This was the third time in twenty years that New York was visited by cholera.'[39] Because of the montage effect, Bay believed that this structure could serve as a more authentic reminder of the housing problem and, although realistic, thought it did not belong to the tradition of mature naturalistic drama. Bearing in mind Bolton's suggestions, all the elements in the New York production worked organically in this more realistic depiction of the issue. The costumes, designed by Rhoda Rammelkamp, differed from the simple ones used in the Vassar production; they were detailed and realistic, portraying characters from an extensive range of professions, classes and historical periods. Also, Lee Wainer's music score was complementary to the action taking place. As the play explored the issues surrounding housing conditions historically, from 1850 to the present moment, it also made good use of projections, showing slides and films of New York City during that time-span.

Where *Power* began with a power cut, *One-third of a Nation* started (and ended) with a fire in the tenement (Figure 3.3). As the curtain rose, the audience observed the daily routine of the people living there until the voice of the Loudspeaker announced: 'February, 1924 – This might be 397 Madison Street, New York. It might be 425 Halsey Street, Brooklyn, or Jackson Avenue and 10th Street, Long Island City.'[40] As soon as that was heard, smoke appeared from the third floor. A crowd of onlookers had gathered but were unable to help. Panic arose among the tenants and a man, Mr Rosen, attempted to enter the flaming building, as his wife and daughter were inside, but was stopped. Then everybody's attention was drawn towards a man who, hanging 25 feet

Figure 3.3 *One-third of a Nation*. Opening and closing scene. Adelphi Theatre, New York, 1938. Stage design by Howard Bay.

from the ground, attempted to use the fire escape but the ladder gave way, thus shutting off any means of escape. The first scene ended with screaming, the noise of the fire brigade's sirens and a cry of 'Look', directed towards the man still hanging but ready to jump in desperation. At that stage, a tableau moment was created, as everybody became motionless and the scene was blacked out.

This introductory scene had a powerfully emotional effect on the audience, who witnessed everything and were aghast. As the search for the causes of the fire began, it seemed that the only participant enquiring and bringing forward the action would be the voice of the Loudspeaker. But Arent again decided to use the generic figure of the 'little man', familiar to the audience from *Power*, Mr Buttonkooper. Mr Buttonkooper was introduced in I, iv, through the auditorium (much to the surprise of the audience), instantly demanding lights, attention and more information on the housing problem. The fact that Mr Buttonkooper and, later on, his wife emerged from the audience again emphasised the importance of the audience's ability to relate to his character and acknowledge in him a potential mirror image of themselves and their conditioning. The enlightenment of Mr Buttonkooper, the generic man, became the task of the Living Newspaper. Thus, it is through the relationship between the voice of the Loudspeaker and Mr Buttonkooper that the spectators became aware of and involved in the housing problem. Similarly, the relationship between the audience and the Loudspeaker became one of student and teacher. The Loudspeaker was no longer the editorial or informative agent of previous Living Newspapers but, as in *Power*, became more instructive. In II, ii, the Loudspeaker invites the little man to take a trip around New York in 1933, a trip that has already taken place in act one.

> LOUDSPEAKER: How about a trip around New York in 1933?
> LITTLE MAN: Wait a minute, wouldn't that be sort of be repeating ourselves? We did that in the first act.
> LOUDSPEAKER: Let's try it. You see, that's the whole point of this housing business. *It repeats itself.* It just goes on and on.
> LITTLE MAN: Well, how are *you* going to stop it?
> LOUDSPEAKER (correcting him): How are *we* going to stop it?[41]

The repetition of events and phrases was instrumental to the language and action of the play and had a double function. Firstly, since the play aimed to raise the spectators' awareness of the housing conditions and provoke protests that would incite changes in the housing legislation, important points needed to be emphasised. In I, iii, a number of prospective tenants bargain with the landowner one after the other for a place on the small green map that he had unrolled; the repetition of the phrase 'a man's got to have a place to live' reflected every man's human right to have a home when uttered by the tenants, but sounded ironic when uttered by the landowner. Similarly, in II, iii, the audience was exposed to a stylised representation of the process the landowner had to go through to construct decent tenements. As he went from builder to builder supplier, from one broker to another, from one contractor to another and each time being faced with a repetition of what the previous character had uttered, the audience was suddenly exposed to the complicated structures of a capitalist enterprise and its inherent absurdity. The second function of this repetition was to instigate protest on the audience's part. When, in the excerpt above, the Loudspeaker corrected the little man, turning the 'you' into a 'we', he immediately asserted the responsibility of the audience to participate in the social action taken to improve the living conditions. This all-encompassing 'we' – reminiscent of Burke's 'we the people' and the humanitarian liberal discourse – becomes symbolic, especially since the play incorporated scenes with people of different religions, nationalities (immigrants) and colour (the 'hot bed' scene remains one of the most memorably effective ones).

One-third of a Nation ended with a repetition of the first fire scene, thus underlining that if the audience persisted in their inertia, the recurrence of such devastating events was inevitable. Both the introductory and last scenes, an amalgamation of trapped and suffering humanity, were symbolic of the emotional tenor that Arent gave the subject. As Goldman had commented, Arent considered that *Power* explored his 'sardonic' side, whereas *One-third* explored his more 'human', empathetic side.[42] The sense of humanity invested in the liberal New Deal rhetoric was shared by Arent and the FTP administration: hence the appropriation of Roosevelt's speech. But what this liberal discourse entailed for the Living Newspaper, as a vehicle of social change and justice, was a turn from a socially based criticism to one based on emotional response. Cosgrove rightly observed that the play's critique of the slum conditions 'sent a wave of moral indignation through depression America' but, by emphasising an empathetic response, the Living Newspaper abandoned its position as 'the formal and political vanguard of the depression'.[43]

The emotional reaction sought from the audience compromised the play's critical approach to the subject and invested more power in New Deal policies with a social agenda. Those were the implications of II, i, for example, which began and ended with the old tenement speaking directly to the audience. It was to the same effect that, firstly, Mrs Buttonkooper made a passing reference to Roosevelt's speech, and later on the Loudspeaker pronounced:

> LOUDSPEAKER: We can't let people walk out of this theatre knowing the disease is there, but believing there's no cure. There is cure! [...] if you can't build cheap houses – and you've just proved you can't – then let somebody do it who can – and I mean the United States Government – for instance.[44]

Following the Aristotelian dramatic principle, Arent presented the American government as a deus ex machina that would enforce order and justice. What *One-third* proposed more clearly than *Power* was that, if social change was to come, it would be possible only via the elected government. In a democratic state, the people's power lay in their vote and trust in the government they had elected, rather than in their own political or social agenda. The legitimate social public agency that *Injunction Granted* proposed was challenged by Arent's script. From its beginnings as an autonomous and experimental form, the Living Newspaper's last production showed signs of conformity and, rather than suggesting public ownership and planning as a cure, it proposed another ineffective legislation change.

The play was enthusiastically received by most critics, especially for its use of a realistic set. Flanagan called it 'the most mature and objective of the Living Newspapers'; Atkinson called it 'the most sensational story on the New York stage at the moment'; Richard Watts found it 'invariably forceful and striking'; and John Mason Brown wrote that 'seeing *One-third of a Nation* is something which becomes every good citizen's Duty'.[45] Others found it 'a representation and a symbol of all slum tenements in which life is degraded', and 'masterly and eloquent', thinking of the fire scene as 'a real triumph of imaginative realism' and 'so realistic, so terrifying [that] it almost sears the spectators'.[46] Whereas the same critics had fiercely attacked *Injunction Granted*, not simply for its politics but for its artistic experimentations (calling it 'hysterical', 'ineffective and anticlimactic'), they felt comfortable embracing the less agitational and theatrically inventive performance of *One-third of a Nation*.[47] However, Mary McCarthy, reviewing this production, commented that it exposed 'a relaxation of standards, a suspension of effort, an aesthetic fatigue'.[48] She went on to criticise the more personalised, stylised and realistic approach, the false illustration of infinite possibilities for self-improvement available under the American system of government, its transformation from an experiment to an institution, and its inability to evoke anything other than an emotional response from the audience, accusing it of being 'the adjunct of an Administration which has exhausted its political resources, itself becoming superannuated'.[49] McCarthy's criticism becomes justified, especially when seen in relation to the play's attempt to incorporate two audiences: the lower-class tenants and the middle-class owners. By representing on stage the problems that each of them faced, the play attempted to generate an understanding between the classes and thus erase the manifestation of social struggle as they knew it. The owners/middle class were no longer part of the problem as such, since their attempt to provide good housing was hindered by capitalist enterprise and not themselves. Providing the middle class as an ally, the Living Newspaper stood between its tradition of subversion and social criticism, and its status as an American institution.

One of the major changes with this Living Newspaper is its sole authorship. Apart from the exclusion of the collaborative effort that characterised previous Living Newspaper productions, the presence of a single author reinstated the 'dramaturgy of pathos'.[50] Arent's creative impetus could no longer rest on the more abstract representation of events. As he commented when writing *One-third of a Nation*,

> the human element was missing. The statements and statistics are flat. We have made no use of the theatre. The next step, then, is the *creative scene*, based on slum conditions as we know them to exist, where instead of one-dimensional characters, speaking the unattractive patois of the politician, we have a man expressing himself in the *warm speech and theatric idiom of a humanity undeterred by the hopelessness of being immortalised in the Congressional Record*. This character represents the one-third of the nation. He is the audience's *identification*, the bridge that leads to an understanding in human terms of the subject of the debate. And the proof of his being is the debate itself.[51]

The emphasis on the representation of the universal concept of humanity becomes problematic, as it obscures a larger understanding of social conditioning by making constant reference to the empathetic and emotional identification of the audience with the character. It thus minimises the critical intervention of flat statements and the representation of the social struggle for justice. Arent's belief in the emotive potential of the human plight did not allow the audience to create a critical distance, and the use of the alienation technique that was present in previous productions was eliminated. By disapproving of the representation of social characters as one-dimensional and thus less human, Arent excluded them from his play, thus reducing the amount of social situations authorised for representation. This new aesthetic approach and moral attitude reduced the amount of effective social criticism and, rather, portrayed the audience as the recipient of its benevolent elected government. Such an attitude was suggested by Roosevelt himself, who, in his second inaugural speech, affirmed that the 'democratic government has *innate* ability to protect its people against disasters once considered inevitable'.[52] The Democratic government's inherent (even 'natural') ability to manage such social and economic issues was meant to reassure the public of the government's policies and, at the same time, to dissuade the public from adopting a more agitational and revolutionary social praxis. As Hopkins adamantly believed, with the coming of the Roosevelt administration, 'the emphasis of government shifted from material to human values', thus making the Enlightenment's humanitarian project clearly visible within American democracy.[53]

The government's 'natural' ability to provide for the American people became apparent in the structure of *One-third of a Nation*. The fact that the play did not pursue the landowners' responsibilities any further than the fact that they own the land, that they were completely absent from the second act, that individuals were to be blamed but not the capitalist economic system as such and that the dangers of slum life emphasised the representation of the victims 'rather than those who profit from it', reinforced the image of the government as a social agent.[54] Such an approach was further emphasised when Mrs Buttonkooper, at the end of the play, specified among the people that would 'holler' for decent housing conditions 'you and me and La Guardia and Senator Wagner and the Housing Authorities and the Tenant Leagues and everybody who lives in a place like that!', thus including with the people and their organisations, the Mayor of New York, a senator and the representative authorities that drove New Deal policies forward.[55] Undoubtedly, the play's ending exposed the insufficiency of governmental agency; at the same time, it undermined the audience's agency by suggesting throughout the action a participatory, rather than an acutely critical (perhaps even agitational), attitude within the democratic system.

One-third of a Nation became the most successful Living Newspaper production, not simply because it ran for 237 performances in New York, but also because its subject matter was suitable for regional adaptations. Most of the regional projects attempted to localise the play by modifying its script to incorporate information about local housing conditions; such productions included Seattle, San Francisco, Philadelphia and Pennsylvania. The fact that the Living Newspaper had finally managed to acquire a nationwide reputation and production by its local divisions manifested Flanagan's ambition to turn the FTP into a national theatre and reinforced her opinion that 'the theatre, when it is any good, can change things'.[56] However, the dramatic change in its politics of aesthetic representation – from displaying a more critical approach to American society's social and economic problems and the governmental agency, into incorporating a more empathetic style of the problems' representation and a pro-New Deal discourse – revealed that the Federal Theatre, in its process of becoming a national agency of expression, had a tendency to legitimise itself. Flanagan's wish to create an alternative theatrical *topos* that would offer a voice to the under-represented classes and question more openly those issues that Broadway ignored seemed to be in direct conflict with her ambition to turn it into a national theatre.

The change in the Living Newspaper's dramaturgy eroded the formal 'dialectic between abstract and concrete', and thus legitimised a certain aesthetics of representation and certain audiences' perceptions over others.[57] That led to the establishment of *One-third of a Nation* as the paradigm of the Living Newspaper-style production. That essential style disapproved of the more experimental and sometimes politically offensive satire of *Injunction Granted* and turned its back on the inheritance of the workers' theatre of the 1920s and early 1930s. Through that style, the legitimisation of a certain audience's struggle took place. The struggle for social justice of the anonymous workers, farmers and unemployed that filled the stage and the pages of *Altars of Steel*, *Triple-A Plowed Under*, *Injunction Granted* and *Dirt*, to name but a few, was replaced by the private suffering of unknown individuals. It was no longer the 'history and social facts' of the problem that mattered, but the 'graphic and personal' depiction of the effects of the problem on an individual that could have been anyone from the audience, anyone who could potentially belong to that one-third of the American nation.[58] By relying mostly on the audience's emotional rather than critical response to the Marys', Sammys' or Joes' plight, *One-third of a Nation* diverted its audience's attention away from the militant unionism of *Injunction Granted* (excluding it from the legitimate public sphere) and closer to the more democratic and humanitarian discourse of the liberal New Deal government.

The canonical status of this Living Newspaper, which is the one most often quoted and discussed, was established when the play was sold to Paramount Pictures and turned into a Hollywood film in 1939 starring Silvia Sidney, Leif Erikson and Sidney Lumet. The proceeds from the sale of the film rights were ironically earmarked for the Federal Writers Committee, a move that signalled serious trouble for the FTP as a prologue to its disbandment. The film bears little resemblance to the original Living Newspaper as a way of both distancing itself from its theatrical tradition of censorship and attracting a new, more attractive audience. They did keep the old tenement and the fire; it is the actual building that dominates the film, as it has now acquired the croaking voice of an old, miserable man. The fire is catastrophic, as in the original script, but with a more personal tone attached to Silvia Sidney, the main protagonist. According to Nugent, the film is not as realistic as the original play but none the less it is 'one that you probably will want to see'.[59]

One-third of a Nation remains an important text and production within the history of the Living Newspaper and the Federal Theatre, both for its merits and its shortcomings. It was a production almost unanimously accepted by all facets of social and political life. The main opposition to the play came from members of the Senate, as some took offence at the fact that they were included in its cast of characters, especially in II, iv, which presented a dramatisation of the Senate debate over the Wagner–Steagall Housing Bill. Senators Harry Byrd, Millard Tydings and Charles O. Andrews felt that, although not misquoted, their presence, coming after 'scenes portraying the evils and miseries of slum life, were fitted in so as to make them villains by implication'.[60] What the Senators' complaint highlighted was the problematics of using such material in a dramatic production, especially by a theatre operating on federal funds. For Flanagan, the critically acclaimed success of *One-third of a Nation* proved the power that theatre had as a means of reform; she commented that 'giving apoplexy to people who consider it radical for a government-sponsored theatre to produce plays on subjects vitally concerning the governed is one function of the theatre'.[61] Although she was confident that the play did not ridicule or satirise any senators, their reaction signified, firstly, their growing dissatisfaction with certain New Deal policies and, secondly, their rejection of a federal theatre as a valuable means of education, information and social change. By locating itself politically so close to the government, the Federal Theatre could not escape the inquisitive eye of the Dies Committee.

4

THE NEGRO UNIT: ELECTRIFYING HARLEM, ELECTRIFYING THE NATION

> The Negro Theatre might be retained as an entity, though drastically cut, on the basis of its sociological [sic] importance rather than theatrical importance.[1]
>
> Harry Hopkins, as quoted in Barry Witham, *The Federal Theatre Project*.

> 'Blackness' is not a material object, an absolute, or an event, but a trope; it does not have an 'essence' as such but is defined by a network of relations that form a particular aesthetic unity.[2]
>
> Henry Louis Gates, Jr, *Figures in Black: Words, Signs and the 'Racial' Self.*

> The plays of a real Negro theatre must be: 1. 'about us.' That is, they must have plays which reveal Negro life as it is. 2. 'By us.' That is, they must be written by Negro authors who understand from birth and continued association just what it means to be a Negro today. 3. 'For us.' That is, the theatre must cater primarily to Negro audiences and be supported and sustained by their entertainment and approval. 4. 'Near us.' The theatre must be in a Negro neighborhood near the mass of ordinary Negro peoples.[3]
>
> W. E. B. Du Bois, 'Krigwa Players Little Negro Theatre'.

ENTER THE SWING: INTRODUCING RACIAL FLUIDITY IN THE FTP

Black theatre and drama existed and were part of American life before the establishment of the FTP. Any time that African Americans performed rituals in songs and music, in storytelling or in church, their mode of expression was infiltrating American culture, whether consciously or unconsciously. So, although the performative expression of drama existed, written African American drama did not appear until the middle of the nineteenth century. But by then, the racially stereotypical representation of African American performers and playwrights as uneducated 'clowns' was strongly established within American culture; many artists felt compelled to leave and sought solace in Europe. The opportunity not only to return but finally to write, produce and act in plays relating their experience of living was ironically provided by the Depression. The establishment of the WPA and the FTP 'proved the open Sesame, providing at once a laboratory and the wherewithal for creative enterprise' for any African American artist.[4]

The theatrical experimentations proposed and the social issues explored by the Living Newspapers discussed in the previous two chapters were not the only exciting aspects of the FTP. Negro units, collectively known as the Negro Theatre Project (NTP), were set up throughout the United States to put into work the many black theatre professionals who were on relief. In the east, there was a unit in New York, Boston, Philadelphia and even Newark; in the south, in North Carolina and Alabama; in the Midwest, in Chicago, Illinois and Ohio; and in the west, in Seattle, Washington and Los Angeles. All these units produced new plays, adapted old ones and experimented with new ways of producing socially engaged and entertaining theatre. They not only provided much-needed economic relief, but also celebrated their localised experience of America with their different customs, linguistic idioms and histories.

Hallie Flanagan was very interested in diversifying both the theatre and the audience that could be reached through the FTP. With the advice and guidance of Rose McClendon, a leading African American Broadway actress and founder of the Negro People's Theatre, Flanagan set up the Negro units in the states mentioned above. McClendon supervised the process of establishing the unit in New York and suggested John Houseman as her co-director during the initial stages. Once more African Americans gained experience in directing, set design and lighting, they would substitute for their white counterparts. In an effort to eliminate discrimination within the FTP, the Emergency Relief Appropriation Act was enacted to combat discrimination in relation to labour but also 'on account of race, creed, color, or any political activity, support of, or opposition to any candidate or any political party in any election'.[5]

Similar to the Living Newspaper units, the Negro units became the podiums for an array of black playwrights and performers to surface for the first time and provided them with opportunities to try different things. Among the regional Negro units, the best known and most active were those in New York, Chicago and Seattle. The New York one was located in the Lafayette Theatre in Harlem and staged over thirty productions. For the first year, it was run by two white directors, John Houseman and Orson Welles. By 1936, they had been replaced by three black ones, Edward Perry, Carlton Moss and H. F. V. Edward. The unit's most popular production remains the 'voodoo' *Macbeth* (1936), an adaptation of Shakespeare's well-known tragedy set in the Caribbean and performed by an all-black cast. The play was directed by Welles and it propelled him to the heart of the American theatrical and film industries. Other famous productions included Arna Bontemps and Countee Cullen's three-act adaptation of Rudolph Fisher's well-known mystery novel, *The Conjure Man Dies* (1936), which enjoyed an extended run.

One of the most unusual productions from the New York unit was *Bassa Moona*, a dance opera that premiered on 8 December 1936. The play was filled with aspects of ritualism drawn from Nigerian life that included war dances, witch doctors and heavy drumming; the African American cast of forty actors and thirty dancers was, unusually, directed by Nigerian immigrant Momodu Johnson. The play was reminiscent of the 'voodoo' *Macbeth* performed earlier in the same theatre, but differed dramatically in its incorporation of dance, both aesthetically and in terms of representing racial issues. Lastly, one should not forget *Haiti* by William DuBois (not to be confused with W. E. B. Du Bois), which appeared in 1938. Subtitled 'a drama of the Black Napoleon', the play takes place in 1802 and dramatised the final year of the twelve-year-long Haitian revolution against Napoleon. The production was seen by a mixed audience of more than 74,000 people, who enjoyed not only its presentation and the struggles for black identity, but also the controversial decision to have black and white actors perform on stage together.[6]

The Chicago Negro unit was headed by Shirley Graham (later to become Mrs W. E. B. Du Bois and personally appointed by Hallie Flanagan) from 1936 to 1939. The unit rivalled the New York one in originality, variety of plays, popularity and controversy. Its most acclaimed production was *The Swing Mikado* (1938), a jazz version of the well-known Gilbert and Sullivan operetta. The gamble of rewriting and restructuring such a popular play paid off and the operetta was very successful in both Chicago and New York. Other successful productions included the *Little Black Sambo* (1937), a children's operetta, and Theodore Ward's drama of the Depression, *Big White Fog* (1938). Prefaced as 'a negro drama', Ward's play followed the Mason family over three generations and their quest to negotiate and situate themselves within a singular culture, either the African one (returning back to their homeland) or the American one (seeking the ideals of the American Dream). The play, relating personal as well as racial, political, economic and social issues, was a success, although its interracial ending was met with mixed reactions from both the black and the white populations.⁷

The Seattle Negro Repertory Unit put on some of the most experimental productions of any Negro unit. Under the direction of Florence and Burton James, the unit fostered new talent, encouraged the writing of new plays and allowed African American playwrights further autonomy and creativity. The unit's repertory was further enhanced by the presence of playwright-in-residence Theodore Browne. Having gained theatrical experience with the Civic Repertory Theatre in Seattle, Browne tried his hand at playwriting. The unit staged four of his plays: *Lysistrata*, an African American adaptation of Aristophanes' comedy; *Natural Man*, a dramatisation based loosely on the folk legend of John Henry, who tests his physical skills against a steam engine; *A Black Woman Called Moses*, a drama about Harriet Tubman and her involvement in the Underground Railroad; and finally, *Swing, Gates, Swing*, which was a musical revue.

For all their differences, these units had something in common: they aimed to expose and explore the social and racial issues and tensions that African Americans experienced. The irony was that such an exposition not only was happening under the auspices of a governmental institution that had no intention of dealing with or solving such a complicated social and cultural matter; it was also taking place with almost exclusively white men in charge of theatres, directing, casting, producing and organising the theatrical experience. At the same time, the same African Americans were fighting among themselves about what this new style or type of theatrical art that the FTP afforded them should look like. Should they follow Du Bois's call for a black theatre about, by and for them, a theatre that would instruct, educate and provide a platform for critically presenting racial issues facing their community? Or, as the hopeful ending of Ward's play suggested, attempt to create a synergy between black and white cultural energies, a new communal coalition of black and white playwrights, directors, artists, actors and audiences that would revolt against racial stereotypes and shift the cultural power paradigms toward a (finally) truly liberal society?

Underneath this dilemma were hidden artistic and personal anxieties: who was the African American artist, and how could a white and even a black director nurture his/her training, culture, experiences and identity? How would the FTP's Negro units fit in with the long tradition of independent African American theatre? Would they be part of a semi-independent, alternative national Negro theatre or part of the FTP establishment? And, by extension, what would constitute an African American audience? As Rena Fraden argues, the impossibility of answering these questions and the reluctance to do so led to the idea of 'a race [. . .] a singular and unified entity, a necessity [. . .] though it also meant ignoring many of the divisions within the Negro audience'.⁸

I would further argue that the divisions Fraden mentioned also existed within the group of African American artists and intellectuals. Not all of them had the access to education, cultural interaction and sometimes privileged upbringing that Du Bois, Shirley Graham and Alain Locke (the latter an African American writer, critic, philosopher and interpreter of African American culture, considered the 'father of the Harlem Renaissance) were afforded. As a result, this idea of singularity within their theatrical community is moot and naïve, and reduces the complexities and anxieties of the debate surrounding their cultural, social and racial identity.

An interesting aspect of this debate among African American artists and intellectuals was their referral to European, predominantly Soviet and Irish, theatres as examples of negotiating a new type of experimental theatre with a great degree of independence. Similar to Flanagan's excitement at the developments of Russian theatre, discussed in the previous chapters, artists and directors such as Raymond O'Neil (director of the Ethiopian Players in Chicago), Anne Cooke (director of dramatists at Spelman College) and Sterling Brown (Locke's colleague and editor for Negro affairs on the Federal Writers' Project) looked to Europe and the Soviet Union for answers to some of the question posed in the previous paragraph. What they deduced either from their experiences of visiting these two countries themselves or from the touring companies of the Abbey Theatre and the Moscow Art Theatre were a sense of constant experimentation and change, a pride in national independence accompanied by a desire to export their theatrical manifestoes, and a firm belief that their 'philosophy of the theatre arts' could bring about change, critically reflect on socio-political changes and reveal to their audiences life-changing ideas.[9]

In this chapter, I will not attempt to discuss the complicated and intricate questions mentioned above. Rena Fraden, John Perpener and Mark Franko's books are excellent sources for anyone interested in starting to understand the complexities surrounding African Americans' quest either to create a culture of their own or to reclaim a space within an already established culture for presenting issues regarding themselves but also society at large. What interests me is how the FTP, with all its restrictions, afforded the Negro units the opportunity to voice these anxieties, frustrations but also dreams and aspirations to such a large audience, both segregated and mixed. I want to examine how, for a brief four years, American culture became more inclusive and politically explosive; how the audience reacted in such a variety of ways to plays, performances, issues and ideas they were never previously exposed to or even had the time and luxury to consider; how, even though racial stereotypical representations were still employed, the Negro units' plays, and their directors, actors and playwrights, found ways to subvert them; and how, in the middle of doing so, there was always a connection with their European predecessors and contemporaries, no matter how slim it was. For me, this connection reaffirms the argument that the interaction between European and American cultural traditions never ceased and, whether it is admitted or not, the experience of Europe by many of the artists and intellectuals mentioned so far deeply influenced some of their ideas and ideals when applied to their version of American culture. Equally, their appropriation of American cultural power fed back to their European contemporaries.

To look at these questions, I will be examining two different plays from two different units, their theatrical experimentations in terms of staging, presentations and representations of racial issues, and conflicts among the units and the federal government, as well as the role of the audience. Starting with the New York unit, I will be discussing the 1936 'voodoo' *Macbeth*, a seminal production in the Lafayette Theatre that electrified not only Harlem but the whole country by making Shakespeare relatable to a much wider and diverse audience. The production used African music, drumming and ritual images of African culture, affecting its audiences and questioning racial representations in different ways.

Concurrently with the New York production, the Seattle unit was preparing itself for Theodore Browne's adaptation of Aristophanes' *Lysistrata* at the Orpheum Theatre. Similar to the way that *Macbeth* had changed locale from Scotland to a fictional Caribbean island, Browne moved the play from Ancient Greece to Ethiopia and used this for a subtle critique of war, power and racial relations. The play described the women of Ethiopia, who withheld sex from their returning soldier–husbands until they stopped waging war. As opposed to *Macbeth*, though, the controversial production was deemed too risqué for Seattle audiences and was halted after only one performance. Whether it was the visible sexuality of the bodies of the all-black cast performing on stage or the change of locale to Ethiopia, the play troubled the federal government. Akin to Rice's failed Living Newspaper *Ethiopia*, it seems that politics – sexual, racial or governmental – once again affected Flanagan and Hopkins's promise of an uncensored theatre.

Practising Voodoo: New York and *Macbeth*

One of the best-known, celebrated and experimental productions by the New York Negro unit remains Orson Welles's adaptation of *Macbeth*. A year or so before the controversies caused by the cancelled performance of *The Cradle Will Rock*, this 'voodoo' *Macbeth* was an instant success for the Negro unit and became a pioneering production because of its innovative staging, interpretation of Shakespeare's canonical work and promotion of experimental African American theatre. Welles, only twenty-one at the time, became an instant celebrity on the American theatrical scene, revered for his ingenious interpretations of canonical works and for his quick identification of his audience's needs and thirst for new theatrical experiences.

The New York Negro unit was established at the Lafayette Theatre in Harlem. The Lafayette Theatre has always been part of African American theatrical history, hosting ground-breaking theatrical performances that entertained and educated their audiences. Although Orson Welles and John Houseman were credited with being there at the unit's inception, it was primarily the influence and presence of Rose McClendon that set the wheels in motion. McClendon was one of the most admired and important actresses of the 1920s. She acted in such contemporary dramas as Paul Green's Pulitzer Prize-winning *In Abraham's Bosom* (1926), Dorothy and DuBose Heyward's *Porgy* (1927) and Langston Hughes's *Mulatto* (1935). She also won the leading role in Countee Cullen's adaptation of *Medea* (1934), written specifically with her in mind, but unfortunately the production never materialised because of McClendon's illness. Wanting to increase the space and presence of African Americans on stage, McClendon acted as a director, playwright and board member of the Harlem Experimental Theatre, and in 1935, together with Dick Campbell, she founded the Negro People's Theatre, which laid the foundations for the FTP's Negro units and was later absorbed by the New York unit. Its first production was an all-black adaptation of Clifford Odets's *Waiting for Lefty* in June 1935, which was attended by more than 4,000 people.

McClendon very clearly stated that she wanted to create 'a new Negro stage ... to develop not an isolated Paul Robeson, or an occasional Bledsoe or Gilpin, but a long line of first-rated actors'.[10] Her views coincided with Flanagan's, who not only believed in the social and educative force of theatre but also wanted to support 'theatrical enterprises so excellent in quality and low in cost, and so vital to the communities involved that they will be able to continue after Federal support is withdrawn'.[11] When the two women met, Flanagan took on board McClendon's advice not only to create a separate Negro unit within the FTP but also to initiate the establishment of similar units in other states. As Flanagan acknowledged, McClendon was instrumental in securing the interest of organisations and individuals such as Edna Thomas, Harry Edwards, Carlton Moss and Gus Smith, and she was invited to head the New York unit. According to Flanagan's memoirs, McClendon initially refused, suggesting that 'since Negroes had always been performers and had had no previous means of learning direction and design, they would prefer to start under more experienced direction'.[12] John Houseman, who was present at the meeting, along with Elmer Rice and Philip Barber, accepted the post of joint head of the unit in association with McClendon.

Houseman was a suitable compromise; he had already directed a black cast in *Four Saints in Three Acts* so would be more approachable and trustworthy for the community. At the same time, he was himself a sort of outsider. Not being American-born, there was a belief that 'he would not have the manifestations of racism' inherent in people born and raised in the USA at the time.[13] With McClendon not being able to assist much because of her illness, Houseman was helped by his two African American aides, Edward Perry and Carlton Moss, who took over the unit when he resigned a few years later. Houseman decided that to be able to use all the performing staff employed by the unit, he would establish two separate, but interrelated, sub-units. The first one would be committed to the performance of plays written, directed and acted by and for African Americans around issues that their communities face. The second would be devoted to performances of classical works in which the 'actors would be the interpreters, without concession or reference to color'.[14] His decision marked the unofficial beginning of the 'voodoo' *Macbeth*.

As soon as those units were established, production started. It was the first unit that went on to produce *Walk Together Chillum!*, which had a moderate outcome, and *Conjure Man Dies* with greater success. But Houseman was more invested in the second unit; having thought of a work by Shakespeare as its first production, he very quickly visited Orson Welles, who eagerly agreed to participate in the project. It was decided that the first production would be *Macbeth*. As soon as their intention was announced, it generated mixed reactions within the Harlem community; although fascinated by Shakespeare's inclusion, some considered the production would bring overwhelming risks for the FTP as a whole. Others thought of it as a 'white man's scheme deliberately hatched to degrade the Negro and bring the Theatre Project into disrepute'.[15] It took a few weeks to audition more than 300 actors and in the end the cast was decided. Jack Carter would be Macbeth, Edna Thomas (replacing the ailing Rose McClendon) his murderous lady (Figure 4.1), and Maurice Ellis and Marie Young the Macduffs; the cast also included a troupe of African drummers that barely spoke English, led by Asadata Dafora Horton.

Welles was aware that the Scottish setting of the play would be inappropriate to situate the all-black cast. While discussing the production with his wife Virginia, she came up with the idea of recasting the play in nineteenth-century Haiti, substituting the witches with voodoo priestesses; the play's action would be amplified with choirs, voodoo drums and music that were appropriate for its time and setting. By researching the Haitian history of that period and the slave revolts, Welles found his Macbeth in the historical figure of Henri Christophe, a key leader of the Haitian Revolution of 1791, who, after liberating the Haitians, turned into a tyrant himself. Another source of inspiration would have been Eugene O'Neill's recasting of similar events in *The Emperor Jones* (1920). The very act of modifying the setting of the original play and the choice of Haiti instantly initiated debates around racial politics. On the one hand, by using the life of Henri Christophe almost as a parable, it appears as if the play was commenting on the conditioned/confused black sensibilities around, firstly, ousting the oppressors and then imitating them. On the other hand, by choosing an existing historical black figure, Welles seemed to encourage

Figure 4.1 Jack Carter and Edna Thomas as Macbeth and Lady Macbeth. *Macbeth*. New York, 1936.

a renegotiation and re-examining of black history and culture. By using such a canonical play and playwright, Welles forced issues of racial identity and culture to the fore of American life, making white audiences, critics and federal government confront their prejudices.

Another issue that predominantly white critics raised concerned the language of the play. Most of the reviews complained about the inability of the actors to speak Shakespearean verse. Percy Hammond wrote 'what surprised me [. . .] was the inability of so melodious a race to sing the music of Shakespeare'; Burns Mantle more explicitly commented that Shakespearean verse 'is not the speech of negroes, nor within their grasp [. . .] with the spoken lines, though they are modestly and sensibly spoken, the coloured Macbeth becomes a good deal like a charade'; and even Brooks Atkinson, although writing a favourable review of the show, commented how it 'missed the sweep and scope of a poetic tragedy'.[16] What these reviewers completely missed, though, was the fact that the decision to let the performers speak as naturally as it came to them and to avoid imitating Shakespearean verse completely came directly from Welles. As Houseman recalls, Welles had strongly insisted on 'the elimination of the glib English Bensonian declamatory tradition of

Shakespearean performance and a return to a simpler, more direct and rapid delivery of the dramatic verse'.[17]

The inclusion of African drummers and witches was received with mixed feelings, with the latter deemed primitive, uneducated and untameable. However, some of them were known to the American stage; Asadata Dafora, for example, was established as a multifaceted artist in the USA. His original 1934 music/drama production of *Kykunkor (The Witch Woman)* combined authentic African music and dance, and is considered a pioneering performance of African American dance. The production's inclusion of rituals, narrative and dance was inspirational and allowed the African American artists to express their own anxieties, creativity and views on performativity by using material directly drawn from their own heritage and by using their own African dialects. Dafora's group of performers, Shologa Oloba, was absorbed by the New York Negro unit, and although not openly acknowledged by Welles or Houseman, Dafora's choreography and Abdul Assen's musical scores bear equal importance to Welles's direction in setting the mood of the show, creating its unique sound and its lasting effect to this day, being a unique example of blending Western European and American with African theatrical forms and traditions. Both Dafora and Assen, and their individual creative contributions to *Macbeth*, were hardly acknowledged by either Welles or Houseman. Perpetuating the racial stereotypes of the time, Dafora is simply presented as the head of the group of drummers, while Assen as the group's witch doctor is credited only with his first name. With their creative output suppressed, both men are almost eliminated from the creative process of the production.

By the time he became fully involved with the unit, Welles had already completed his adaptation of the play. He reduced the length of the original script almost by half; changed the banquet into a ball; revised and increased the role of Hecate (the goddess of magic and witchcraft, and traditionally a woman), played by Eric Burroughs in the production; enlarged the role of the three witches by adding a group of voodoo men and women and three drummers; changed the setting; and made significant use of lighting, sounds, costumes and masks, the latter designed by Nat Carson (Figure 4.2). Welles's inclusion of Hecate, the voodoo group led by a witch doctor and the drumming were instrumental in his interpretation of the canonical work. Up to that point, most productions of the play predominantly emphasised the psychological and physical effects of seeking power at any cost for one's own sake. While not disregarding this interpretation completely, Welles wanted to expose and capture the dual power of emotional fear of and fascination with the supernatural upon which Shakespeare's play lightly touches. Reacting against the early twentieth century's conventions of representing the witches as rational beings or caricatures, Welles wanted to re-establish their relevance but also to investigate a new avenue for exploring the play. Rather than rationally try

Figure 4.2 Nat Carson: designer of the set, costumes and masks for *Macbeth*. New York, 1936.

to explain and restrain the power of the supernatural, Welles decide to let it explode on stage, its flamboyant theatricality taking over the actors, the audience and the streets of Harlem and New York.

The setting equalled Welles's treatment of the supernatural in flamboyance. Designed by Carson, it involved a castle set with tower, battlements, staircases and a massive central gateway. But it was during the scenes in the jungle that the setting was transformed. Covering the set were massive backdrops, one of which presented luxurious vegetation coiled into the shape of a resting human skeleton. When the voodoo drums, chanting, thunder, wails and bells filled that scenery, the backdrop became so alive that it seemed to be part of the action. Equal to the setting in creating the play's atmosphere was the use of lighting. In the script there are seven pages with very specific instructions regarding each aspect of lighting; they include which side of the set would be illuminated, which character and at what stage of their speech, at what angle they would be lit, and even how many watts each bulb and projector should be. Abe Feder was responsible for the lighting and his contribution to Welles's vision of the performance was crucial. His lighting cues emphasised the theatricality of the production, adding to the supernatural atmosphere Welles intended to create; as Flanagan commented, Feder's lightning '[bathed] the whole affair in an unearthly glare'.[18] Its usage in an almost cinematic format, dissolving and fading, directed the audience's eye exactly where Welles intended it to go. Interestingly, then, his technique bears similarities to those used by the Living Newspapers, discussed in the previous chapters, thus implying a creative continuity and connection among the different units and performances of the FTP.

Welles's changes to Shakespeare's play can be seen from the very beginning. In the synopsis, his script interchanges the setting of each act between palace and jungle: one scene takes place in the jungle, the following in the palace. And it all begins in the jungle. Before the audience even sees anyone, its sense of hearing is engaged with the sounds of the trumpets, first booming, then mimicking the roll of thunder; then the sound of rain comes and slowly fades to silence. Macbeth's first line of 'So foul and fair a day I have not seen' draws the audience into the perpetual duality present in the play of jungle and palace, night and day, dark and light, ballroom music and voodoo drums, self and other, natural and supernatural.[19] Macbeth and Banquo have hardly exchanged any words when they notice Hecate and the group of witches. They are both bewildered by their presence and their out-of-this-world appearance, which is accompanied by the sound of thunder and drums; Macbeth is ready to move on and stops only when they pronounce their prophecy regarding him and Banquo, which partly comes true when Ross enters to announce his ascension to the position of Thane of Cawdor. When all three men exit the stage, Hecate, with his bull whip, and the witches take centre-stage. He instantly chastises them for letting Macbeth know of his future and for not including him in the process. Their presence on stage is accompanied by screeching, and the sounds of hooves and chanting. The scene ends with Hecate and the witches casting their spell on Macbeth as the 'charm's wound up'.[20]

The greatest contrast between the play's two worlds take place in act two. Scene one begins in the palace; after Duncan's murder, and Macduff and Malcolm's escape, Macbeth pronounces himself king. Instead of a coronation ceremony, Welles decided on a court ball, which presented an excellent opportunity for the costume department of the FTP to produce some brilliantly colourful outfits. The scene constantly mixes and weaves together the contrasting sounds of the waltz and the drums. It begins with Macbeth in his regal attire, surrounded by his court of noblemen and women. As the couples waltz to the music (choreographed by Clarence Yates), Banquo enters; the couples drift away and the confrontation between Macbeth and Banquo takes place to the sound of drums. Banquo's murder occurs and Hecate and the three witches appear, with their cackling filling the air. As Hecate starts his spell and the witches chant 'fair is foul and foul is fair' – almost quoting Macbeth's first line in the play – the waltz music starts again, very faintly.[21] The chanting begins to fade and the waltz increases. Hecate, having completed his spell on Banquo's ghost, starts dragging his body off the stage, while simultaneously the music

Figure 4.3 The 'cauldron' scene, in which the witches can be seen. *Macbeth*. New York, 1936.

grows louder and the stage is again populated by the dancing figures and other dignitaries, all greeting the Macbeths.

Macbeth is informed of Banquo's murder and joins Lady Macbeth at the ball, mixing with his guests; but Welles does not let Macbeth or the audience relax, as they are both suddenly confronted by Banquo's ghost. Visible only to Macbeth and the audience, the ghost not only disrupts the experience of the ball but sets in motion the events of scene two. Macbeth's behaviour becomes erratic and neither Lady Macbeth nor his guests can comprehend it. As the ball slowly dissolves, the guests leave and Lady Macbeth cannot bring Macbeth around. He is left slumped on the step, filled with guilt and apprehension; it is at this stage that the voodoo music is slowly introduced. As Macbeth's invocation to Hecate and the witches grows louder, so does the music. A tremendous burst of thunder is heard simultaneously with Macbeth's plea of 'answer me!' and Hecate appears, beckoning Macbeth to follow him into the jungle.[22]

Scene two of act two remains one of the most powerfully directed and choreographed scenes of the play. It takes place in the jungle; the voodoo men and women surround a cauldron that is smoking and the three witches are suspended in mid-air, already in a state of ecstasy before Hecate and Macbeth even appear (Figure 4.3). Standing behind the three drummers, with their fantastically designed headbands, isolated by lightning against the painted backdrop of palm branches and the human skeleton, the three witches captivated the audience. Even Brooks Atkinson, who was not greatly impressed by the company's overall acting, could not but comment:

> The witches have always worried the life out of the polite tragic stage ... But ship the witches down into the rank and fever-stricken jungle of Haiti, dress them in fantastic costumes, crowd the stage with the mad and gabbing throngs of evil worshippers, beat the jungle drums, raise the voices until the jungle echoes, stuff a gleaming naked witch doctor into the cauldron, hold up Negro masks in the baleful light – and there you have a witches' scene that is logical and stunning and a triumph of theatre art.[23]

The scene's vibrancy, the chanting, wild dancing and drumming, all added to the spectacle that Welles wanted to create. Macbeth is given the prophecy that 'none of woman born / Shall harm Macbeth' but he is also cursed by Hecate.[24] The scene is set for the third and final act, where Macbeth's downfall is witnessed by the audience, Lady Macbeth's madness and demise materialise and Macduff, fulfilling Hecate's prophecy, rids the kingdom of Macbeth. Welles also adapted the end of the play; similar to its beginning, the play ends with the sound of drums, music and voodoo voices. Unlike in Shakespeare's original ending, Welles finishes his version with Hecate, putting a spell on Macduff this time, setting in chain almost a recurrence of events similar to the ones already witnessed. Order is restored but the power of the supernatural is firmly established.

Welles cut many of the witches' lines from the original play but what he sacrificed in speech he recovered by theatrical means. He moved Hecate, the witches and the voodoo celebrants from the periphery to the centre of the play; they were all on stage when the curtain rose. Welles made sure that all three were presented, even when silent, in all but two of the production's eight scenes. And even in their silence, their presence was a constant reminder of the human struggle with the supernatural. One could argue that, by emphasising their roles, Welles's interpretation of *Macbeth* took away from Shakespeare's play the human agency, the lesson in morality and responsibility; instead, it seems to suggest that voodoo and the supernatural drive the development of events. Welles's interpretation invited the audience to a theatrical experience focused on the spectacle rather than on a possibly moral tale (Figure 4.4).

This experience of a spectacle was introduced to the audience even before they stepped into the theatre. On opening night, 14 April 1936, the Elks Lodge band, dressed in their light blue, scarlet and gold uniforms, took over the streets of Harlem with two huge banners announcing the production. Houseman spoke of 10,000 people surrounding the band as it approached the

Figure 4.4 Macbeth surrounded by the voodoo men and women. *Macbeth*. New York, 1936.

Lafayette Theatre, which was illuminated and crowded with people from both uptown and downtown society. Among them one could find Rose McClendon, Hallie Flanagan, Philip Barber and Jimmie Daniels. The mixed reactions from the press did not deter the audience from seeing the performance; it played in front of sold-out audiences for ten weeks before moving to the Adelphi Theatre.

Houseman and Welles's production of *Macbeth* has always been a point of contention amongst the African American literati regarding its iconic status. On the one hand, it did exemplify the richness and diversity of the artistic cohort and provided an antidote to the stereotypical roles the actors and actresses had to portray. On the other, it was the 'child' of Houseman and Welles, two white men, who, in self-promotional mode, would choose to produce something controversial and experimental, as the buzz generated around their names would do them no harm. The literati had placed so much expectation on the Negro unit as a space of education for its black audience, for providing a safe and experimental space for actors, directors and producers, a space for the wider black community, a space that would be voicing the agonies, anxieties, worries and injustices they faced because of their race, colour and class: in short, a space of their own.

The hope was that, ultimately, from the Negro unit of the FTP, a new, distinct and legitimate theatrical space would be created and sustained for the African American artists. And although these hopes and aspirations were dispelled, the production did exactly what it was supposed to do for Houseman and Welles. Welles became an instant celebrity and expert on Shakespeare. Houseman supervised one further project for the unit, the politically and racially charged *Turpentine*, about the history of black labour in the South. But as they both wanted to work more with classical texts, they were allowed to leave the Negro unit and start their own FTP unit to continue with their theatrical experimentations. With federal funding, their Project 891 was established; their first production was Christopher Marlowe's *Tragical History of Dr. Faustus*, which Welles directed and in which he played the leading role. It was followed by *Horse Eats Hat* in 1936, and in 1937 by *The Cradle Will Rock*. As discussed in Chapter 2, the controversies surrounding the production of the latter led to Houseman being fired and Welles resigning from the unit. But it was not long before they set up the acclaimed Mercury Theatre and more creative opportunities came their way.

But what about the original unit and its actors, creative and technical staff? How about the community and its audience? It was decided that the unit would have three directors, all African American: Gus Smith, who had co-written *Turpentine*, would be managing director; Harry Edward, a West Indian intellectual, was in charge of administrative services; and Carlton Moss was head of publicity.[25] At the same time, the Negro Dramatists Laboratory, organised by George Zorn, intended to train new African American playwrights to provide for 'the need of better written plays by Negroes for Negroes' but the venture did not succeed.[26] The new directors were faced with a problem similar to Houseman's regarding both the quality and the themes of future plays and performances. And even when plays were written, they were not produced. *Liberty Deferred*, a 1938 Living Newspaper by Abram Hill and John Silvera on the subject of race, never received a performance. Intended to challenge the way white audiences view and experience the history of race, the play was deemed too political and the Negro unit's directors were not powerful enough to push for its production. It is quite telling that Moss claimed 'it would have taken a Houseman to get it through'.[27]

For the contemporary academic cohort working on issues of race within the American theatrical tradition, the 1936 production of *Macbeth* represents many challenges. Benjamin Hilb makes a strong argument as to how the misappropriation of the religiousness of *Vodou* for the sake of 'voodoo' in the play has furthered the misunderstandings surrounding the religion, promulgated its ritualistic, supernatural power of suggestion and evil, and established it as a permanent marker of 'blackness', regardless of ethnicity. Stephanie Batiste has claimed that the term 'voodoo' 'conflated blackness with a wild, mystical, and dangerous primitive contrasted against Western civilization', and Marguerite Rippy suggested that 'while the vision of Haiti Welles presented was more fantasy than fact, the drummers gave the performance a dimension of authenticity'.[28] All three critics' arguments highlight different aspects of the production not previously considered in depth, or perhaps allowed to be discussed so openly and polemically in an accessible platform.

The production followed the Harlem riots of 1935 and the harsh realities of racism, poverty and social inequality. Thing were no better by 1936, but it is my opinion that Welles never intended to use this production as a means of political commentary on the social, economic and historical situation of African Americans. What attracted Welles was the opportunity for making something 'new', for shocking and experimenting with his favourite playwright, and for creating a name for himself. He was not actively involved in the political and social possibilities that new experimental theatre could present, nor did he aspire to Flanagan's desire for a socially inclusive American theatre. He saw an opportunity for having his most daring theatrical experiments, ideas and dreams realised with the financial backing of the American government, an opportunity that would not have presented itself in any other circumstances. Therefore, the 'voodoo' *Macbeth* was more of an experiment in new dramatic forms than a political or social statement. This argument is not intended to minimise the strongly influential dialogue conducted among the critics mentioned above but simply to add a further perspective on this exciting and complicated narrative that the production, the Negro unit and the FTP in general activated within American culture.

Flirting with the Greeks: Seattle and *Lysistrata*

Apart from the Negro unit in New York, the Seattle Negro Repertory Company was another unit that produced exciting plays, allowed new playwrights' works to be performed and attracted large audiences to its performances. Although not originally listed as an FTP unit, by joining it eventually, the Seattle Negro unit was afforded the opportunity to produce the plays that its African American ensemble wanted to produce, experiment with genres previously prohibited to them, expand their theatrical experiences and, in the process, avoid commercial and racial prejudice. The group's origins are not as straightforward as the New York one's, but it is closely tied up with the tremulous relationship between Glenn Hughes and Burton and Florence James.

Glenn Hughes, head of the Division of Drama at the University of Washington in Seattle from 1930 to 1961 and regional director of the FTP for the Northwest, had been instrumental in proposing a new experimental aesthetic for the American stage. Having completed his Guggenheim fellowship in 1928, which he spent in Europe meeting W. B. Yeats, Ezra Pound, D. H. Lawrence, Sinclair Lewis and T. S. Eliot, he returned to the USA with renewed interest and enthusiasm. One of his first decisions was to appoint Burton and Florence James as technical director and director of acting. Burton and Florence James were New York theatre artists who were proponents of art's social mission and wanted to make theatre socially relevant to American society. Greatly influenced by the classical European theatrical tradition, the Jameses saw European theatre as the source of revolutionary praxis and the newly socially informed American theatre (Broadway excluded) as its fulfilment. In pursuit of this goal, they were enticed in 1923 to Seattle and the prestigious Cornish College of the Arts. While there, they established a reputation of working with modern plays and displayed a commitment to producing experimental performances of Ibsen, Chekhov and Shaw. However, their artistic and socially focused political commitments brought them into direct collision with the college's conservative board of directors. After their resignation, they established their own group, the Seattle Repertory Company.

The Jameses operated the Seattle Repertory Playhouse from 1928 till 1951 as a forum for both classical and socio-politically informed theatre. During this period, their relationship with Hughes became antagonistic, culminating in the University of Washington owning the Playhouse building from 1951 onwards.[29] At the same time, the Jameses maintained a tentative relationship with Seattle's affluent class, upon which the Playhouse depended for support. Although it was happy to participate in and support productions of classical plays, resentment grew when the Jameses proposed more socially critical productions and enthusiastically sponsored the Negro Repertory Company (NCR) under the FTP. It was that 'betrayal' of Seattle's dominant social and cultural codes, along with their political commitment to engaged theatre, that led to the Jameses' persecution by the anti-Communist Canwell Committee hearings and forced them to give up their playhouse and theatre.

Similar to the New York Negro unit, the NCR represented another case of white directors in charge of African American actors, playwrights and technicians. Although the Playhouse had some experience of working with actors, the majority were amateurs. Among them was Theodore Browne, who had moved to Seattle from New York and had gained theatrical experience with the community-based Civic Repertory Theatre. When the NCR was established, he was named assistant director in an effort to allow for some fluidity and racial coherence within the unit, as mentioned earlier; Flanagan reportedly referred to him as 'our only playwright'.[30] He played the title role in the NCR's first production, *Noah*, and the leading part in its sensationally successful labour drama, *Stevedore*.

The NCR's productions allowed for the envisioning of alternative theatrical forms and expressions beyond the periphery of the American cultural hierarchy. Nowhere is this vision more clearly observed than in its most famous and briefest production. *Lysistrata* opened to a sell-out audience on 17 September 1936 to generally positive critical acclaim. The play was adapted by Browne, who mostly stayed faithful to the original; he set the action in Africa, hoping to emulate some of the New York 'voodoo' *Macbeth*'s success, and at the same time allow the audience to draw parallels with the events occurring simultaneously in Ethiopia. The play was cancelled indefinitely by Don Abel, the state WPA director, the following day and was never revived. Similar to *Ethiopia* and *The Cradle Will Rock*, the Seattle *Lysistrata* has been mythologised within the history of the FTP. But what were the reasons behind this abrupt cessation? How could a classical play performed over centuries embarrass Seattle's social sensibilities? Was the NCR's flirtation with a canonical text a piece of hubris deserving punishment? Did the NCR, like Icarus, fly too high and aspire to greater theatrical, social and cultural inclusivity? Or was it a question of how Aristophanes' comedy had been presented and appropriated by contemporary American culture?

Since the first production of *Acharnians* in 1886 by the faculty and students of the University of Pennsylvania, Aristophanes' comedies had become a regular choice for American university productions; professional productions soon followed, among them *Lysistrata*, which remains by far the most popularly interpreted Aristophanic play. Its main theme is the intervention of Lysistrata to stop the Peloponnesian War taking place between Athens and Sparta. In her efforts to do so, she successfully mobilises the women of Athens and Sparta, and draws support from women all over Greece. Their actions put significant pressure on the men; not only do they withhold sex until the war's conclusion, but they also occupy the Acropolis, which housed the treasury, thus preventing any further funding for the war. The occupation of the Acropolis bears further significance: a primarily emblematic space of male dominance, power and government becomes a female space of resistance that redefines democracy and participation within a public area. It is the combination of both sexual and political components of the play, the physical with the radical, the private with the public, that determines the public and artists' continual fascination with it.

During the first two decades of the twentieth century, the play's interpretations within Europe tended to focus on one of the two themes, sexuality or politics. And the US stage tended to approach the play through the lens of a Broadway musical production. However, this attitude changed on both continents with the 1923 Soviet production directed by Vladimir Nemirovich-Danchenko of the Moscow Art Theatre (MAT). A co-founder of MAT, Nemirovich-Danchenko worked tirelessly to promote its vision of a new theatre within Soviet culture. Swept up in the Russian Revolution and very in tune with the new avant-garde trends in theatre, he established the Musical Theatre of the MAT in 1919 (renamed the Nemirovich-Danchenko Musical Theatre in 1926). With this theatre he wanted to respond to the aesthetic and ideological challenges that the new revolutionary regime posed for the artist and for culture in general. Focusing on Constructivism's emphasis on the three-dimensional aspects of an object, on the non-representational theatre of

Meyerhold, and his emphasis on the utilitarian function of the actor's body and movement, and on Alexander Tairov's synthetic theatre, which incorporated the actors' singing, acting and dancing abilities into the design aspects of a performance, Nemirovich-Danchenko aimed to create a synthetic theatre for the lyrical stage, freeing it in the process from the old clichéd performative principles.

Among the plays that were chosen for this new synthetic theatre was *Lysistrata*. Rehearsals began in the autumn of 1922, after Stanislavsky and the main company of MAT had left for their renowned tours of Europe and the United States. MAT's position within the new revolutionary reality was still precarious but Nemirovich-Danchenko saw in the play a comedy of 'exceptional social, moral and political relevance'.[31] As Kotzamani's detailed discussion of the 1923 production demonstrates, he chose to limit the sexual element and instead concentrate on the female political praxis of stopping the war and occupying the Acropolis. In doing so, though, he moved away from the apolitical stance that MAT and Stanislavsky still represented; once in favour of such apoliticism, he was now advocating that '[artists] should not keep away from life, nor claim we are apolitical. Total apoliticism, what absurdity! ... The artist lives with his time. Moreover, it is interesting to respond to the demands of a new audience.'[32]

Nemirovich-Danchenko entrusted his artistic vision of the play to the dramatist Dmitry Smolin. Smolin's version is more political than comic; the sexual instinct so prominent in the Greek original and the comic effects it has on the events leading to the war's resolution are muted. Instead, the resolution of the war is presented as 'the outcome of mediated and carefully implemented political scheming'.[33] As both Athenians and Spartans assure Lysistrata at the end of the play, 'Our woes have made a unit of us. / We are all parts of one large body, / Aching and crying for peace and love.'[34] It appears, then, that the women's sexual ban has served its didactic purpose of awakening the men to the need for change, to the need to embrace the new reality and morally unite in such acceptance. This political message of change is further emphasised by Smolin's arrangement of the choruses. Aristophanes' play is a rare example of the choruses being divided from the beginning but reconciling in the end, thus promoting the message of peace and resolution. Smolin keeps the two choruses, and although the male one, represented by old men, remains intact, the female one undergoes much restructuring. It is not represented by a singular entity of old women but by a polyphony of female voices, some organised in small groups, others anonymous, some young and others old; some lines are also reserved for the characters of Myrrhina and Lampito. The women's polyphony becomes pronounced when they openly taunt the old men's chorus: 'Our numbers overawe you? ... What you see is only a thousandth part of us!'[35] Juxtaposing the polyphony of a vibrant, age-defying female chorus with the monotony of an elderly male one, Smolin appears to comment on the contemporary Soviet reality: on the one hand, the new progressive revolutionary reality, steeped in action and change; and on the other, the remnants of the old guard, clinging to a past reality that is no longer applicable.

To complement his vision of the play, Nemirovich-Danchenko commissioned Isaac Rabinovich to create the set and costumes. In designing the set for *Lysistrata*, Rabinovich chose an abstract, practical rotating stage, influenced by Constructivism. The design involved a few high, serpentine, white columns furnished with semicircular stands in an attempt to evoke the idea of the Acropolis and the Parthenon. In the spirit of Constructivism, Rabinovich combined the recognisable columns with more abstract spaces for the actors to perform in, such as rotating platforms linked by staircases. The design's simplicity and plasticity allowed for versatility in terms of performing the drama, the chorus, the songs and the more physically choreographed movements. In one of them, half of the female chorus is situated on one of the platforms, pouring water over the men below them; in another, Lysistrata is positioned on the top platform, watching over the old men's stampede. And in a third, both male and female choruses address the audience, vying for their favour – but it is only the female one that occupies the platform.[36] In all these documented photographs, it is only the women that occupy the upper platforms and stairs, representative of the Acropolis, the centre of political power, governance and money. Men are reduced to sitting, being heckled and observing the actions on the bottom stage. This transferral in the gendered use of space and its representation of power is facilitated by the way that Rabinovich enabled Constructivism's focus on the multidimensionality of an object to affect the rotating set design.

The play's success allowed it to be transferred to the American stage. *Lysistrata* opened at Jolson's 59th Street Theatre in New York on 4 December 1925, before moving to Chicago in the spring. The play was performed entirely in Russian with English subtitles; the translation was conducted by George and Gilbert Seldes, whom Oliver Sayler oversaw. Having established himself as an authority on revolutionary Soviet theatre, Sayler went to great lengths to emphasise the production's artistic merits, divorcing them completely from its ideological context. In his eyes, the play was revolutionary, as it dealt with the universal issues of war, peace, sexual desire, and the power struggle between men and women. What he purposefully left out was a critical consideration of this production, coming out of a revolutionary country that had, and was still negotiating, issues surrounding the power struggle and change of regime, with new and innovative ways of expressing these debates. The production was received very warmly and excitedly by the American public, and as a result of Sayler's influence, the artistic aspects of the production received all the attention.

The considerable public interest it generated and the critical acclaim it received firmly situated the Russian *Lysistrata* within the American theatrical sensibility. One of the play's translators, Gilbert Seldes, recognising the play's potential for attracting and appealing to contemporary audiences, decided to write his own American version. Greatly influenced by Nemirovich-Danchenko's adaptation and using it as a model, Seldes constructed a distinctively American version of the play by synthesising both avant-garde and more popular elements of singing, dancing, humour, farce and burlesque. The production was very successful commercially, as well as aesthetically, and influenced the staging of *Lysistrata* within the USA until the early 1960s, including the 1936 production for the FTP.[37]

As Seldes himself acknowledged, the project was 'an attempt to create *Lysistrata* in the terms of the American theatre'.[38] Seldes was approaching American theatre from a very particular angle; he chose to work on the Russian adaptation that he himself helped translate, rather than opting for the Greek text or any English translations of his time. Reading his adaptation of the Russian text, one cannot help but compare and contrast; whereas, in the Russian version, Lysistrata's individual actions are considered not on their own merit but as part of the overall female group, the American version creates a heroic Lysistrata, whose leadership skills overshadow all the men's and set her apart from the other (especially young) females, who are portrayed as more free-spirited, sexually promiscuous and somewhat unruly.[39] Although influenced politically by the Russian adaptation, Seldes's approach was emphatic of the American core value of individual liberal identity.

The set design was constructed by Bel Geddes. Similar to Rabinovich's, Geddes's design was architecturally influenced by the Acropolis and there was no formal curtain. As Kotzamani comments, though, the set design gave the impression of verticality: the minimalistically designed citadel was directly associated with modernist architecture and the vertical towers closely resembled the New York skyscrapers.[40] Unlike Nemirovich-Danchenko's directions, Geddes chose to place the women on a fixed point in and before the citadel, not moving in any direction, while the men were slowly but steadily moving upwards, trying to reclaim the citadel space as a way of consolidating their status and power. Although both set designs were similar in their use of modernist forms of representation, they were used in distinctively different ways to promote different ideological and cultural readings of Lysistrata's actions.

Another difference between the two productions involved the female costume designs. Whereas Rabinovich dressed the women characters in simple, comfortable costumes that were not sexually provocative, the same cannot be said for Geddes. Designed by Mildred Orrick, they were 'elegantly constructed of sheer chiffon' with 'flesh-colored undergarments [that] simulated nudity'; a dancer 'opted for bare breasts slightly veiled by a transparent chiton', whereas 'the courtesans wore jewels in their navels and painted their nipples'.[41] The emphasis on the sexuality and sexualisation of the female body seemed to reinforce the reading of the play as a provocative yet entertaining battle between the sexes, dealing with the basic human desires of peace, prosperity and sexual intimacy. The play and production invested in the aesthetic appreciation of the spectacle, with its modernist, sculpture-like set design and the beautifully designed female clothes. Added to that, the humorous, burlesque and slapstick moments guaranteed that the play was a success with its audience and most critics.

The prolonged impact of Seldes's adaptation, which lasted until the early 1960s, signifies, in my opinion, the production's popularity in terms of aesthetics. The production became a popular contemporary spectacle that successfully amalgamated a modernist set design with farcical and burlesque acting. But in terms of reworking and reimagining the play's intended message, both Seldes and Geddes failed in their utopian social theatre. For two people who had expressed their intention to create a new form of theatre that would align avant-garde and pop culture with a social agenda in mind, it seems that their *Lysistrata* fails to do so. It took six years between their production and the NCR's to try to rework Aristophanes' comedy to awaken and challenge the American stage socially and racially.

Browne's *Lysistrata*, subtitled an 'African version', was not the first attempt by an African American playwright at adapting Aristophanes' comedy. When discussing the unavailability of socially conscious plays to follow on from *Macbeth*, Houseman mentioned a new play written by Zora Neale Hurston. Her play was a Negro *Lysistrata* updated to a fishing community in contemporary Florida, 'where the men's wives refused them intercourse until they won their fight with the canning company for a living wage'.[42] The play, addressing black labour issues, shocked everyone within the Negro unit, whether on the left or right of the political spectrum, because of it 'saltiness'.[43] Although at opposing ends, both parties concluded that Hurston's adaptation presented dangerously explosive working-class issues regarding working conditions and wages. As a result, Houseman had to abandon Hurston's ideas and her original script has been lost. Judging from her interest in socially, racially and culturally invested issues, as well as her flair for weaving humour into her narrative, one can only assume that Hurston's *Lysistrata* would have exposed and explored said issues combined with laughter and wit.

Browne started working on his adaptation as soon as the performances of *Stevedore* were completed. He never explained why Aristophanes' play was chosen over other plays, but it presented an alternative to the huge success of the New York 'voodoo' *Macbeth*. As he himself explained,

> We were going to do [*Macbeth*], and I'll tell you what happened there [. . .] We had a lot of trouble in getting the people to learn those lines.

The lines were unfamiliar to them. This is Shakespeare, you see, and we had that trouble [...] You had to have material that they could handle. As I said about *Macbeth*, they couldn't handle it. It was a nice idea, but it was just out of the question [...] And then there was *Lysistrata*. I designed it with them in mind and wrote it.[44]

Although he never mentioned which version he based his adaptation on, the final product remains mostly faithful to Aristophanes' original script but was also greatly influenced by Welles's *Macbeth*. To begin with, the play takes place in the African locale of Ebonia, although he keeps the names of Acropolis, Athens, Sparta, Boetia and Corinth as in the original. The group of men and women are dressed in native African costumes, he makes both biblical and voodoo references, there is drumming in each act, a female witch appears in act two, and the language spoken facilitated a comfortable identification with Seattle's African American communities and culture. Each act begins and ends in the dark – as opposed to Seldes's and Geddes's production, which was enveloped in multicoloured lights. As in *Macbeth*, there is a drummer located on the extreme right downstage, who repeats the same beats/message, which in turn is repeated by the female chorus and an off-stage drummer. The other similarity is the old woman, located on the extreme left side of the stage and dressed in native African costume, who is stirring something in a large cauldron, presumably keeping time with the beats. The positioning of the male drummer and the female witch at the extremes of the stage may symbolically indicate the distancing between men and women in the play in terms of intimacy and their views about the war. The fact that their actions mimic and complement each other is indicative of the final reconciliation and peace.

Browne kept the main theme of the original play intact – the women of Athens and Sparta would abstain from any sexual action until their husbands and lovers signed a peace treaty. But this was the first time that the stage would be overtaken by the power and sexuality of black bodies. The audiences, up to that moment, were used to seeing only the sexualised white female and male bodies appropriating the stage. But at this production, the viragoes' bodies were black, exuding sensuality, intelligence, determination and strength. The combination of these qualities and their exhibition by the black female body not only was revolutionary but also challenged the position of the African American woman, within both her own community and American society overall. Whether intentionally or not, Browne's choice of play brought to the fore racial issues involving whole strata of American society, but also gender issues and behaviours among African American communities. If the black man and his body were considered inferior, primal and insignificant within America (apart from their monetary value), the black female and her body's beauty, value and presence remained subordinate and unacknowledged, even within her own community. In this play, the black women and their bodies address their position within their communities and American society in general, and assert their radically indispensable intelligence, sexuality and authority.

From the very beginning of the play, Lysistrata is trying to mobilise the rest of the women to disprove the men's opinion that 'we are incapable of thinking or doing anything for ourselves'.[45] Forcing the subject further, Lysistrata's exchange with Calonice confronts some of the stereotypical gender views on women's abilities and place within society:

> CALONICE: Just what do women know about running a country? They can't even run the men!
> LYSISTRATA: If the women assemble, those from the Boetian and Spartan tribes, and we women of Athens – in one united front – we can save our country from war. I'll bet you, and you can take all the odds you want.
> CALONICE: War is a man's business. Not ours. I don't want to get mixed up in some silly war!
> LYSISTRATA: (rises to her feet, argumentative) War concerns us just as much as it does the men. Our family life and marriage relationships are broken up. We bring children into the world – for what? – to be used for cannon-fodder. And you say war is man's business?
> CALONICE: Well, don't our statesmen take care of all that for us?
> LYSISTRATA: They sure do! And what a hell of a mess the country's in right now![46]

Calonice's views run congruent with the way that females – and, in this case, black females – are viewed societally. She believes in the clearly defined boundaries that the patriarchal community has established, perceiving her ability to become actively involved in politics and war as unnatural, prohibitive and even uncomfortable. But Lysistrata moves past these boundaries. She questions the efficacy of the male-dominated political system to propose and provide a solution to the war, and pushes women to reflect on their abilities, and their positions within their community and their individual families. She invites them to awaken to their intellectual powers, their social responsibilities for taking action and proposing change.

The play's powerful feminist and political messages were enveloped in comedy and satire. Following the above powerful speech and after the Athenian women have assembled, Lysistrata must prepare them for the imminent arrival of their enemies, the Boetian and Spartan women. For their movement to have the desirable effect, Lysistrata is aware that she needs to enforce a peace treaty among them first. When she announces her invitation, the Athenian women are aghast, calling them 'savages' and 'dummer', with Myrrhina most clearly expressing their sentiments when she comments, 'I think the whole affair is outrageous, ridiculous! I resent having to hobnob with those tribal hussies who live in the bush. They're heathens, all of them, uncivilized and they still practice voodoo.'[47] She continues to insult Lampito (the head of the Spartan women), commenting how her physique resembles that of a 'cow' as a result of working in the fields pushing a 'plow'. Lampito and the other women do not hold back, accusing the Athenians of sitting 'on your fat rump and warm[ing] up chairs', being 'cream-puffs' and thinking 'they're the cream of Ebonia just because they happen to live in the capital'.[48] Although their heated exchange (which ends up in a short-lived brawl) might be read as another stereotypical representation of females pitted against each other, it can also represent a way of exposing racial tensions and attitudes within the African American communities themselves.

Hill suggests that Browne's inclusion of all the above insults points to the 'shifting demographics of the 1930s black population' and the increasing divide between them.[49] One of the outcomes of the booming economy of the 1920s was the desertion of the countryside and the agrarian lifestyle by many African Americans in pursuit of a different life in the city hubs. However, that move was resented by those already occupying the cities, as it presented a major threat to their equilibrium, an almost existential crisis in their cosmopolitan lifestyle. The conflicts between these communities intensified after the Great Depression, with jobs becoming scarcer and standards of living declining. Browne's text does not shy away from confronting such issues; to the white audience, the African American communities represented one uniform group but *Lysistrata* explores these divisions for both white and black audiences to experience and acknowledge. Using comedy and satire and appropriating the 'cow' lines from the original Greek text legitimise Browne's exposé of the inherent tensions among the African American communities and didactically inform the white audience of their misconceptions regarding the homogeneity of said communities in terms of attitudes, class, power and social presence.

Although revolutionary in this way, Browne's text is careful not to employ any language or terminology that might associate it with leftist politics. Possibly aware of the controversies regarding the production of *Ethiopia*, discussed in Chapter 2, as well as rising antileftist sentiments, Browne's text uses the terms 'comrade' and 'Communism' only once and in different acts. In a sense, the utterances cancel each other out, thus rendering moot any allegiance with the American Communist Party or leftist ideology. The first instance is spoken by Lysistrata in act one, when she is finally allowed to address all the gathered women and unfold her plan: 'very well, comrades, I will now mention it'.[50] The word is used more in a reconciliatory manner, to bring the previously brawling groups of women together, rather than as a term that portrays a common ideology. The second instance is uttered by the Committeeman, near the end of the play. Having realised that the Athenians and Spartans are close to making peace and are calling on Lysistrata to lead them, he exits the stage with the rest of the old men, shouting 'Communists! Treason! Anarchists! Revolution!'[51] The Committeeman's utterance – written within a parenthesis – in presented as the last attempt of a delusional, shrieking man who is unable to accept the decision that has been made. Carrying on from the way he is presented in act one, the Committeeman occupies the role of the irrelevant buffoon, who leads an equally irrelevant group of old men who make fools of themselves, have no arguments to present and are stuck in their archaic status quo. Read this way, these two statements clearly reveal Browne's reluctance to promote a politically ideological narrative in his *Lysistrata*.

As argued above, his *Lysistrata* reveals more aspects of the African American females' lives, concerns and status within their own communities and within American society as a whole. Unlike Aristophanes' play, which focused primarily on married women, Browne's adaptation introduces single females into the discussion, along with their concerns regarding sexual relationships with their partners. By examining the dialogue between two couples, the married Myrrhina and Cinisias and the unmarried Melistice and Leonidas, one can see a variety of attitudes towards African American women. In the first instance, Cinisias attributes Myrrhina's rejection of his sexual demands to Lysistrata's influence:

> CINISIAS: [. . .] What has Lysistrata got that I haven't got?
> MYRRHINA: Brains!
> CINISIAS: Brains! I hate these females with brains! They can't get along with their own husbands, so these miserable creatures go around breaking up other people's homes! You listen to me, Myrrhina. Stay away from that woman. She's not your kind. She's touched in the head from reading too many books.
> MYRRHINA: I think it's nice for women to read. You've never encouraged me to read.
> CINISIAS: I know what's good for you, that's why. (rages) I'd give my right eye to see that Lysistrata!
> MYRRHINA: You've seen her and you still have your right eye![52]

In this exchange Cinisias is eager to establish his male authority within the relationship; when Myrrhina resists, he readily reaches the conclusion that she has been morally and intellectually corrupted by Lysistrata. He is promoting the stereotypical representation of a married woman as the silent partner within the marriage, the one who does what her husband tells her and does not need to have access to any further knowledge or literature. This regressive view of women, although used for comic effect, does signify its persistence within the narrative of the power relation between male and female. At the same time, it highlights the racist attitude that makes education unavailable to African Americans, and this attitude works on two levels: both between the dominant white American male and the African American male, and between the African American male and his contemporary female. When Myrrhina refuses to follow blindly, Cinisias's rage flares up – possibly hinting at the physical abuse that African American women experienced within their marriages. His last resort is their child, playing on Myrrhina's motherly instincts, but his plan backfires as Myrrhina sees through it; instead, she follows Lysistrata's plan of teasing him and leaving him wanting.

Melistice and Leonidas's relationship develops differently. Melistice's main argument against intimacy is that they are not married:

> MELISTICE: No! – In the first place, we are not married.
> LEONIDAS: But the whole village knows we're engaged. Besides, I believe a man should know something about a woman before he marries her.
> MELISTICE: That means you don't trust me.
> LEONIDAS: No, it doesn't, Melistice. It's just logic.
> MELISTICE: Logic he calls it.
> LEONIDAS: You're practically mine already.
> [. . .]
> MELISTICE: There still the balance due before I'm lawfully yours.
> LEONIDAS: I'll pay the balance in cash from my army bonus.
> MELISTICE: I hate being married on the instalment plan![53]

If the married African American female had some standing within her community, the single or even betrothed one had close to zero. In the exchange above, Browne allows the latter's concerns finally to be uttered and enter the public domain. He acknowledges her precarious social position and the realities around her circumstances. By painting a more realistic picture of the diversity within the African American community, Browne encourages his audience to reflect on their constrictive views of said community. Recognising the tensions, different attitudes, beliefs and behaviours dispels the over-simplified views of society and community, and awakens them to the complexities of reality and life.

Lysistrata opened to a sell-out audience in the Moore Theatre on 17 September 1936. But that was its only performance, as the following day its abrupt closure was announced by Don Abel – the state supervisor – although they were sold out six months in advance. Although he did not see the performance himself, he heard rumours that the show was indecent and vulgar. There are different versions of how those rumours were circulated but in all of them it appears that only two out of all those in attendance on the night of the premiere made the above allegations. This begs the question, why was a production of a play that was approved and rehearsed for weeks with no objections from any official quarters cancelled so swiftly because of two discontented spectators? What could possibly have led to this new act of censorship and what were the consequences of such an act for the Seattle NCR, but also for all the Negro units functioning within the FTP?

It is indeed extraordinary to consider that the rehearsals for *Lysistrata* had gone ahead with no real difficulties. Even Flanagan, when considering the history of the FTP, underlined the importance of the play; she recounted how 'in *Lysistrata*, *Stevedore*, and *Noah* we present plays whose universal theme remains the same regardless of race or creed'.[54] What makes the play's termination even more preposterous is the fact that Harry Hopkins had visited Seattle the week before the opening night but there are no reports that he noticed anything damaging in the Seattle FTP project that could create serious issues for the WPA as a whole. Abel's decision was supported by J. Howard Miller, Flanagan's western regional director, who travelled to investigate the dispute. Although he did not find anything to justify the accusations of 'indecency and bawdy', Miller was not happy with the overall quality of the production. Writing to Flanagan, he found the play 'badly cast, badly directed, cheaply costumed and had no focal point'.[55] Abel's decision stood and *Lysistrata* was cancelled for good with no plans to reproduce it in another theatre. Ironically, although Flanagan mentioned the play's importance in *Arena*, as quoted above, she spent little time dwelling on or explaining the reasons behind the production's cancellation. Unlike *Ethiopia* or *The Cradle Will Rock*, *Lysistrata* received little attention and the imbalance in the treatment of censorship that each play faced needs to be addressed, researched and questioned.

A number of modern commentators, when addressing the act of censorship, highlight as one key factor the white anxieties regarding black female sexuality.[56] Flanagan herself suggested that the play offered too much 'spice' for the Seattle audience.[57] And as historians Errol G. Hill and James Vernon Hatch remarked, 'a sex comedy played by Blacks had become in the white gaze, pornographic, even though the costumes, language, and physical action were designed not to be provocative'.[58] Although Browne was careful not to exaggerate the play's overt sexuality, the presence of black male and female bodies on stage displaying their eroticised nature seemed to detract from the play's socially conscious ideas. Compared to Seldes's production, in which the oversexualised female costumes were accepted as part of the production and seen as 'normal', the black *Lysistrata*'s celebration and sexual acknowledgement of the black male and female bodies incited the deeply seated discomfort of a socially repressed white eroticism. Whereas the white body was associated with a normalised sexuality, the black body represented both a forbidden, repressed desire and an uncomfortable acknowledgement of its existence and presence as equal to white ones. The black body's enactment on stage, its entrance to the public (voyeuristic) space, legitimised its existence and forced its entry into the culturally protected area of what is standard and normal for the white. It was no longer standing on the periphery of society, being disregarded, abused and raped, but took centre-stage in an acknowledgement of its vitality, virility, sexuality and beauty.

By placing the black body at the centre of the stage, Browne redefined and reconstituted what was culturally normal, accepted, beautiful and lawful. Coupling these ideas with the revolutionary peace politics of Aristophanes, the play exemplified a significant threat to the social, political and cultural strata of Southern America. If the black body could legitimately occupy the public stage and space, then further issues of racial behaviours, economics, political power, social positioning and civil rights could be addressed. Instead of being disenfranchised, the African Americans took centre-stage, their concerns acknowledged and voiced, their intellect growing and their bodies finally seen for their materiality, expressiveness and sexuality. Their existence need no longer serve any purpose other than that of being. But American society was in no way ready for such socially altering revolutionary politics and neither was Flanagan. Although she was sympathetic and empathetic to the plight of African Americans and wanted to provide an expressive podium for them, she was not prepared to fight local WPA officials, Senators or Congress for this production. Witham suggested that, with the nationwide opening of Sinclair Lewis's *It Can't Happen Here* only a few weeks away, Flanagan would not entertain a confrontation with the WPA for a singular production in a remote part of the FTP network.[59] Witham's argument is very valuable but it also highlights the inadequacies of the concept of a national theatre for the USA, as well as the inherent contradictions of the FTP's dual status as both a relief and a creative agent.

Creating and attempting to establish a national theatre for the whole of the USA was not a feat for the faint-hearted. The complexities of such racially, historically, socially and economically diverse communities were not easily addressed or accommodated from the very beginning. Flanagan perhaps thought that she would have had more than the four years the project lasted to address them; she probably considered this venture a life-long enterprise. But the reality was that the very existence of the Negro units within the FTP, 'the idea of autonomous Negro units, leading to a national Negro theatre or a fully integrated American theatre, including whites and blacks equally, threatened the status quo'.[60] Cultivating and raising the consciousness of African Americans through theatre was a bold undertaking, one that drew considerable fire from Congress and contributed to the FTP's demise. Although not openly objecting to the existence of the Negro units, the Dies Committee was very suggestive of the connection between African Americans and 'un-American' behaviour and Communist tendencies. Relying heavily on the testimonies of Hazel Huffman and Sallie Saunders, the committee exploited the links that these women made between race, sexuality and politics.[61] Huffman's testimony included references and rested on detailing twenty-six 'un-American' productions that included a good number produced by the Negro units; she made very specific mention of 'Negro songs of protest' when referring to How Long Brethren?[62] Sallie Saunders's testimony also claimed racial tolerance that went beyond 'acceptable' societal norms. In a carefully choreographed session, Dies makes it clear that the committee wants to examine the issue of race 'insofar as it forms a vital part of Communist teachings, practices and doctrines'.[63] Saunders's testimony relates an incident when a fellow African American employee asked her out on a date. Her complaint to her supervisor was met with tolerance and acceptance, promoting what Dies called 'social equality'.[64] She ended her testimony by positively confirming Dies's question that social equality and the merging of races are parts of the Communist programme.[65]

This implication placed the FTP firmly within the parameters of what constituted 'un-American' behaviour and was added to further charges relating to the Living Newspaper productions discussed earlier. But at the same time, it further reveals white anxiety that interracial mixing automatically constituted interracial sexual relations and placed African Americans in a precarious position. Although *Lysistrata* was not mentioned in any of the testimonies, its abrupt cessation and the lack of clarity regarding the reasons behind its censorship point to the aforementioned societal and political anxieties and to the whole project's failure to adhere to its mantra of free, adult and uncensored theatre. But it appears that the FTP was, consciously or unconsciously, mirroring the attitudes of its governmental patron.

While the Roosevelt administration promoted with enthusiasm women in leadership roles, its track record on race was disappointing. Similarly, while Hallie Flanagan's story and her efforts to remake the American theatre, are focal, present and accounted for, Rose McClendon's work has been mostly suppressed, erased and discarded. Du Bois's observation that 'the problem of the Twentieth Century is the problem of the color line' seems fitting.[66] His comment, made as early as 1900, pre-empts the artistic struggle between the white administration and African American artists, writers and performers. This tension was evident primarily to black actors; as Sarah Oliver Jackson, an active member of the Negro Repertory Theatre (NRT) in Seattle, remembered, 'all through the Negro Theatre, the head people in the theatre were white, and, of course, it was their type of idea of what the Negro theatre was about'.[67] The African American performers were caught up between their vision of theatre, drama and performance and Flanagan's national policies. The segregated theatrical industry, reflecting contemporary societal attitudes, could not permit any more revolutionary politics. Experimental theatrical techniques and Socialist politics from white men were barely tolerated but allowing racial politics and concerns to take centre-stage was strongly undesirable.

When studying or reading about both 'voodoo' *Macbeth* and black

Lysistrata, one cannot help but become deeply involved with the politics of gender and race. Both plays had all-black casts; both took well-known, classic plays and transported them to an African context; both made use of African cultural traits such as music, drums, voodoo and costumes; and both positioned the African American performers on central stage, as the main protagonists. But the two plays did not enjoy the same fortunes: the first was proclaimed a masterpiece, has been positioned within the pantheon of experimental and forward-thinking performances and contributed greatly to Welles's career. *Lysistrata*, on the other hand, has, until recently, been largely ignored, omitted from any serious consideration of the history of the FTP and closed after one performance. Both plays were adapted and directed by men, one white and the other black. Both dealt with strong leaders and characters, one a man and the other a woman. And both dealt with important social and political issues, the one through tragedy and the other through comedy.

Viewing the plays in such a dialectical manner does not intend to assess which one was better than the other, but it does highlight societal expectations of the time regarding their performance and the failure of the FTP to extend its proposed theatrical experimentation to issues of gender and race. Watching the rise and fall of Macbeth and the intricacies of power with a dollop of African voodoo to make the African experience more 'authentic' was more acceptable than *Lysistrata*'s explosion of empowered black female bodies on stage. *Lysistrata*, visually, thematically and performatively, pushed societal sensibilities beyond its self-prescribed limits. Watching strong women, confident in their bodies and sexuality, taking over the stage, gaining control of a dramatic situation, and dispelling the myths of male power, order and hierarchy was intolerable. And it was intolerable predominantly because the female body was black.

The Negro units remained an important and invaluable part of the FTP until its disbandment in 1939. Both units in New York and Seattle went on to produce further productions that attracted large audiences. The New York unit found it hard to replicate the success of the 'voodoo' *Macbeth*; the NCR unit produced *An Evening with Dunbar* in 1938, based on the life of poet Paul Laurence Dunbar. With diminishing funds, racial prejudice, the gathering pace of the constant opposition of the WPA, Congress and the Dies Committee, the Negro units found it hard to sustain themselves. But for all the difficulties they faced, they remained exceptional groups, comprised of talented performers, who worked tirelessly and creatively to produce plays, whether existing or newly written, that promoted social, political, racial and gender concerns.

5

THE CHILDREN'S THEATRE: PLAYING WITH PINOCCHIO AND THE BEAVERS

> These [public theatres] gave added impetus to the theatre for children. They developed new uses for theatre talents in the field of education, therapeutics, diagnosis, social, and community work.[1]
>
> Hallie Flanagan, *Arena*.

> If I had a real wishing stone, [. . .] I would wish that everybody in the whole world was nine years old.[2]
>
> Saul and Lantz, 'The Revolt of the Beavers', I, i, 129.

CHILDREN'S THEATRE IN THE USA

During its short existence, the FTP – as already discussed in the previous chapters – was not afraid to delve into new theatrical territories, explore controversial issues and foster new creative and collaborative relationships with people from all walks of life. Therefore it can come as no surprise that it also established a Children's Theatre unit with regional units throughout, employing out-of-work playwrights, designers, puppeteers and vaudeville actors. The Children's Theatre unit produced new and adapted plays that were both entertaining and educational. The plays attracted massive audiences and were enjoyed equally by children and grown-ups. But not without its controversies, the unit did manage to upset a few Congressmen; particularly, the production of *Revolt of the Beavers* was accused of educating children in Communism. The controversy was picked up by Senator Dies and was included in his arsenal against the FTP.

It is impossible to determine chronologically exactly when it began but theatre for children, as Stuart Bennett describes it in terms of professionally scripted plays, started some time in the late nineteenth century in Europe in the form of 'touring companies with dramatisations of folk and fairy tales'.[3] In the UK, J. M. Barrie's 1904 *Peter Pan* is the first widely recognised play that conforms to this description. Bertha Waddell formed the pioneering Scottish Bertha Waddell's Children's Theatre in 1927, giving performances of plays written especially for younger audiences. And in 1935 Peter Slade founded the touring company the Parable Players to perform medieval plays in schools and other venues. Children's theatre bloomed further in the UK after the end of the World War II with the formation of several children's companies (such as John Allen's Glyndebourne Children's Theatre), which produced original plays written for specifically child-based audiences. Other European children's theatres included the Moscow Theatre for Children, established as early as 1918 and best known internationally as the birthplace of Sergei Prokofiev's *Peter and the Wolf*. The theatre (initially run by Natalya Sats from the age of fifteen till her prosecution by Stalin) was established right after the October Revolution and is considered the world's first professional theatre for children, specialising in music, dance, acrobatics and drama. Its stylistically inventive productions combined fairy-tale elements with contemporary social issues.

Meanwhile, in the USA, there was a parallel growth. The first children's theatre was the Children's Educational Theatre, founded in 1903 by Alice Minnie Herts and established at the Educational Alliance, a community centre located on the Lower East Side of New York. Herts, a social worker, had witnessed how drama attracted the interest of both children and adults of the mostly Russian–Jewish immigrant community. As the existing drama club was made up of adults, Herts decided to set one up exclusively for children that would offer them a means of creatively expressing themselves while simultaneously learning the language and customs, and integrating themselves within American society. Its first production, *The Tempest*, opened in October 1903 and was hugely successful. The pattern of using a theatrical project to involve migrants within their community, enhancing language acquisition and cultural integration, was used extensively within settlements in the USA.

The Children's Educational Theatre folded in 1909 but other leagues and communities carried on its ideas. For example, the Karamu House in Cleveland, Ohio (1915–75), had young migrants creating and performing theatre that broke the boundaries of race, sex, culture and language whilst providing learning experiences for all involved.[4] Universities also became influential in creating programmes specifically for children's theatre. Among the people involved was Winifred Ward, nicknamed the 'mother of creative drama', who founded the field of creative drama at Northwestern University and established the Children's Theatre of Evanston in 1925. Her book,

Creative Dramatics, published in 1930, established theories and activities relating to children's theatre that still influence contemporary practices. Ward observed children and their attitudes, use of imagination and play, and her programmes for creative dramatic training rested on the goal of educating the whole child. Resonating with the 1920s progressive educational movement, Ward's theories and training proclaimed that 'the child could achieve an understanding of self and society', and that drama was the discipline through which this goal could be achieved.[5] Ward saw drama as an art form that could foster collaboration and participation, expand the imagination and expose children to the processes of creating, producing and performing. Her theories and ideas were influential on other children's theatres set up by universities and communities, as well as the FTP.

As soon as the FTP was formulated, Flanagan was invested in setting up a children's theatre, as she was aware of the need for one during the Depression period. The theatres would be organised independently from the adult ones, would be formed all over the country into a national network to reach as many children as possible, and would perform plays suitable for children. They were particularly encouraged to develop new plays and new performing techniques to go hand in hand with the established repertoire and traditional acting methods. These units were formed in New York City, Los Angeles and Cleveland, Ohio, carrying on from the work of Herts and Karamu House. In other cities, such as Chicago, Boston, Newark, Norwalk in Connecticut, Miami and San Francisco, to name but a few, adult units performed children's plays on a regular basis. Marionette companies and amateur groups also performed for children, as the demand was ever increasing. Like other FTP productions, the children's theatre ones were to be put on at the lowest possible cost without compromising their quality; they also offered tickets at the lowest price for all children, as well as free admission for the under-privileged. In this way, children who had never experienced theatre before (and who may never have had the chance without the FTP) were encouraged and included in all the performances.

The only exception to this structure was the Gary Theatre in Indiana, whose actors were exclusively children. The Gary was set up in a community of (mostly) European immigrants and was based on a project initiated by Betty Kessler Lyman in 1932. Lyman and her husband, seeing the need of children to experience theatre, laughter and life, and to respond creatively to their daily reality, turned their house into a workshop and a theatre. They worked with children in composing, writing, acting, choreographing and staging their own plays. According to Flanagan, Walt Disney was informed of this venture and supported it; he also gave permission for the children to name their theatrical group the 'Mickey Mouse Players'.[6] The Gary Theatre suffered during the Depression but was taken on by the FTP, which set up a project for ten people.

The well-equipped theatre became a community centre for children aged between four and eighteen, who wrote, rehearsed and performed their own plays, as well as established ones. Among them were classics such as *Rip Van Winkle*, *Robinson Crusoe*, and Mark Twain's *The Prince and the Pauper* and *The Connecticut Yankee*; original plays developed by the children included *Reycoch* by Croatian children and a Greek play using masks by Greek ones.[7] The Gary project was suspended in 1938 due to Lyman's pregnancy and was never reopened, but during its short life it gave 179 performances for 66,980 children free of charge.

The New York City Children's unit was set up as a model for the rest of the units and spent many hours setting up play lists and productions for them. As part of its administrative duties, it conducted research and sent out questionnaires to schools, settlements and educators to determine the children's preferences and theatrical knowledge. They also requested research information from the Moscow State Central Theatre for Juvenile Audiences; their research had produced certain standards for productions, based on the age of the children, and they had also compiled suggested reading lists for children, according to their age. The material was studied, distributed and consulted but there is no evidence that the Children's units adhered to the Moscow Theatre's classifications. None the less, the information they received did help Flanagan and the rest to crystallise their vision for the new children's theatre.

As early as 1935, Flanagan had developed her vision for the Children's theatre. In her instructions for all the projects, she eloquently wrote:

> Children's theatres, with adult actors, may be organized as independent producing units or as supplementary units to operate in connection with another unit of the Federal Theatre Project. Plays and presentations for children should not cling to the often sentimental production in children's theatres of the past. Rather, their subject matter and presentation should be as simple, eloquent, and imaginative as the terms in which the modern child reacts to the world around him. Wherever possible members of a children's theatre unit should write their own plays, drawing on history and folklore of the past, legends and stories of the locality, and modern invention and discovery in which the child is interested.[8]

In Flanagan's guidelines, one can see the importance and emphasis the FTP placed on cultivating and educating its new audience, as well as tailoring plays to its interests and imagination. Considering the contemporary realities and living conditions, plays for children would provide both entertainment and new perspectives for experiencing life. Two general types of play would be presented. Firstly, there were those that were imaginative and fantastical in nature, such as *The Emperor's New Clothes*, *Cinderella*, *Hansel and Gretel*, *A Christmas Carol*, *Treasure Island* and *Jack and the Bean Stalk*. These well-known fairy tales and fiction stories were produced in new and exciting ways, with new settings and costume designs, and integrating marionette, puppetry and vaudeville with live acting. Their imagery was not obscured, thus allowing children to experience them as performative happenings in which they could participate visually, orally and imaginatively.

The second type of play involved a more realistic depiction of their lives. Jack Rennick, managing director of the whole Children's unit, reported in 1936 that this type – which had been consistently neglected by previous children's theatres –

> is the play with a heightened sense of realism which will help the child to an awareness of himself and his place in the world about him. In all plays, there must be an educational and cultural value, and above everything else, the play must be presented to attract and retain the interest of the child.[9]

Reiterating Flanagan's instruction quoted above, Rennick's comments further emphasised the need to propose a different theatrical experience for children. Reminiscent of Brecht's 1930s *Lehrstücke* plays, these educational works ranged from subjects such as safe driving and good nutrition and hygiene to contemporary issues such as war and the Depression itself. Among the latter plays were *A Letter to Santa Claus*, *Bullets and Babies*, *The Revolt of the Beavers*, *Flight* and *The Boiled Eggs*. These plays were ultimately accused of promoting social mobility and revolutionary ideals, and of being subversive and un-American in intent.

Another objective of the Children's unit was broadening its audience. The middle-class children had access to many productions performed on Broadway and in other mainstream theatres. Like the Living Newspapers, the Children's unit aimed to attract children whose parents were working-class, low-waged and frequently immigrants. Lacking opportunities to experience theatre, working-class children were deserving of the same rights to its educational and entertainment values. For the FTP and Flanagan, children were an integral part of the audience they wanted to address; adults and children alike would share the same experience of both enjoying live theatrical productions and becoming educated and informed about contemporary realities: 'In all productions it must be remembered that the young auditor is deserving of the best only, and that if we are to have an intelligent and discerning audience tomorrow, we must build it today.'[10] Rennick's view reflected the FTP's overarching aim of developing an educated audience for a permanent National Theatre in the USA. And that audience would invariably encompass children and young adults.

CHILDREN, POLITICS AND ROLLER-SKATING:
THE REVOLT OF THE BEAVERS

In late 1936, during an informal policy board meeting with Philip Barber, Walter Hart, Jack Rennick, Frank Merlin, Helen Tamiris, Virgil Geddes and Morris Watson, Flanagan argued that the predominant issue for the FTP should be to 'do all kinds of plays and we should be using our minds to find them, and if they don't exist we'll have to write them'.[11] Flanagan's call was answered by New York's Children's unit, which produced nine plays and three festivals. Putting on successful performances of classical tales, such as Charlotte Chorpenning's *The Emperor's New Clothes* with Jules Dassin in the leading role of Zar, the unit also produced *Horse Play*, an original script by Dorothy Hailparn, written for children between the ages of five and eight, as well as *Flight*, a Living Newspaper on the history of aviation. Targeting a junior-high age audience, *Flight* was dramatised by Oscar Saul and Louis Lantz using Charles Lindbergh's 1927 transatlantic crossing as a framework. It was presented in twenty-eight quickly moving scenes and employed formal elements used in previous Living Newspapers like spotlights, a loudspeaker narrator and blackouts.

The next production to follow was *The Revolt of the Beavers*, an original script by Saul and Lantz about anthropomorphised beavers; a supposedly harmless play about animals, *The Revolt of the Beavers* caused political and social furore, and like *The Cradle Will Rock*, was used by the Dies Committee to attack the FTP. The play opened in New York in May 1937 at the Adelphi Theatre during a turbulent period for the FTP. There were rumours about impending cuts in personnel and the more unionised members were organising strikes and demonstrations, resulting in accusations that the FTP was openly fostering leftist and Communist political ideologists. With *The Revolt of the Beavers* the FTP wanted to propose a new way of approaching children's theatre, a new way of appropriating fairy tale, folklore and fable; it wanted to bring together form and content in a more imaginative, colourful, musical and involved manner. But mixed reviews from the critics, protests from adults and the direct involvement of the Dies Committee – as opposed to the more positive reactions of the children – led the FTP to close the show on 17 June 1937 after only seventeen performances and to the children's theatre being labelled as a site of ideological struggle.

The Revolt of the Beavers narrates the dream adventure–journey of Paul and Mary, two impoverished working-class nine-year-olds, from their unnamed city to the forest of Beaverland by Windy (Mr Wind), and their ensuing involvement in Beaverland's life. The play is comprised of two acts, each with three scenes. The play opens to the scene of an industrial city, an image very familiar to most of the audience. Enter Paul and Mary on their way back from school and in the middle of an argument. Their argument centres on a story their teacher told them and the two different belief systems they have. Mary believes that truth can be found in the teacher's story, but Paul thinks it is a fairy tale. Angrily, he claims that 'because we're nine years old he can tell us fairy tales. Well, I don't like 'em and I don't believe 'em. I like real stories about cops and robbers – and cowboys and Indians . . . .'[12] The opening lines of the play set the tone for the argument between fairy tales and real stories. Which ones are the most important? Which ones are the most relevant to one's life? Which ones are more valid? And which ones should we believe? Are fairy tales the domain of children / childhood and reality the domain of adults? In Paul's mind, fairy tales – and, by extension, childhood – are associated with lies; they are used to enforce forms of deception on children, thus keeping them away from the realities of life, which are perceived as a realm exclusive to adults. By pitting fantasy–reality and children–adults against each other, a rigid binary system of belief is proposed where the two do not interact. This binary argumentation of holding a clear position for or against one or the other will be challenged as the play unfolds, but will be reinforced by the way that the whole play was received by the critics and the grown-up public.

Although Paul craves a more realistic world, he fails to see the fantastical narrative behind the 'real' cops and robbers, cowboys and Indians. Yes, these people really existed (as opposed to a talking beaver), but Paul's knowledge of them is based on narratives he heard from his peers or adults, who, in turn, heard them on the radio, read them in the newspapers or saw them on film. Cops and robbers, cowboys and Indians are physically real, but the narrative behind them is based on fiction, on somebody else's use of imagination and fantasy. The reality that Paul desires is not as clear as he claims, and he soon reverts to fantasy. When challenged by Mary as to the three wishes he would have if he found a wishing stone, he quickly participates in the game. Whereas Mary would ask for everything she wants, for her father to get a job and a big piece of chocolate, Paul's imagination runs wild:

> If I had a real wishing stone, I would really wish for a blue sweater and a pair of skates, and I would wish that everybody in the whole world was nine years old. Then I'd never be sad, 'cause then I could go to the candy store, and just imagine. Mr. Berger would be nine years old, and I would say: 'Mr. Berger, I haven't got no penny, gimme a piece of candy, will ya,' and he would give it to me, because he would know how I felt if I didn't have any candy.[13]

Both Paul and Mary's wishes address the reality and effects of the Depression for adults and children alike. The children are acutely aware of how their parents' employment affects their livelihood and their desires. In Paul's dream, granting one wish – everybody being nine years old – would inevitably and positively affect his whole life. In this scenario only Mr Berger at the sweet shop could experience the devastating effect of wanting but not being able to have some sweets. The simple and innocent wants of children act as a subtle introduction to the economic conflicts and class divisions, but also as a reminder of the truth and reality concealed behind a fantastical wish.

Paul resumes his rejection of fairy tales when Mary pushes him further to go looking for the talking beavers of which their teacher spoke. To his exasperated query as to how fairy tales can be real, Mary replies that 'the teacher once told me, that some real stories are so full of lies that they're fairy tales, and some fairy tales are so full of truth that they're just like real stories'.[14] The repetition of the teacher's comment, appropriated by Mary, has relevance, as it hints at a level of perception with which we normally do not associate children. The comment blurs the lines between fairy tales and reality, discrediting the above binary structure, and instead revealing the complex relationship between these two strands. If the fairy tale had been used in the past as the predominant narrative associated with childhood as a means of providing a blueprint for moral behaviour, it can no longer sustain this function. If there are lies in real stories that border on fantasy and if truth can be found within fairy tales, then the latter is not an escapist genre that can shield children from reality. Nor can it impose morally appropriate behaviour if lies are incorporated within it. By blurring the line between truth and lies, fairy tales and reality, the teacher allows Mary to broaden her views of these concepts.

Even the reluctant Paul begins to perceive this new approach. As he is about to fall asleep in the woods next to Mary, he cannot help but

> wonder could there be a real fairy tale, like the teacher said? Huh, just imagine, a beaver comin' out of the woods, wearing pants, an' a blue sweater, and even skates. That would be a real fairy tale. A real fairy tale![15]

Paul projects in his speech the desire and wishes he expressed a short while ago. At the same time, the conflation of the two seemingly opposing worlds – real and fairy-tale – into one opens the space for query and debate further. Can the real and the fantastical co-exist? How does a real fairy tale work? And how does this co-existence influence the children and adults' belief systems that tend to promote one over the other? If fairy tales have been created by adults to protect children's innocence of the real-world order and living conditions, Paul's real fairy tale presents an antidote to this imposed narrative through which children were expected to understand and perceive the world. A real fairy tale empowers children's perception, voice and knowledge, as it promotes a critical synergy of two belief systems, thus allowing a broadening of consciousness, and new ways of experiencing life and gaining perspectives. A real fairy tale promotes children's independence, and accepts their innocence

Figure 5.1　Paul, Mary and Windy in *The Revolt of the Beavers*. Adelphi Theatre, New York, 1937.

as a powerful – rather than limiting or simply vulnerable – aspect of childhood that facilitates their intellectual growth.

And, as if by magic, Paul and Mary's wish of experiencing a real fairy tale comes true. They come across Windy, and after much haggling, he agrees to take them to the woods (Figure 5.1). Having chosen medium wind, as opposed to hot or cold, the children are transported to Beaverland. They are very excited to meet their first real live beaver, asleep on a pedestal, who turns out to be the Professor. The Professor is quick to shut down any romanticised views Paul might have had about having a good time; he informs them instead that there are 'no more good times. The chief is making everybody sad.'[16] Once the Professor realises that they are human beings, he tells them to get out of Beaverland quickly, as there is a lot of trouble and they 'might get right in the middle' (Figure 5.2).[17] Without realising it, the Professor is ironically commenting on Paul and Mary's choice of a medium wind, as well as his occupation of a pedestal in the middle of the woods. While singing a song before fully waking up, the Professor inadvertently reveals his intellectual weakness, his inability to choose a side or commit to an action. In the song he claims,

Figure 5.2 Paul, Mary and the Professor in *The Revolt of the Beavers*. Adelphi Theatre, New York, 1937.

I sit on the left and I sit on the right
But my favorite spot is the middle.
I like to get up in the early dawn,
I'm fond of the morning light,
There's nothing I like as much as the morn,
But the beautiful, beautiful night.[18]

This insistence on occupying the middle, this inability to express a preference, has landed him in a compromising position but his biggest weakness lies on his inability to recognise the process that led him there. Soon, though, he will be forced to recognise it, reclaim his intellectual strength and act upon his beliefs.

Having established that all the beavers are nine years old, the Professor proceeds to explain why he holds said title. Smarter than a teacher, he is the biggest professor, 'the best story teller, too. I could tell you a million stories, that could last forever, almost.'[19] When challenged, he also reveals that he cannot work, as the Chief has closed all the schools. While they are talking, another beaver, Oakleaf, comes out of hiding but everybody soon must hide from the Whistling Clubs. Once they are gone, Oakleaf reveals that the Whistling Clubs, the Chief's gang, have been instructed to chase him out of Beaverland, and if caught, to 'hit him till he cries'.[20] The reason behind this action is Oakleaf's direct disobedience of the Chief's orders. He tells them how he could no longer stand the beavers being sad, so he decided to make a club to become glad. And although all the beavers were in favour, the Chief expelled him because of his defiance. Oakleaf's heroic actions counterbalance the Professor's indecision but also propel him to act. The Professor, along with Paul and Mary, is going back to Beaverland to 'tell the chief a story. Not a plain story but a story with a moral. And then that'll show him how mean he is, and then he'll turn into a good chief.'[21] Oakleaf leaves them to go into exile but his last words anticipate the failure of the Professor's plan and the eventual revolt: 'some day the beavers'll get very, very sore and they'll wanna do something big against the chief. And then they'll call me back because I'm on their side, and I got a lot of schemes.'[22]

The audience's first visual introduction to Beaverland occurs in scene three of act one. The first thing the audience sees is the enormous wheel, the hub of the city, that is constantly moving; it is fully connected with the Chief's house and the belt where the beavers are busily working. As the curtain rises, the audience sees the sad and overworked beavers singing their 'Busy, Busy' song. Through their song, the audience is informed of their working conditions and the reason behind their sadness. The beavers collectively chop the trees and chip, stack and pack the bark, but they are all unhappy since

> The chief of all the beavers
> He gets all the bark we make
> All he does is pull the levers
> While we work until we ache.
> So we're poor unhappy beavers,
> Working busy as the bees,
> While he sits and pulls the levers
> And gets richer if you please
> While we strip, strip, strip
> And we don't like it. Would you?[23]

As the song ends, the audience finally meets the Chief. Dressed in a beaver's frock coat with a blue sweater over it and on skates (like in Paul's wish), the Chief makes sure that the beavers have all been staying obedient since Oakleaf's departure; his General and the Whistling Club oversee them closely. With lunch time approaching, the beavers stop working but there is no bark for them, as all is reserved for the Chief. The beavers wish for the Professor to be with them, to argue with the Chief and make him realise how badly he is treating them. And their wish comes true as the Professor, Paul and Mary arrive on stage.

The Chief is instantly interested in Paul and Mary, and invites them to ask questions about Beaverland. Paul, very openly and confrontationally, asks him why he is making the beavers sad, why he keeps all the bark himself, and why he is so fat as opposed to the other skinny beavers. But these questions make the Chief cross, and when the Professor declares that it is the Chief himself who is creating all the trouble and destroying Beaverland by being greedy – and not Oakleaf, as he argues – the Chief throws a temper tantrum, ordering the Whistling Clubs to 'hit 'em, even the girl!'[24] When one of the remaining beavers, Birch, dares to criticise him for his actions, the Chief responds with anger and threats. He calls for the Barkless Beavers to come back to Beaverland, daring the working ones, 'Who wants to be the first Barkless Beaver? Where is he? Let him say something. Go ahead. Who wants to get wise? Go ahead!'[25] With these threats, the frightened and bullied working beavers return to work on the Wheel while the Professor, Paul and Mary, expelled from Beaverland, find themselves in the woods.

Act two begins with the three in the woods at night. The Professor, deflated and unable to see a viable way of proceeding, of making the beavers happy, decides to leave. Paul and Mary are disappointed by his action and choose to stay 'right in the middle of the story and [do] the best [they] can'.[26] As soon as Paul and Mary are on their own, a group of beavers, led by Birch, arrive, looking to stop the Barkless Beavers who are approaching Beaverland to threaten their livelihood. As the Barkless Beavers arrive, so does the Professor, who comes back to warn them. The Barkless Beavers are portrayed in absolute dejection; they are destitute, their clothes are torn and their heads hang. When the two groups of beavers start talking, they both realise how unhappy they are and how they do not want to fight each other. On Paul's suggestion, the Barkless join the working beavers' sad club, each promising not to work on the Wheel without the other. Paul then assembles an owl to find Oakleaf, inform him that all the beavers have joined his club and urge him to come back to lead them. As the owl disappears, though, the Chief, his General and the Scaly Brothers appear, demanding that the Barkless Beavers march to Beaverland (Figure 5.3). Paul blurts out that they are all now members of Oakleaf's club and the beavers refuse to resume their status. The Chief almost explodes with anger when he hears this, ordering his gang to kill Oakleaf while teaching the Professor, Paul and Mary 'the biggest lesson there is' by 'killing them tomorrow lunch time'.[27] In the face of these threats and with the Professor, Paul and Mary captured, the Barkless Beavers depart and the working ones start marching back to Beaverland.

With the Chief unaware that Oakleaf has secretly returned and is conspiring with the working beavers on a scheme against him (scene two), scene three opens with the Professor, Paul and Mary tied to a stake, jailed and awaiting their fate. Just before all are awake, Blubber – a working beaver – approaches

Figure 5.3 The Chief and his gang confronting the Barkless and working beavers in the woods. *The Revolt of the Beavers*. Adelphi Theatre, New York, 1937.

and has a short conversation with Porky, one of the Scaly Brothers. In their brief exchange Blubber notifies Porky that 'the Chief's gonna tell you to fight beavers today, what are you gonna do?'[28] Porky quickly dismisses Blubber's suggestion but seeds of doubt have been planted regarding the Chief's behaviour. When the Chief appears, he intuitively knows that Oakleaf has entered Beaverland. Trying to elicit information from Paul, he is met with disdain and outright refusal. When the working day begins, the beavers appear as usual, carrying their empty lunch boxes. But once they start work, they proceed to build a barricade between themselves, the Professor, Paul and Mary and the Chief with his gang. When they are ready, Oakleaf appears carrying the flag of the sad beavers' club. Instantly he challenges the Chief and rallies the beavers:

> Chief, the wheel is the most wonderful thing in Beaverland, and you been a wise chief long enough, always skatin' around on your ball-bearing skates, with a blue sweater, and playin' potzie, and never lettin' the beavers have a good time. The beavers are sad and they need the wheel – it belongs to them. What do you say, Beavers?[29]

The battle begins; the beavers produce their 'Zippo guns' from their lunch boxes (stolen previously from the Chief) and appoint Paul as their general. The Chief, enraged, orders the Scaly Brothers to kill the beavers. But Porky defies the Chief: 'we're supposed to kill wild animals of the forest, not beavers. Fair is fair', to which Oakleaf exclaims 'it worked – it worked – the scheme worked!', revealing to the audience that the plan has always been to take the Wheel back for all beavers, the Barkless, workers and Scaly Brothers included.[30]

Porky is led to be executed for defying the Chief, but he is saved by Blubber. With the Scaly Brothers and the Barkless beavers joining them, the working beavers are victorious. The Chief and his gang flee Beaverland and everybody joins in the celebrations. The play's final song is full of joy and optimism:

> O' sing the beavers happy song / The beavers sing it all day long,
> To all the beavers now belong / All of Beaverland.
> Every day we'll work and play / Work and play, work and play,
> Clip, clip, clip and strip away / Bark for Beaverland.
> There's bark for every beaver / Who swings a cleaver / Or pulls a lever,
> There's not a barkless beaver / In all of beaver's Beaverland.
> We'll be building every day, / Each one helps in his own way.
> Every beaver has his say / In building our new land.
> Always helping one another, / Every beaver like a brother.
> All the beavers help each other / In our Beaverland.[31]

With the beavers all now equal, happy and without an oppressive Chief, Paul and Mary's time comes to an end. Although they are invited to stay, both children feel they have accomplished their intention of helping the beavers be happy again. As if by magic, Windy appears, ready to take them back home; choosing once again a medium wind, the children bid their farewell to their friends. The beavers begin skating around Windy, Paul and Mary, to gather momentum, and they all shout 'Wheeeee'. The stage darkens, lightning flashes, thunder roars and the hurricane wind blows as the curtain falls.

The play was an enjoyable, imaginative and energetic performance. Its simple costumes, the beautiful use of make-up to portray the beavers and the use of roller skating equipped it with a playfulness rarely experienced. At the same time, the setting was beautifully crafted, accommodating the fantastical but also engaging the children's imagination. But for all its artistic and acting merits, the play received mixed critical reactions for its subject matter, and the controversy it created continued to haunt Flanagan for the next two years. The New York critics, although in agreement regarding the social significance of the script, disagreed about the overall production and its impact on its audience of children. John Harkins considered it a 'comic strip as much as it is fantasy ... the settings are bright, ingenious and decorative. The direction is imaginative, and acrobatic to a kid's delight ... If there is any underlying significance to the story, the children probably will not see it.'[32] Douglas Gilbert found it an 'unclever production ... the piece is so devoid of imagination, charm and sensitivity I could endure only one act', whereas *Life* magazine's review included a child's opinion – 'I like the Chief because he made me laugh but I didn't like the way he treated the beavers' – as a way of including the voice of the play's intended audience.[33]

The biggest assault on the production came from Brooks Atkinson. In his review, he called the play 'Mother Goose Marx', and accused the FTP of conscientiously producing 'a revolutionary bed-time story', 'a primer lesson in the class struggle' that 'unformed minds accustomed to innocent play in the streets may not grasp the Marxian dialectic'.[34] His seething irony is expressed in the comment that the play should definitely improve the diplomatic relations with the Soviet Union. Atkinson ends his review in the same political tone that he started it:

> The style is playful; the mood is gravely gay and simple-minded. Many children now unschooled in the technique of revolution now have an opportunity, at government expense, to improve their tender minds. Mother Goose is no longer a rhymed escapist. She has been studying Marx; Jack and Jill lead the class revolution.[35]

Atkinson's polemical review framed *The Revolt of the Beavers* as outright Communist propaganda with an underlying anti-American sentiment, now targeting young children. The characters of the beavers (apart from the Chief and his gang) are all seen as anticapitalist revolutionaries (and, by extension, anti-American), whereas Paul and Mary are described as 'children of the proletariat'.[36] In constructing this narrative, the actions of the beavers – when they take out their Zippos and guns – are seen in the light of the violence inherent within a revolutionary movement. Nowhere in his review does Atkinson deal with the oppressive nature of the Chief, or the bullying and terrorising techniques or physical violence inflicted upon the beavers and the children as well. At the same time, Atkinson's framing of the play as a piece of dangerous moral teaching presupposes its audience / the children to be vulnerable and naïve recipients of the propagandistic message, impressionable and in danger of imitating the actions witnessed on stage. What underlies this framing is the fear among politicians and the American middle class that plays such as *The Revolt of the Beavers* perform an assault that reveals the true nature of the American capitalist way of life. The play exposes the fundamental brutality and inequality that exist within capitalism, and its effects on the quality of everyday life, and very simply but powerfully introduces children to contemporary economic and labour realities.

The Children's Theatre officials tried to address some of the public's concerns and contain the negative reactions. A detailed survey was conducted on the thoughts of children who had seen the play. After a series of interviews and questionnaires, the research team concluded that the children saw a moral to the story, not its political or 'class' implications. However, the view of the play as purely propagandistic, as damaging and corrupting to children, proliferated and could not be contained. The play closed after a few weeks but the furore it caused did not quieten. When called in front of the Dies Committee in 1938, Flanagan was prepared to answer questions about this play. Regretting that Atkinson and the police commissioner were disturbed by it, Flanagan emphasised that 'we did not write the play for dramatic critics, nor did we write it for policemen. We wrote it for children and I wish to write in to the record what the children thought about the play.'[37] To Congressman Starnes's accusation that the play was poisoning the minds of youth, Flanagan juxtaposed in great detail the afore-mentioned survey. She produced for the committee a number of questions and answers provided by the children that ranged from 'the play teaches us never to be selfish because you don't get anything out of it', 'that it is better to be good than bad' and 'how the children would want the whole world to be nine years old and happy' to 'how a boy and a girl can make beavers be happy'.[38] When pressed on what Mr Atkinson or the commissioner's reaction was to these answers, Flanagan reiterated that, in this instance, it was the children's reactions that she and her officials mostly valued.

Flanagan continued to defend the play, even after her testimony. In the detailed brief she had prepared for the committee she reiterated that the Children's unit produced only two types of play:

> Those which are imaginative, humorous, and fantastic in character; and those which give a sense of realism to the play, and so help the youngster gain a greater awareness of himself as a personality, as well as a realization of his particular relationship to the world in which he lives.[39]

To emphasise her point further, she cited a children's magazine editor who denied the play's politically subversive message. Alice K. Pollitzer claimed that the play was 'no more Communistic than Christian. The moral of the play is just that entrenched greed and cruelty are not desirable. That is the theme of many old, classical, accepted fairy tales for children.'[40] Lastly, Flanagan addressed the accusations in her memoir. In a long paragraph, she claimed that she never had the impression that the play was actively disseminating Communism:

> In almost all fairy tales the poor child, Cinderella, the Jack-and-the-Beanstalk, is abused by the selfish stepmother or the bad giant; always the hero or heroine triumphs in the end. It seemed to me natural that in the fairy tale pattern brought up to date the beavers had a bad beaver king whom they drove out so that all the beavers could eat ice cream, play, and be nine years old.[41]

Flanagan's defence of the play relies on the premise that its subject matter is located within the realm of the fairy tale or fable. Historically, fairy tales and fables have been used to instruct children on acceptable societal behaviours and values. However, the play is not a simple, fantastical and moral fairy tale. It is a combination of the two types described by Flanagan above. *The Revolt of the Beavers* fused the imaginative and fantastical with the contemporary and the real. It combined the talking, roller-skating beavers with the economic realities of the Depression. It also wove together the familiar punishment of the villain in a fairy tale with the political realities of what happens in a dictatorship. Because of these combinations, the play transcended the traditional artistic and socially accepted perimeters of a fairy tale.

Flanagan was not naïve when attempting to defend the play as a fairy tale; she knew that it delved into uncharted territories, artistically, educationally and societally. But as one of the premises of the FTP was to respond and be relevant to its contemporary realities, the Children's unit could not fall behind. Children from low-income and working-class backgrounds experienced daily the harsh realities of economic deprivation on a financial, social and emotional level. *The Revolt of the Beavers* offered entertaining escapism from that reality but at the same time voiced the children's contemporary experiences. In an era of rising anti-Communist paranoia and of growing mistrust of the liberal economic strategies that were (and still are) the backbone of American life, Congress and critics like Atkinson could not allow a government-funded project to 'corrupt' future generations. The play was dangerous: dangerous because it spoke the truth, because it proposed an alternative way of living and acting, and primarily because it recognised and engaged its child-audience with America's economic and social realities. The play closed after only a few performances, but it stayed vividly in the minds of the children for its roller-skating beavers and for its earnest desire for everyone to be happy, have ice-cream and be nine years old.

'You're really very bad, you know': *Pinocchio* and the Final Curtain

Pinocchio by Yasha Frank opened on 23 December 1938 at the Ritz Theatre in Manhattan and proved to be the most successful production of the New York Children's Theatre. Frank, director of the Los Angeles Children's Theatre unit, had already produced the play successfully there. His version of *Pinocchio*, based on Collodi's 1883 original story but altered significantly to reflect Frank's contemporary social realities, as well as his understanding of childhood psychology, which he had studied at university, greatly influenced Disney's 1940 full-length cartoon adaptation of the same story. Before his version of *Pinocchio* became an integral part of Disney's fantastical world, though, Frank moved to New York in 1938 to work on the play's production and adaptation there.

Frank and Flanagan had met previously and discussed in detail what a children's theatre and its fundamental principles should be. According to Flanagan, Frank was passionate, enthusiastic and a bit melodramatic on the subject, but his views found Flanagan in agreement. In a long extract in *Arena*, Flanagan cited his opinions as examples of how dramatists, playwrights, performers and producers needed to approach children's theatre. According to Frank,

> Children are by nature dramatists and actors. They intuitively prepare themselves for their impending conflict with society by dramatizing their problems and fortifying themselves with the aptitudes thus arrived at. Children love to learn but hate to be taught – so all we have to do is to frame our plays in such a way that we never tell them anything but just evolve, with as much participation as we can get from them, the behavior patterns we want them to follow [. . .] Education has to be dramatized – everybody knows that – but the theatre is letting the school win this great potential audience [. . .] Children's settings should be reduced to the essentials – but never bleak, always provocative [. . .] ethical values . . . use of vaudeville technique . . . repetition . . . broad comedy . . . primary colors . . . We must train children to cope with emergencies . . .[42]

Frank implemented his views on all his productions; the settings and costume designs were colourful, playful and attractive, but more importantly, he structured his adaptations in such a way as to elicit children's active participation and, through that, an awareness of behavioural patterns that could be used at home, and in interpersonal relationships and societal situations. The behavioural patterns encompassed a critical understanding on the part of the audience, as the children, through participation in the action, had to reflect on which pattern is appropriate for each event, why it was right or wrong, and how further relational, social or financial complications, based on how the characters behaved, occurred.

Frank's adaptation of *Pinocchio* was a visual and musical extravaganza. The play consisted of three acts, each having three scenes. A great advocate of vaudeville, fast-moving action and music, Frank incorporated all these elements in the production; not afraid to experiment further, he also developed a circus scene (II, iii) that ended up containing a real circus on stage. In his adaptation, Frank decided to do away with the complexities of Collodi's story. In the original story, Pinocchio is initially portrayed as wilfully mischievous. His nose begins to grow as soon as it is carved (as a sign of his inherent lying nature), he kicks Geppetto as soon as his legs can move, runs out of his home as soon as he can walk, has Geppetto arrested by the police, and accidentally kills (by throwing a hammer) a talking cricket that warns him of the consequences of his thoughtless actions. It is only through a vast array of repeated mistakes, lies, failures and reflections that he finally understands the error of his ways, starts making amends and is granted a human form. Seen as an allegory of the human condition, Collodi's story offered a complex narrative that incorporated issues around morality, human behaviour, development of the self and child-rearing in contemporary socially and economically deprived realities.

Frank's version simplified the original story by doing away with some of Pinocchio's experiences but predominantly by altering his start in life so that he is a 'good' (as opposed to mischievous), playful and naïve boy. The play opens in Geppetto's cottage; as soon as it begins, the audience is confronted with pantomime and slapstick humour, as well as the rhyming language that expresses playfulness and is more easily received by children. Geppetto is busy preparing dinner for himself and his cat. The cat, played by a grown-up actor in full make-up, dashes to the cupboard to get his bib, which has the word 'CAT' spelled out on it. Having devoured his milk too quickly but still feeling hungry, the cat decides to catch some mice using a piece of cheese. But the mice outsmart him, grab the cheese and drop a cuckoo clock on his tail. This fun, playful and fast-paced first scene sets the tone for the rest of the play.

After a visit from a new father to pick up a cradle, Geppetto is struck by the idea of making a puppet or child out of wood: 'Children are not made of wood? / Great heavens! I wonder if I could.'[43] Fully assembled, Pinocchio is taught by Geppetto how to walk; whereas Collodi's Pinocchio kicks Geppetto and leaves his home, Frank's dutifully accepts Geppetto's help in learning how to walk and falls to sleep to a lullaby. The following morning, Pinocchio finds his voice, to his father's delight, and promises,

> I shall be most dutiful
> And good as I can be!
> I'm sure that if I'm very good,
> We'll some day know the joy
> Of actually seeing me
> Become a proper boy.
> With flesh and blood and meat and bones
> And with a stomach, too,
> And so, I pledge myself to try
> To be a son to you.[44]

Full of filial love, Pinocchio is eager to fulfil his father's desire that he be a 'good' boy. Should he succeed, then his reward will be his incarnation as a 'real' boy. From the very beginning of the play, then, Frank sets a morally educational tone by associating good behaviour – complying with societal norms, being vulnerable, lovable and at the same time in need of protection – with a reward. This sets up a transactional relationship between child and parent, and, by extension, between child and society. If the child behaves in a morally good way, and avoids causing grievances or making a mess, then s/he is rewarded with what s/he desires (toys, books or even attention and acceptance). However, Pinocchio's intentions and this transactional pattern are soon challenged because of his actions.

The following two scenes are both acted in pantomime, which made for an engaging and entertaining sight. On his way to school, Pinocchio comes across the puppet show and very soon he is entangled in it. Captivated by the pretty female puppet, he joins her in a dance while also attempting to repair her broken strings (Figure 5.4). Although all the children head to school, Pinocchio is still transfixed by the girl and remains there till the puppeteer bellows at him angrily and drives him off to school. So, the first act ends on a note of almost carnival fun, with a wooden puppet fascinated by a puppet show and figures that bear close a resemblance to him in terms of their functionality and purpose. Pinocchio does not pause to consider this conundrum, nor is the audience made explicitly aware of it, but one cannot help but wonder what differentiated Pinocchio from the other puppets. Was it the strings that were attached to them? The freedom that Pinocchio is allowed? Geppetto's belief in Pinocchio's intention to be a 'good' boy? Or perhaps a sense of responsibility? None of these queries is examined; instead, scenes two and three are a visual masterclass in pantomime, choreography and vaudevillian acting.

Act two, scene one begins with Pinocchio's encounter with the beggar women at the crossroads between school and Boobyland. Begging for money and unhappy that Pinocchio swallowed it (rather than hand it to them), they capture him and '*gleefully string him up [a tree]. Being made of wood, he dangles there harmlessly.*'[45] It is at this moment that the blue-haired Fairy Queen, Pinocchio's self-proclaimed guardian angel, appears and the women disappear. In a long speech, she reproaches his behaviour, revealing the two women as evil spirits and issuing him with a warning:

> Let me once more sum up your case;
> This is the problem that you face.
> You will see me twice again –
> Remember! Only twice! And then
> If you have not, by word or deed,
> Conquered all trace of Human Greed,
> You'll never, never know the joy
> Of being a living, breathing boy.
> A wooden puppet's all you'll be
> From then throughout eternity.[46]

The Fairy Queen's stark warning regarding his behaviour and future, as well as the reminder that one of his three chances has already been missed, barely registers with Pinocchio. He instantly comes across the cat and the fox, who trick him into giving up his four pennies (Figure 5.5). With his realisation that

Figure 5.4 Pinocchio and the Pretty Puppet dancing. *Pinocchio*. Ritz Theatre, New York, 1938.

Figure 5.5 Pinocchio, the Cat and the Fox. *Pinocchio*. Ritz Theatre, New York, 1938.

he has been deceived, Pinocchio's second chance is also spent. The Fairy Queen reappears, reprimands him, repeats the warning about greed but also offers him one last piece of advice:

> Share your pennies with the needy.
> This is the lesson of the penny:
> some have too few; some have too many;
> And there are some who haven't any![47]

In these few lines, the play puts forward its own subtle message regarding children's economic and social realities, a message that they can easily pick up, understand and critically process. But no sooner has she left than Pinocchio is once again derailed. Mesmerised by the group of singing children and the Jolly Coachman's promise of Boobyland as a place of freedom, full of toys, fun, games and no meddling adults and teachers, Pinocchio follows them and is taken prisoner. As his transformation into a mule takes place, Pinocchio is sold to the circus's Ringmaster to replace his old mule. The second act of the play ends with a spectacular circus scene in which the audience is invited to witness Pinocchio's first performance (Figure 5.6).

Figure 5.6 The Circus. *Pinocchio*. Ritz Theatre, New York, 1938.

Before Pinocchio's appearance, the children are treated to an array of entertaining tricks. They see a lion hypnotising his trainer and an accomplished musician who 'can play anything from bicycle pump to a toy balloon', while the clowns' antics constantly interrupt the flow, making everyone laugh.[48] And, of course, they watch the fearless Mademoiselle Fifi perform a death-defying act that fascinates everyone. When Pinocchio appears, he successfully executes a series of difficult tricks until he falls and breaks a leg. At the Ringmaster's command, Pinocchio is to be shot! What follows this decision is a series of mishaps that delay Pinocchio's execution (the clowns are confused, the rifle barrel goes limp and the cannon brought on fails repeatedly to fire), until an exasperated Ringmaster declares, 'Ladies and Gentlemen, the grand circus finale!'[49] This sees the clowns, positioned on a high cliff, throwing Pinocchio the mule into the sea. Although a fast-paced and comical scene, it none the less encompasses the violence inflicted on the puppet's wooden body. Seen from a critical distance, the violence that Pinocchio's wooden body suffers throughout the play almost acts as a commentary on the hardships that contemporary children experience at the hands of adults, at the hands of a society that is set up based on the needs and aspirations of grown-ups. It is the same society that constructs the behaviourally moral code for children, and the punishment for failure is both brutal and instant. By inflicting this violence on a wooden body, the play up to this stage aims at the non-identification of the children with Pinocchio. A closer relationship with or understanding of him is to come in the last act, in his reunion with Geppetto and in his incarnation as a real, material boy.

In act three, Pinocchio is found at the bottom of the sea. In scene one, he is transformed back to his original form, shedding the mulish skin. He encounters many species of fish and is having fun playing around with them when he is suddenly swallowed by a whale. Scene two begins in the stomach of the whale, where Pinocchio is reunited with Geppetto, who narrates his quest to find and rescue him from Boobyland. It has been a year since Pinocchio's disappearance and Geppetto has been imprisoned in the whale's stomach for most of this time. Resigned to their fate of living inside the whale, as it never sleeps, Geppetto sings a lullaby to his son, which luckily results in the whale finally falling asleep. Geppetto's act allows them both to escape and finally to return to Geppetto's cottage, where it all began.

The final scene of the play sees Geppetto reunited with his cat (who now has four kittens) and helping Pinocchio and the cat make amends and become friends. Excited at the prospect of Pinocchio becoming a real boy, Geppetto is preparing his birthday party. Before leaving for market, he hands Pinocchio four pennies to spend them as he likes, probably buying a toy. Pinocchio is once again in possession of money and is instantly faced with a dilemma. When an old beggar woman knocks on the door, asking for help, Pinocchio does not know what to do – in his ambivalence, he turns to the audience and, prompted directly by the children, hands out all his money. The beggar is revealed as the Fairy Queen and, through his act, Pinocchio fulfils his fate and is assured that he will become a boy. The next day, everyone arrives for Pinocchio's party. As he blows out the candle on the cake, the Fairy Queen appears, making good her promise:

> You've learned the lesson of the penny;
> Some have too few – some too many –
> But give to those who haven't any,
> So let the bells proclaim our joy.
> While you become a human boy
> And since you've been so very good
> I'll free you from your bonds of wood.[50]

As his wooden limbs fall away, Pinocchio rejoices in his new human form, starts dancing, and is joined in celebration by Geppetto, the Fairy Queen and the entire company.

The New York theatre critics were kind in their reviews of the play, unlike those of *The Revolt of the Beavers*. Although initially complaining that the press were not allowed to see the play during the first week of production, Atkinson concedes that what they saw was 'a finished and fully equipped performance'.[51] He further called the equipment 'stupendous', commenting on the regiment of actors, dancers, clowns and musicians, on the spectacular scenery and on the 'lovely' musical score, particularly the 'beautiful lullaby'.[52] He was satisfied with the acting, in particular Allan Frank's, whose portrayal of Geppetto had a sincerity that captivated the audience. Lastly, he could not but comment on how *Pinocchio* was an improvement over *The Revolt of the Beavers*, a better, more satisfying work and more worthy of 'Uncle Sam and the Federal Theatre'.[53] William Cobb of the *Wall Street Journal* called the play a 'complex and intricate bit of stagecraft', was particularly impressed with the work vaudevillian actors did and thought that the overall production was 'beautifully paced, full of wit and sheer belly laughs'.[54]

Overall, *Pinocchio* was much better received, as it offered a vision of childhood closer to the ideals of a progressively liberal middle class. Frank's version emphasises how the moral development of children rests on their own shoulders. They are given advice and pointers but what allows them to enter society as fully functional children is their own choice. However, the play does not offer any other alternative to this freedom of choice or any answers. All the mishaps happen to Pinocchio while he is still a marionette. What would have happened if Pinocchio had not overcome human greed at the moment he did? Would he have missed his chance of ever becoming a real boy? Would he not have a further chance in life? Is Geppetto's love for Pinocchio based purely on the latter manifesting as a real boy? How about when he first made him – was Pinocchio not made of love? The play does not consider any of these questions; its intention is to demonstrate to the young audience that the benefits of good behaviour lead to a fulfilling life, a life within a loving family, a life embedded within a joyful and caring community. The play affirms the values of parenthood; at the same time, it acts as an allegory of how to navigate modern realities. Children, burdened with contemporary social and economic anxieties, can, like Pinocchio, navigate them if they are armoured with the moral advice and ethical behaviour passed on by their parents or guardians. Although they might lose their ways at times (seeking cheap thrills, as in Boobyland, or quick ways to make money, as with the Cat and the Fox), they can always regain control of themselves and their future. The play's message was equally satisfying for children and adults, thus earning a loyal audience that came back to see it more than once.

Pinocchio Is Dead! The End of the Children's Theatre Unit

Pinocchio's successful run was suddenly interrupted on 30 June 1939, when the entire FTP project was terminated, after being performed 197 times in New York alone. Before this interruption, *Pinocchio* was playing to crowded houses, had received a colour spread in *Life* magazine and was chosen as the first children's play to be used for television.[55] When news of the FTP's closure was announced, Frank provided a new ending for *Pinocchio*'s last performance. Having conquered selfishness and greed, Pinocchio does not turn into a real boy but remains a puppet. Instead of a birthday party, a funeral takes place. As a gunshot is heard, a voice proclaimed that Pinocchio is dead, and the curtain rose to reveal the lifeless puppet lying on the stage.

> 'So let the bells proclaim our grief,' intoned the company at the finish, 'that his small life was all too brief.' The stagehands knocked down the sets in view of the audience and the company laid Pinocchio away in a pine box which bore the legend: BORN DECEMBER 23, 1938; KILLED BY ACT OF CONGRESS, JUNE 30, 1939.[56]

Then the crew and cast members, followed by the members of the audience, formed a funeral procession and took Pinocchio's coffin out on the streets of New York. This theatrical event was reported heavily in the press, and although it did not alter the decisions already taken, it was live theatre, produced spontaneously, and bringing together the hopes, dreams and aspirations of both the professionals making up the FTP and the audience that followed the FTP's adventures all the way.

Being an integral part of the FTP's mission from the very beginning, the Children's Theatre unit revealed the importance that Flanagan placed on having the children's voices, dreams, anxieties and lives represented, challenged and reinterpreted on stage: a stage dedicated exclusively to them; a space where they felt safe and energised, and could participate fully and playfully; and a space where they were encouraged to be creative, reflective and themselves. Before the Federal Theatre, children's theatre did not receive any widespread professional theatrical attention. There were puppet and marionette shows, and the telling and retelling of traditional fairy tales, but there were no new plays or new ways of addressing children's creative needs and realities. What the FTP brought into play was an awareness that children also needed access to theatre and drama, that, through them, it had a chance of shaping a new audience and contributing effectively and positively to the educational aspects of performance.

From 1935 to 1939, the Children's Theatre prioritised children's needs. Faced with the economic hardships resulting from the Depression and experiencing their parents' social and economic anxieties, children felt lost and confused. Although most of the plays stayed away from politics, it was impossible to escape poverty or inequality, impossible not to promote community spirit and togetherness, and impossible not to explore new moral teachings. From *The Emperor's New Clothes* to *A Letter to Santa*, *The Story of Little Black Sambo*, *The Revolt of the Beavers* and *Pinocchio*, the plays presented children's contemporary realities, struggles, wishes and dreams. At the same time, they became a forum for the young audience to exert its agency and reimagine a more hopeful and energetic future that had been marred by the Depression. In ending the FTP, its political critics terminated this avenue for future adult generations to imagine a better reality and to participate actively in building it morally, educationally, economically and socially.

But apart from its emphasis on children's emotional, educational and social development and entertainment, the Children's Theatre played an important role in terms of the FTP's relief status. Flanagan wrote to the Dies Committee, citing *Pinocchio* as a prime example of this two-fold venture. She invited the committee to see the play,

> not only because it represents one of our major efforts in the field of children's theatre, but because it is a visualization of what we have been able to do in rehabilitating professional theatre people and retaining them in new techniques. In *Pinocchio* we use fifty vaudeville people who were at one time headliners in their profession and who, through no fault of their own, suddenly found themselves without a market. Now they are artists in a new field and I feel certain you will find that this recreation of theatre personalities is no less exciting than the presentation of the play itself.[57]

Flanagan's impassionate argument summarises what the unit tried to achieve from an administrator's point of view. Not only did it introduce children and communities who had never had access before to live, frequently free-ticketed theatre, but it also retrained theatre professionals, thus providing employment and hope for a large group of people left devastated by the Depression.

The Children's Theatre unit had a great impact on all the children that saw its performances or participated in theatrical, dance or puppet-making workshops. From South to North, and East to West, the directors of children's units and community theatres were all in agreement: because of these units, live theatre was attracting new audiences, children were engaged in acting and play-making, libraries were used more heavily, sales of plays were rising and drama was emerging as a new, creative and participatory outlet for economically and socially disadvantaged groups. Because of these federal ventures, America was on the verge of creating its own unique and native take on theatre that could produce plays with national subject matters at heart and simultaneously champion a universal and international outlook. But the disbandment of the FTP meant that children's theatre once again returned to its previous premise of reproducing canonical fairy tales and myths, of promoting specific systems of moral behaviour, of neglecting contemporary social realities and anxieties affecting children, and lastly, of making theatre less accessible to those with few pennies. *Pinocchio*, a play that came to symbolise the FTP – especially with its rewritten ending – may have taught children the dangers of greed and the gift of sharing and helping those in need, but it failed to extend its message to the widespread adult community and to Congress.

6

THE FEDERAL DANCE PROJECT: DANCE, RACE, GREEK TRAGEDY AND HELEN TAMIRIS

> The dance of today must have a dynamic tempo and be valid, precise, spontaneous, free, normal, natural and human.[1]
> Helen Tamiris, 'Tamiris in Her Own Voice: Draft of an Autobiography'.
>
> A skilled worker at work invariably reminds me of a dancer; thus work borders on art.[2]
> Vsevolod Meyerhold, as quoted in Braun, *Meyerhold on Theatre*.
>
> the more deeply embodied bodies [are] the female body, the radicalised body, [and] the working body.[3]
> Mark Seltzer, *Bodies and Machines*.

INTRODUCING THE FEDERAL DANCE UNIT

When the WPA was initiated by President Roosevelt, its aim was to provide work for all the artists that had been affected by the Depression. As previously mentioned, the WPA consisted of the Federal Music Project, Federal Art Project, Federal Writers' Project and FTP. There was no mention of a separate Dance unit; instead, in early January 1936, Elmer Rice, the New York regional director, approved the formation of three dance units within the project. Flanagan was very excited about it; she was quoted saying that 'it is impossible to think of the modern theatre without thinking of the dance [. . .]

it is necessary for the director to learn the hard lessons of the dancer – how to emphasize and distort line, how to assault by color, how to design in space'.[4] However, this arrangement did not sit well with Helen Tamiris. Being fully aware of what modern dance had accomplished within American culture, she was adamant that a separate Dance unit should exist within the WPA. Tirelessly working to have the dancers recognised as a group entity rather than a mere part of the FTP, Tamiris persistently waged a campaign with both Harry Hopkins and Flanagan for the creation of a Federal Dance Unit.

Tamiris, born Helen Becker of Russian Jewish immigrants, had a hard and difficult upbringing but found solace and strength in dance. A contemporary of Martha Graham, Doris Humphrey and Charles Weidman, Tamiris never established a dancing school or distinct dancing style as they did. In trying to find her method and develop her technique, she travelled to Europe, and worked the American scene in nightclubs and commercial theatre. She discovered that she wanted to be a concert artist, fusing music with choreography (with the two interdependent rather than the choreography being an interpretation of the accompanying music) and mindfully expressing through her art her country's contemporary issues. Her dances would be of and for America, sincere and simple; they would have 'a dynamic tempo and be valid, precise, spontaneous, free, normal, natural and human'.[5] Her dedication to the American spirit, her independence from past dancing styles and forms, and her desire to explore and expose contemporary social issues set Tamiris apart from the rest of her contemporaries.

Before her involvement with the FTP, Tamiris experimented with Negro spirituals; they formed part of her recitals and reflected her view that it was necessary for an artist not simply to understand his/her place within the contemporary social, political and cultural reality but also to 'recognize his role as a citizen, taking responsibility, not only to think, but to act'.[6] Their commitment to action and recognition of the need for such action were, for Tamiris, signs of an artist's maturity and of human significance. The world of the Negro spiritual accommodated Tamiris's desire for a socially conscious art. Their history and stories of oppression, racism, hardship, slavery, pain and faith gestured at genuine expressions of the human condition that American culture and society had, for a long time, ignored; the time for serious, conscious and creative consideration within a white-dominated American society had arrived and Tamiris was eager for such subjects to be developed further within a separate Dance unit funded by the WPA.

Flanagan did not take much persuading; she herself could see the validity of a separate modern Dance unit that was of its time, expressed contemporary ideas, displayed social consciousness and experimented with new ways of representation combining dance with theatre. Tamiris's statement that the validity of modern dance is rooted in its ability to express modern problems (and some of these are social problems), to touch modern audiences into sympathetic awareness of social conditions, even to excite them into wanting to do something about them

could not have been closer to Flanagan's ideas and the goals she had set for the FTP.⁷ Flanagan and Tamiris's efforts were successful and in the middle of January, 1936, the Federal Dance Project (FDP) was born. Its first director was to be Don Oscar Becque and the executive committee included Tamiris, Doris Humphrey, Charles Weidman, Felicia Sorel and Gluck-Sandor; Genevieve Pitot was also named as an associate. The FDP was given a budget of 155,000 dollars to cover the costs of the first six months; during those months, the project was to employ 185 dancers and stage eight productions. The original plans included Humphrey's restaging of *Suite in F*, Weidman's new version of *Candide*, Tamiris's extension of the original *Walt Whitman Suite* into *Salut au Monde* and Gluck-Sandor's revival of *The Prodigal Son*. Sorel worked on Strauss's *Till Eulenspiegel* and Becque himself on a piece entitled *The Young Tramps*.

Things did not go according to plan, however, and Becque's reign, between 1935 and 1937, was plagued by continuous problems. Many dancers did not like him and were suspicious of his qualifications in modern dance. From the beginning, they rejected his two aims for the project: firstly, the development of a 'common denominator' modern technique that all dancers and choreographers would follow; and secondly, the expansion of modern American dance (in terms of both form and content) into full-length theatrical dance works.⁸ Both aims were controversial among dancers since they restricted their diverse creative individual styles and geniuses, as well as carving out a direction for American modern dance that was too prescriptive. But the first issue that Becque and the FDP faced had to do with personnel rather than with an actual performance. Although the project was to employ 185 dancers, on 5 March 1936 registrations halted, with only 85 hired. There was an instant reaction to the decision, with petitions reaching Becque's office demanding that he fulfil the government's quota obligations. From petitions, the protests escalated to the dancers picketing his office and being arrested in the process; these events resulted in a trial that took place on 22 April 1936, at which all charges were dismissed. As Grant Code commented, the April trial was 'the first recorded public performance of the dance project'.⁹

The frustrations escalated further, with a petition requesting Becque's removal being circulated to Hopkins, Flanagan and Barber. By that point, the project's choreographers had also added their voices to the dancers' complaints. Their inclusion in the debate further intensified the feud between Becque and the choreographers, with Becque primarily accusing Tamiris of manipulation. In November 1936, a public hearing was called to discuss and address issues of mismanagement but Becque chose not to attend. During the hearing, many of the dancers and choreographers openly questioned his practice of re-auditioning dancers who had already worked on previous productions put on by the project; it was suggested that he used auditions as 'an instrument against the dancer'.[10] But what drew the most criticism was Becque's insistence on imposing the common denominator dance technique. Tamiris was quoted as arguing at the hearing that 'there is no single choreographer who has given years to the development of her own technique willing to allow a Don Oscar Becque to change the course of their teaching at his will or whim'.[11] Voicing the sentiments of all the project's choreographers, Tamiris's disclosures added to the already long list of grievances against Becque, who resigned in December.

Becque was replaced by Lincoln Kirstein, whose reign was also short-lived, as he himself fell short of embracing the more democratic, socially conscious and experimental vision of modern dance. It has been documented by both Flanagan and Schlundt how, in his attempt to compliment Tamiris, Kirstein ended up offending her. While meeting her to discuss his ideas on his first project – a panorama of the history of American dance – Kirstein suggested that Tamiris could dance Isadora Duncan, to which Tamiris, eyeing him coldly, asked, 'And who will dance Tamiris?'[12] Shortly after this incident, Kirstein resigned and was replaced by Stephen Karnot, a member of the Shock Troupe and a director of the Workers Laboratory Theatre, who had studied under Meyerhold in Moscow. Perhaps his knowledge of biomechanics, his expertise in group rehearsals and his wife's knowledge of dance allowed him to have a better understanding of the complexities of the FDP, the needs of the dancers and the choreographers. and the direction that modern dance wanted to take within American cultural life. Karnot stayed in the role till the end of the project.

Tamiris was assigned twenty dancers to work with, some of whom were founding members of her company. One of her dancers, Pauline Tish, who first started out with Martha Graham, described how each day would start:

> with basic movement taught by Tamiris or her assistants . . . There was a conscious avoidance of anything resembling ballet. The legs were never turned out! Legs and body were thought of as one piece, used freely, with no pressure on the joints . . . Rocking, movement and combination were part of the technique. Turns, jumps, and leaps were also included. Excerpts from Tamiris' choreography and improvisation with new material usually ended the session. Some of these excerpts became parts of future dances.[13]

Tish's description reveals a group that worked hard, rehearsed together and respected their choreographer. Tamiris, being a good listener and great speaker, was able to articulate clearly to her group her vision of modern dance, and the social responsibilities of the dancer that underlined such a vision. As Tish further commented, it was only after she opened up herself to the economic realities of the Depression and the social relationship between art and life that she was finally able to understand Tamiris's importance to and influence on the growth of modern dance within the USA.[14]

Tamiris's first production for the FDP was a revision of the successful *Salut au Monde*, which opened on 23 July 1936 and run till 5 August. In her revision, Tamiris choreographed five dance episodes based on Walt Whitman's poems; this time, the dance was accompanied by an actual narrator. Arthur Spencer, of the Experimental Theatre in New York, served as the production's narrative voice, introducing each dance. The music was composed and arranged by Genevieve Pitot and the textual adaptation was done by John Bovingdon and Winthrop Parkhurst. In *Salut au Monde*, Tamiris investigated issues of struggle, racial inequality and oppression – themes that would be further explored in her next production, *How Long Brethren?* The narrator was used as a representative of the American everyman (similar to the Living Newspaper's everyman or Mr Buttonkooper) and the performance was a representation of how he viewed the world around him, how his future looked and the struggles he was to face. The press release for the production started by quoting part of Whitman's poem and went on to pronounce:

> This theme is particularly fitting, and expresses the attitude of America, in these days of racial distrust. It is significant that the dance is the vehicle for the expression of a vital social concept. 'Salut au Monde' illustrates the aim of the Federal Dance Theatre to bring the concert dance out of the realm of the esoteric and introduce it to the wide mass of people as an expressive medium for presenting living ideas.[15]

Then, it described in some detail the five episodes of the performance. The first and the last were solos, danced by Tamiris herself (Figure 6.1), whereas the middle three were performed by her group. The group dances were instrumental in representing to the American audience the struggle and dissonance that persisted among the different races. Their main aim was to bring the audience to an awareness that, despite their cultural and ethnic differences, they all experienced the same level of suffering, struggle, racism and poverty. The social message – the need to unite to fight poverty and racism, to allow and cultivate an understanding that poverty and racism are common problems among the people of the world, even though they are ethnically different – was repeated and accentuated in Tamiris's concluding solo. In it, she danced until the group – which had previously fallen back when she entered – stood up and joined her call to work together, unite in peace and combat inequality and racial prejudices.

Figure 6.1 Helen Tamiris in *Salut au Monde*. New York, 1936.

Tamiris's *Salut au Monde* dealt directly with the melting pot of America. Taking her cue from Whitman's vision of the individual man/woman as part of a larger international community, Tamiris could not resist his call:

> Each of us is inevitable
> Each of us is limitless – each of us with his or her right
>   Upon the earth,
> Each of us allowed the purports of the earth
> Each of us here as divinely as any is here.[16]

Only photographic evidence is available of this performance but Pauline Tish's article, in which she details Tamiris's work ethic, the way she choreographed and her socially infused agenda regarding modern dance, remains a much-quoted and referenced source. In it, she described how, by joining Tamiris's group, she was instantly exposed to the idea of the choreography and the dance movements being intrinsically linked with the poetic text (as opposed to simply enhancing the text). She was also exposed to improvisation; as she described, 'Tamiris encouraged us to develop movements of other culture and then put ourselves into the movement, thus discovering "the other".'[17] This

THE FEDERAL DANCE PROJECT

new form of collaboration worked on a variety of levels; firstly, the dancers were allowed to tap into their own creativity, into their past training, and bring it forth to the present; secondly, they were faced with the creativity of their fellow dancers, and thus encouraged to discover the 'other' both within themselves and in the body of their fellow dancers; and thirdly, in participating in the creative process of the specific choreography, they were able to explore the 'other' in terms of different cultures, ideas and movements. All the different interpretations of 'otherness' that these dancers could have come up with required a rigorous cognitive and creative process, firstly, to interpret such movement and then incorporate it within the whole choreography.

Tish was cast as part of a circle of women (Figure 6.2) that held hands and never let go, representing the world and its people. Describing their dancing, Tish remembers how they 'pulled and pushed and undulated, gradually moving downstage until some of us were off the platform and on the floor downstage, our feet tucked under us, our hands still clasped'.[18] *Salut au Monde* was well received by the critics and the audiences. And equally importantly, it was well received by Flanagan, who found 'the first offering of Tamiris and her fiery cohorts' dynamic, experimental and appropriate.[19] The use of the word appropriate to describe it, though, was quite ambiguous. Similar

Figure 6.2 The circle of women in *Salut au Monde*. New York, 1936.

to the FTP, the FDP's ideals and purpose within both American cultural life and the economic relief project were not clearly articulated or even defined. Was the project a form of relief for the unemployed dancers or did it undertake the heavy task of creating a distinctively American national dance theatre? This ambiguity attributed partly to its downfall; for the time being, though, the FDP was finally ready to produce exciting performances that would challenge audiences' perceptions of modern dance and their beliefs in the founding values of American liberalism and exceptionalism, and make them question the representative portrayal of American life and realities.

Race and Dance in *How Long Brethren?*

Tamiris's first major success, both commercially and experimentally, was *How Long Brethren?* Riding on the success of *Salut au Monde*, relying on the Negro spirituals she had devised and performed in her first solo concerts and continuing her mission to present socially conscious and experimental theatre, Tamiris and her group of twenty dancers were ready for the premiere on 6 May 1937. Tamiris's project was staged along with Charles Weidman's *Candide* at the Nora Bayes Theatre in New York. It remains the undisputed hit of the whole FDP, enjoying critical acclaim and a longer run than any other dance production. It played to packed theatres from May till early July – a run that was unprecedented for a dance performance – and attracted an audience of over 24,000. According to Lloyd, it won the first of the *Dance* magazine awards for choreography, it reached and enthused a general (rather than a specialised) audience, it deviated from the dance conventions of its time in terms of subject and performativity, and it 'made social comment that took'.[20] It fulfilled on all levels what Flanagan aspired to achieve with modern theatre and dance within American cultural life: to be experimental, relatable to the general public, informative on social issues, daring and willing to expose difficult truths and realities.

Tamiris choreographed the dances, both solo and group, to seven African American spirituals: 'Pickin' Off de Cotton', 'Upon de Mountain', 'Railroad', 'Scottsboro', 'Sistern an' Brethren', 'Let's Go to de Buryin'' and 'How Long Brethren?' The music score was provided by Pitot, and Feder was responsible for the lighting. These songs, among others, were originally collected by Lawrence Gellert. For over a decade, Gellert had been collecting and documenting songs of protests, race and class from African Americans residing in the South. And in 1936, a slim book containing his collection, entitled *Negro Songs of Protest*, was published by the American Music League, which was affiliated with the American Communist Party.[21] The print release of these songs forced the primarily white readership to face the true, honest and unabashed feelings of discontent and agitation experienced by their fellow African Americans. Tamiris, who was always fascinated with exploring issues of race, class and equality through the Negro spiritual (as opposed to her own background as a poor Jewish immigrant), was quick to pick up on the publication; she chose the seven afore-mentioned songs and, along with her female dancers, worked hard to represent social injustice and racism through their choreography.

As is the case with most productions by the FDP, as well as the FTP, there is no film evidence of how the choreography actually looked, how the stage and lighting worked or how the audience really behaved throughout the performance. Therefore, the reconstruction of this performance is primarily based on photographic material, archived notes and playbills, interviews with and articles on some of the participating dancers, and also on other academics' reconstructions of this material. One major addition to and difference from not only *Salut au Monde*, but also her previous Negro spiritual concerts, was the inclusion of a large African American choir and a full orchestra. The inclusion of both the choir and the orchestra, as well as the employment of twenty dancers, was in keeping with the policy set out by Flanagan and the WPA: that the majority of the budget should be spent on employing unemployed artists. As photographs of the production will demonstrate (Figure 6.3, for example), the scenery was sparse and the costumes were simple but elegant.

Figure 6.3 Tamiris in *How Long Brethren?* New York, 1937.

The choir of fifteen, directed by Bob Moman, was made up of the Federal Theatre Negro Chorus, and the collaboration between white female dancers and an African American group was a rare occurrence. As discussed in Chapter 4, the co-existence of both groups within the same theatrical and public space was not something that was encouraged. Contemporary critics have commented on how the choir was positioned in odd places within the stage (seated in boxes at one side of the stage at the Nora Bayes Theatre and at one side of the orchestra pit at the 49th Street Theatre), making them visible to the audience but also keeping distant from the dancers, whose performance was meant to embody what they were singing. At the same time, the choir's individual members were not named in the first printed programme (unlike the individual dancers), something that was rectified in the subsequent revival and performances of the production.[22] Both of these comments raise the important question of why Tamiris chose an exclusively female white cast to experiment with and represent racial angst, inequality and protest. Was it, as Manning argues, that Tamiris's commitment to leftist politics and their social message was more crucial to represent than explicitly using a black body to manifest the songs' anguish and despair? Was it because Tamiris's choreographical and experimental vision could not accommodate and incorporate a dancer's black body? Was it because the audience was not ready to accept the mingling of a white and a black body working together and co-existing within the public space of a theatre? Or was it a matter of resources, there not being enough good-quality African American dancers around who could perform in her productions? No definitive answers can be provided to these pertinent questions, but some interpretations will be attempted.

The seven dances that made up the performance told stories of poverty, starvation, injustice and death; the audience directly faced the struggles of African Americans and empathised with them. At the same time, Tamiris's choreography represented a change from what she had devised for her 1928 concerts. Whereas the latter were based on elegiac songs of slavery, expressing resignation to current living conditions and hope for a better life in Heaven, the current songs were more polemical, more direct, expressing anger and demanding a betterment of living conditions in the here and now. Tish recalled how the choreography mirrored the said anger, oppression and call for action; the steps were slow, the feet shuffling along the ground – representing heaviness and burden – while the back, arms and torso were held in angular positions with the body in general bending and straightening.[23] The song lyrics provided the narrative pretext for each episode and for the overall choreography, but Tamiris did not simply use dance to interpret or demonstrate the narrative; instead, the choreography and dance amplified their meaning and promoted to the audience a different artistic vision and aesthetic.

Figure 6.4 'Pickin' Off de Cotton' from *How Long Brethren?* New York, 1937.

Each episode built from the previous one, and the whole piece moved from 'desperation to a certain amount of defiance', from low-key lighting to a march into 'a red dawn'.[24] The first episode, 'Pickin' Off de Cotton', depicted the labour of cotton picking that most African American slaves had to endure. Tamiris's choreography employed the motion of moving forward and backward, using angular positions for the legs and bending the torso to mimic the actual movements that cotton pickers made (Figure 6.4). There were also fast running steps, with the dancers starting and stopping, and finally falling down on the stage due to exhaustion. Episode two, entitled 'Upon de Mountain' (Figure 6.5), was a family scene, with Tamiris taking the role of the mother; the theme of the song is starvation, brought about by unemployment. While the dancers were portraying their protest, the chorus was singing

> Upon de mountain chillum call,
> Cain't make a dollah, save mah soul.
> Chillun hungry, nothin' to eat,
> Git no money, walk in de street.
> Ast man Cap'n cain he use a man.
> Use a man, not a skeleton.
> How cain ah make, Ah don' know,
> Tired of starvin', won' starve no moah![25]

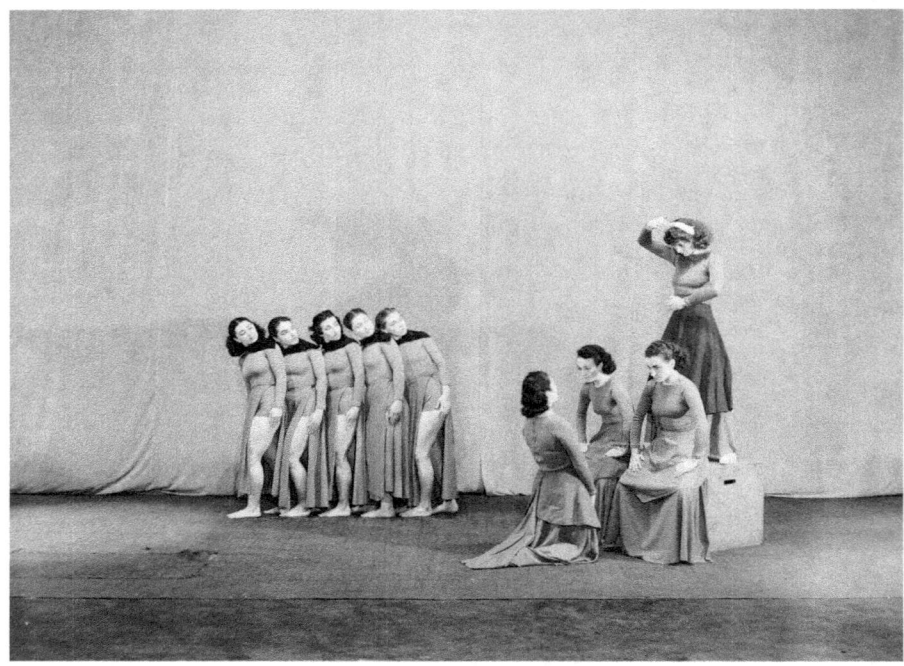

Figure 6.5 'Upon de Mountain' from *How Long Brethren?* New York, 1937.

Although the song talks of a man, the matriarch Tamiris and the female body took centre-stage. Two groups of dancers represented the despair and rebelliousness pouring out of the lyrics. On the one hand, Tamiris, situated in a box to elevate herself, was surrounded by her three children, whom she is trying to embrace and protect. As the dance progressed, one of her children fell on the floor in a contraction of hunger. On the other side, there was a group of dancers, at first standing close together. But similar to her child, as the dance progressed, one by one they stepped out of line, 'raising an arm as if demanding food'.[26] This formation was also repeated in the concluding section of the performance to reiterate the message of solidarity and protest in light of such poverty, inequality, brutality and racism.

The third episode, 'Railroad', again depicted the difficult working conditions, and the destitution, exploitation and disposability the people experienced. The dancers on stage were performing their choreography to the choir signing:

> Workin' on de railroad – fifty cents a day.
> De boss at de comp'ny sto' sign all I make away.
> Mammy po'ly write, 'Please send some money, son.'
> But I ain't got no ready made money [. . .]

> Railroad it completed, cars arunning on de track.
> No mo' work for me here abouts, -
> No mo' work for me – here abouts.
> It's time for packing up de ol' raggety gripsack [. . .]
>
> Walkin' 'long side de track – hungry, wantin' to eat.
> Dog dead tired – Shoes wore out – Dog dead tired –
> Shoes wore out and Lawd, burnin' blisters on my feet.[27]

The fourth episode did not shy away from taking on actual historical events, casting a critical eye over them and exposing the inherent racial attitudes of American society. Entitled 'Scottsboro', it dealt with the events surrounding the Scottsboro boys, nine African American boys aged 13 to 20, who were accused of raping two white females on a train in 1931. Only six years after the original trial, with retrials on the way, the 1931 events had become infamous for their lynch mob, an all-white jury, the speed with which the trials were organised and the unproven testimonies of the two women. One can understand how the African American population of the South created a song to express their feelings of frustration, pain, anger, injustice and rejection at this example of miscarriage of justice in the legal system.

This episode marked an important shift within the whole production in terms of the narrative and the message it was putting forward. Whereas the previous three episodes expressed the dual burden of, firstly, the lack of proper and constant employment, and secondly, the physically punishing work available to them, in 'Scottsboro' the feeling moves towards actual protest, demanding action and change. The choir's strong, harmonised voice would sing:

> Paper – come out – Done strewed de news
> Seven – po' chillum, Moan deat' house blues.
> Seven – po' chillum moanin' deat' house blues.
> Seven nappy head wit' big shiny eye
> All boun' in jail and framed to die
> All boun' in jail and framed to die.
>
> Messin' – white woman Snakely – in' tale,
> Hang an' burn And jail wi' no bail
> Dat hang an' burn – and – jail wit' no bail
> Worse ol' crime in white folks lan'
> Black skin coverin' po' workin' man
> Black skin coverin' po' workin' man.
>
> Judge – an jury All in – de stan'
> Lawd, biggery name Fo' same lynchin' band.
> White follks and Darkie in great Co't house

Like cat down cellar wit nohole mouse,
Like cat down cellar wit' nohole mouse.
Paper – come out, Done strewed de news.
Seven po' chillum Moan deat' house blues.
Seven – po' chillum moanin' deat' house blues –[28]

While the choir sang these lyrics, the dancers would appear on stage, each one taking her place on one of the five boxes meant to represent the jail cells that the Scottsboro boys occupied. In one of the most iconic photographs from the performance (Figure 6.6), one can see how the five dancers were blindfolded, a direct and pronounced commentary on the racism and injustice surrounding the trial. The remaining two, also blindfolded, were moving among the boxes, representing the executioners. In a caustic comment on the American legal system, the executioner's blindfold reminded the audience of Lady Justice, whose blindfold is meant to represent impartiality – that everyone is equal in her 'eyes', regardless of wealth, gender, race or power. How untrue that was for the Scottsboro boys, whose trial served as another reminder of the way African American were treated and considered as lesser people because of the colour of their skin. To represent the execution, Tamiris's choreography had the dancers hold their bodies as if hanging from trees (another image

Figure 6.6 'Scottsboro' from *How Long Brethren?* New York, 1937.

familiar to the audience from lynching), 'their jerky torso movements indicating a modicum of life left in them'.[29] As the photograph depicts, seeing these movements projected as shadows on the backdrop deepened the audience's experience of reliving the trials, the injustice suffered and the perpetual torture, both physical and mental, that the boys endured.

Following this episode was 'Sistern an' Brethren', which showed two groups of dancers with their heads and faces covered with black veils, representing mourners (Figure 6.7). As Tish remembers, one group stood in the back, motionless, whereas the one in the front rocked repeatedly back and forth; the dance was meant to satirise the passivity of prayer for the dead.[30] It was as if this episode was commenting on the events described in the previous one. No longer was the song about praying for the soul of the young African Americans, for finding peace and their rightful place in heaven; the tone of this song was more confrontational, expressing exasperation, anger and a demand for change:

> Sistern and brethren, Stop foolin' wid pray. Sistern an' brethren
> Stop foolin' wid pray. When black face is lifted, Lord turnin' way [. . .]

> We's burying a brudder De kill fo' de crime. We's buryin a brudder
> Dey kill fo' de crime. Tryin' to keep what was his al de time [. . .]

Figure 6.7. 'Sistern an' Brethren' from *How Long Brethren?* New York, 1937.

> Yo' head tain' no apple Fo dagglin' from a tree, Yo'
> Head tain' no apple Fo daglin' from a tree, Yo'
>
> | | |
> |---|---|
> | Stand on yo' feet, – | Club gripped 'tween yo' hands. |
> | Stand on yo' feet, – | Club gripped 'tween yo' hands. |
> | Spill dere blood too, Show em | yo's a man's.[31] |

The choreography and lyrics forced the audience to confront their shared responsibility in the perpetuation of racism, but it also invited them to witness the change in sentiment. Praying to the Lord was no longer enough, and describing the unimaginable racism and torture their minds and bodies endured was already proven; now change was demanded in their daily lives, realities and communities. This song also offered a direct commentary on their cultural heritage; African Americans had all grown up singing spirituals to express their hardship but these songs presented an evolution in terms of how they approached their racial past, how they negotiated it and also how they moved on to action. Singing about slavery, torture and racism was no longer enough – a recognition that action and change were long overdue had enthused the African Americans' soul.

The last two episodes were 'Let's Go to de Buryin' and 'How Long Brethren?' The former was a celebration of life, death and rebirth. Tamiris's choreography juxtaposed vernacular dance steps with angular movements. Despite the macabre lyrics, Tamiris transformed the song into an energetic dance that took over the audience. The choir was singing

> Come on, – come on, – let's go to de buryin' . . .
> Wayover in de new buyin' groun.' . . .
> Heah a mighty rumblin', let's go to de buryin' . . .
> Wayover in de new buyin' groun.' . . .
> Cap's kill my buddy, let's go to de buryin' . . .
> Wayover in de new buyin' groun,[32]

to which Tamiris's dance responded with a life-affirming force. Tish recalled how Tamiris came out

> In an almost swash buckling sideways pattern of arms and legs. She chewed up the space in full-bodied movement phrases, not dancing to the music so much as embodying it, Pitot providing the air under the dance with her music. Tamiris' chugs and struts moved as quickly as if on air, while digging into the ground at the same time. She seemed to say, 'Here I am. Come and join me wherever I go.' As the audience responded with wild applause, we danced Tamiris' phrases, coming and going on and off stage.[33]

The energy that Tamiris put into that dance focused the audience's attention more on the choreographical elements of the work, the way the body could mould itself into angular movements, and how modern dance combined everyday movements with more experimental structures. 'Let's Go to de Buryin'' was all about the body, it was all about Tamiris, as a representative of the modern dancer, being able to transform herself and her body into the life force that the song implied and to make the audience feel that energy and become part of it.

With the exception of the afore-mentioned dance, the audience was, up to that point, bombarded with the realities that African American faced in their everyday lives. The last song and dance, the homonymous 'How Long Brethren?', forced the audience's attention to revert to those realities, bringing along a clearer call for action that was firstly introduced in 'Sistern an' Brethren'. The lyrics of the song were explicitly demanding action:

> How long brethren, how long mu' my people weep and mourn?
> How long, how long brethren, how long?
> So long – my people been asleep,
> White folks plowin' darkies soul down deep.
> How long, how long brethren, how long?
> Too long, brethren too long –
> We just barely miserin' long.
> Too long, too long, brethren too long.
> White folk he aint Jesus
> He jes' a man grabbin' biscuit out of poor darkie's hand.
> Too long, too long, brethren, too long.
> So long – brethren.
> So long – Darkie keep asingin' de same ol' song.
> So long –, so long, brethren, so long.
> Darkie he jes' patch black dirt,
> De raisin' part of de white man's earth. –
> So long, so long, brethren, so long.[34]

The episode began with Tamiris alone on stage, with her feet on a lunge and her hand extended, in a curve, her fingers pointing forward. The dancers would then slowly enter the stage in groups of four, gradually forming one line, one snuggled against the other, with their fists clenched, their heads slightly turned and their gaze fixed on their leader (Figure 6.8). The dancers' eyes were focused on Tamiris until they left the stage, 'marching into a red dawn'.[35] The ending of the episode, the whole performance creating unison between the dancers and their leader, and the symbolic use of the colour red could not but point to a historically Socialist/leftist-inspired call to action. The message was clear: leaders are needed and are necessary but change and action can be

Figure 6.8 'How Long Brethren?' from *How Long Brethren?* New York, 1937.

effective only when driven by the people, not by individuals. The necessity for political and social change and the power to enforce it lay within the collective; it would be inner strength, combined with the joining forces of 'brethren' and 'my people', that would bring about justice, freedom and equality.

As mentioned earlier, the performance was received enthusiastically by the majority of critics, who enthused about her choreography and also picked up on Tamiris's call for action and social awareness. Jerome Bohm's report stated,

> in *How Long Brethren* Tamiris has accomplished the finest composition of her career . . . the most thrilling episode, 'Let's Go to De Buryin',' with its frenzied emotional climax heightened by Tamiris' superb dancing, aroused the audience to a state of high excitement.[36]

At the same time, Margaret Lloyd commented that

> [these] modern songs of protest from the present-day deep South . . . focus attention on Negroes, not only as Negroes, but as a symbol of all the oppressed peoples of earth. It may be racial oppression, or religious, or political, but thus focused on one aspect of contemporary life, [the production] becomes in its singularity a poignant reminder of a universal problem.[37]

Henry Gilfond commented on Tamiris's success in attracting a general public – 'rarely have audiences responded so wholeheartedly and rarely have dancers deserved such ovations' – as well as her on performance, since 'Tamiris turned back to her jazz rhythms – richer for all her long work with themes of basic social import [. . .] she has captured the rhythms as they have come up from hard folk experience'.[38] And lastly, John Martin praised Tamiris for employing, particularly in 'Let's Go to De Buryin', 'vigorous and sustained movement patterns and ... succeed[ing] in topping the massed effect of orchestra and voices'.[39]

There can be little doubt that most contemporary critics were able to recognise Tamiris's experimentations with movement, the female body and choreography, and that spectators were able to recognise her Socialist politics. What was missing from their consideration was the irony of having an all-white female cast to represent and speak for racism against and oppression of African Americans. This absence was picked up by Ellen Graff, a researcher of leftist dance, whose work attempted to contextualise the racial casting of the work in relation to the cultural tradition of dance that American modern dance inherited. Graff pointed out that most New York African American dancers and actors were employed at the Negro Theatre in Harlem's Lafayette, and that any efforts to recruit black dancers did not materialise.[40] But one of the main restrictions was the FDP's self-definition. The unit was set up to offer work to any dancer trained either in traditional ballet or in any of the emergent modern dance schools. Current bibliography on American modern dance has testified to the racial discrimination and difficulties accessing proper dance training that many African American dancers had endured.[41] In particular, regarding ballet training, John Martin's characterisation of the 'European outlook, history and technical theory of ballet' as alien to the black dancer 'culturally, temperamentally and anatomically' was considered true by many and prolonged a stereotypical and racially restricted attitude towards them.[42]

The main criticism of Tamiris's use of exclusively white bodies has come from Susan Manning. In her work, Manning recognises Tamiris's contribution to American modern dance and discusses her focus on primarily redefining and mixing gender with radical politics. For Manning, Tamiris wanted to challenge the status quo of the female body of the dancer as a sexual object for the heterosexual gaze. At the same time, though, this challenge was accompanied by her desire to diminish her own Jewish ethnicity in an attempt to embrace universalism. Tamiris was aware of the immigrant Jews' conflicting desires to be accepted as American 'whites' and assimilate to the established culture. By enabling Jewish female bodies on stage to represent the struggles and racism of African Americans in both Negro spirituals and *How Long Brethren?*, Tamiris displayed the power, fierceness, malleability and potentiality of the female body (as opposed to its regular representation as an eroticised object), as well as enabling it to stand in as a representative of the body politic. This 'metaphorical minstrelsy', wrote Manning, 'conferred "whiteness" – aesthetic legitimacy – on the female body' while the African American performer 'still labored under the limitations of representing white folks' images of black folks'; at the same time, her casting 'conferred social legitimacy on the immigrant, working-class, Jewish body'.[43]

Mark Franko contested Manning's thesis, arguing that Tamiris sympathised with popular front ideology and therefore identified with the African American experience as part of a larger class struggle.[44] Franko's point becomes more explicit when considering Tamiris's radical politics, her desire to raise social awareness among both her dancers and the audience, to create a form of dance malleable to many kinds of political agenda. She wanted to ensure that her dancers had the opportunity to experiment with new forms, challenge established bourgeois notions of art and dance defining the female body, and become confrontational in their presentation of new ideas and movements. In choosing to work and concentrate on issues of racism and struggle experienced by African Americans, Tamiris expressed many leftist artists' identification with them because 'they believed they were members of the same class and because Negro protest songs echoed their determination to take control of their economic lives'.[45]

It is difficult to find a definitive answer as to why Tamiris did not use any African American dancers since she did not address the subject in her unfinished biography; nor did the people closer to her (such as her husband, Daniel Nagrin) have any inkling. She must have been aware of black dancers who may have performed in either Asadata Dafora's highly acclaimed *Kykunkor* or Welles's *Macbeth*, and other African American dancers performed some Negro spirituals that took place after Tamiris's 1928 solo.[46] However, I believe that Tamiris did not exclude African American dancers on purpose or because they did not have any formal ballet training. Speculating on her life project, I tend to conclude that her primary objective was to combine gender with leftist politics while redefining American modern dance. As a feminist, she wanted to challenge the way the female body was displayed on stage; in order to do that, she had to create new dances not only in terms of movement but also in terms of themes. As a creative force wanting to encompass modernity but unveil the pluralism of American culture, she explored American sources, including African American spirituals. And as a radical leftist thinker, she wanted to cultivate a social awareness in both her dancers and the audience on issues of race, injustice, poverty and working conditions.

Tamiris's choreography in *How Long Brethren?* succeeded in its aim. It masterfully approached the issues of racism, lynching and poverty, and loudly (as well as proudly) voiced the call for action and change. In hindsight, yes, it did fail in not recognising the irony of discussing the plight of African Americans whilst simultaneously excluding them and their bodies from being physically present on stage. And yes, it did expose the limits of cultural pluralism within modern dance. But it did not conceal the brutality experienced by African Americans, it did not absolve the audience of its social and cultural responsibilities or its racial tendencies, and it did awaken a passionate response in terms of both aesthetic appreciation and social responsibility. For all its limitations, *How Long Brethren?* remains an admirable example of American modern dance's experimentation with form and technique, combining a new appreciation of the female body with contemporary social, political and economic issues, with the female body becoming the expressive instrument of action and change.

Experimenting with the Greeks: *The Trojan Incident*

By the spring of 1937, rumours had started circulating about more personnel cuts that directly influenced both the Dance Project and the Federal Theatre. The more embattled New York dancers decided to act and started picketing. One of the most memorable and effective picketing incidents took place after the 17 May 1937 performance of *Candide* and *How Long Brethren?* According to Flanagan, at the end of the performance, audience and cast joined 'in an all-night sit-down demonstration against cuts, while 44th Street was filled with marchers'.[47] Despite the demonstrations, hunger strikes, picketing and arrests, in October 1937 the budget cuts were enacted and the once autonomous Dance unit was incorporated within the FTP. These events caused considerable confusion and distress to the dancers, as some of them had to be laid off. The ones remaining in employment had to adjust to new demands, as they now had to combine their dancing with speaking and acting.

Although disappointed, Tamiris did not give up and threw herself into the next project, which was to be *The Trojan Incident*. Based on Euripides' tragedy *Trojan Women* and Homer's works (the *Iliad* and *Odyssey*), this play marked the first and last attempt of the FTP to stage and experiment with classical Ancient Greek tragedy. This ambitious project was doomed from the beginning, as any attempt to restage Greek tragedy would be, firstly, scrutinised for its closeness to the original text (thus judged on its 'authenticity'); secondly, compared to previously successful ('classic' by now) productions; and thirdly, reviewed for the way it portrayed the democratic nature of Greek tragedy and the tensions between its thematic development and American ideology. All the above were present within the intellectual circle of the theatre and dance critics, as well as commercial theatre, but the debate was also exploited within the political arena, with Senator Martin Dies's committee using the play as part of his prosecution and eventual disbandment of the FTP.[48]

For this project, Flanagan herself was personally invested on an intellectual, academic and professional level. The play was adapted by her husband, Philip H. Davis – a renowned professor and scholar of Greek at Vassar. At the same time, it marked the second time she would work with Euripides, the first being her own production of his tragedy *Hippolytus* at Vassar in 1931, in which Davis played Hippolytus. More importantly, though, this production would test her belief that theatre was democratic, open to all people, relevant to its time and a medium of free expression. Having travelled to Greece in 1934, explored the ancient theatre sites and read the classic tragedies, Flanagan had concluded that theatre was part of the institution of democracy within Ancient Greece; if America was to establish itself as the new democratic force of the world, it had the moral and institutional obligation to make theatre the space through which social and political issues would be investigated, exposed, satirised, debated on and made relevant to the people. After all, if Euripides' *Trojan Women* could expose the absurdity of war, the disillusionment with victory and the moral invalidity of the Greeks' arguments, and still survive the test of time, why could the FTP and American theatre not become that force in the twentieth century?

Trojan Women was first produced and performed in 415 BC, during the Peloponnesian War, and was a direct commentary on the events surrounding the island of Melos and Athens' transition from a democratic to a tyrannical and imperialistic power. In 416 BC, Melos had adopted a neutral position during the war; when pushed by the Athenians to side with them, Melos declined. In return, the Athenian assembly decided to invade the island, slaughter all of its male population and sell all the females as slaves. The play formed part of a trilogy about the Trojan War, although the previous two tragedies (*Alexandros* and *Palamedes*) were not directly connected with each other (as opposed to Aeschylus's *Oresteia* trilogy, for example). In terms of content, it followed the fate of the women after the fall of Troy. Once a community, the women are slowly separated from each other and their motherland, sold as slaves to the Greek captains and condemned to a life of slavery. The play concentrates on the matriarch Hecuba, her oracle daughter Cassandra and her daughter-in-law Andromache, enslaved by Odysseus, Agamemnon and Achilles' son, Neoptolemus, respectively. It ends with the ritual burial of Andromache's murdered infant son, Astyanax. Throughout the play, the chorus, made up of Trojan women, is the powerful voice of lament, loss and sorrow, and provides the audience with points on which to reflect critically.

The first two well-known instrumental productions of *Trojan Women* on the American stage were both instigated by European (specifically, English) actors, directors and entrepreneurs. In 1913, the Chicago Little Theatre, co-founded by Englishman Maurice Browne and his American actress wife, Ellen van Volkenburg (after being encouraged by Lady Gregory during the Abbey Theatre's 1911 visit to Chicago), decided on *Trojan Women* as its first production. In 1915, Gilbert Murray's 1905 version of the play was also adapted for the American audience. Directed by Harley Granville Barker, the play was performed only in education institutions (Yale, Harvard, University of

Pennsylvania, City College of New York and Princeton); it reached large audiences, but primarily targeted those of a certain educational and financial standing. Both Browne and Barker's productions aimed at re-establishing poetic drama within the American theatrical tradition, employing new stagecraft observed by the likes of Gordon Craig, Adolphe Appia and Max Reinhardt to create focused and unified performances that would make 'Euripides a contemporary'.[49] The timing of both productions was no coincidence, as World War I had already started and pre-dated the USA's 1917 involvement. *Trojan Women* became the antiwar play par excellence at the beginning of the twentieth century, but its popularity waned after the end of the war. Browne and Barker's productions – despite the latter's mixed Anglo-American cast – still represented European efforts to initiate a new approach to Greek tragedy within the American theatrical space. Native efforts in this new approach were to follow, but not for *Trojan Women* until the 1938 FTP production.

Unlike Murray's translation and adaptation, Davis decide to approach Euripides' text more liberally and to adopt passages from Homer's texts as well. For this, he was instantly accused of hubris by classically trained academics, actors and theatre impresarios; these accusations were also mirrored in the play's reviews. As mentioned previously, Davis was a professor of Greek; he had travelled to Greece extensively and had studied their writings on democracy, community, life, art and war in depth. Apart from acting in *Hippolytus*, he had not displayed any further interest in performance, but his archived personal writings exposed his passion for theatre and new theatrical techniques. Similarly to Browne's views when adapting Euripides' text, Davis wanted to make him contemporary and further emphasise the play's antiwar message. As opposed to faithfully reconstructing the old performances and paying homage to the playwright's intentions, Davis believed that the knowledge he had gained from studying the texts should be used to inform contemporary realities. His text's intention was to 'wake in the audience emotions akin to those awakened by Aischylus, Sophokles, and Euripides', as opposed to simply representing a mirrored reality.[50]

The play was conceived as a dancing antiwar theatrical performance and Davis's adaptation reflected this combination of dance with acting. Tamiris, along with Harold Bolton, co-directed it; she choreographed all the group and solo dances, as well as playing the role of Cassandra, which required her both to dance and to act. Howard Bay designed the setting and the costumes to reflect modern reality but also to allow the fluidity required for the dancing to occur. Wallingford Riegger, who had previously worked with Martha Graham, Hanya Holm and Doris Humphrey, composed the music, and the chorus of twenty-three singers was conducted by Pitot. Unlike previous productions, this one had two choruses: a singing one and a speaking/dancing one. Whereas the first was presented as a unified ensemble, the latter was to be strongly individualised. The play's production notes clearly emphasised the importance of the singing chorus as the core of the play; they also stressed the 'powerfully individualised' female characters of Hecuba as a powerful matriarch, Andromache as passionately devoted to Hector, Cassandra as the prophetic voice of the future and Helen as the epitome of a femme fatale.[51] Davis situated the play in a 'timeless' but recognisably contemporary world in which all external references to places (apart from Greece and Troy) were removed. By putting side by side the defeated women of Troy and the triumphant men of Greece, Davis's adaptation proposed an allegorical reading of war as self and other, past and future. Although defeated, the women of Troy exhibit the courage and knowledge they are trying to instil in the men; but the men, assured in their victorious arrogance, are not willing to learn these lessons. It is up to the audience to make the connections, to listen, experience and understand the atrocities of war, and situate the knowledge gained within contemporary reality. As Davis wrote in his notebook regarding Greek drama, 'our business is to learn what we can of the ancient Greek theatre . . . and the expectations of the audience, and to use the knowledge . . . for our contemporary world'.[52]

The play's press release described the

> story of what happened to the women and children of defeated Troy as fresh as today's bombing . . . The production combined the most interesting and exciting technique of ancient and modern theater in a fusion of drama, dance movement and music.[53]

Davis began his adaptation, unlike the original text, by taking away the gods. The speech between Poseidon and Athena is replaced by a scene in Odysseus's tent, with him, Menelaus and Agamemnon present. During the scene, the three generals debate the length of the war but also revel in their successful deception, which will lead them to conquer Troy. Within the space of a few lines, the true motivation behind the war is revealed; reclaiming Helen was but a pretence, as, in reality, 'we wanted war, not Helen. We wanted the Dardanelles, Menelaus,' proclaims Odysseus.[54] Davis painted a different picture to the Homeric Odysseus; in his play, apart from his resourcefulness, Odysseus also displays his more duplicitous and murderous side. When Thersites breaks into his tent and confronts the three generals with the Greek army's grievances, Odysseus initially seems to understand them and side with the demand to leave, enraging Menelaus and Agamemnon in the process. But as soon as the troops have quietened and left, Odysseus reveals to the other two his real plan to send the boats back to Troy as soon as the horse is inside. Thersites, though, overhears his speech and comes out in full force, confronting their lies. Whereas, in Euripides' play, Odysseus ridicules and brutally attacks Thersites to reinstate order, in Davis's he orders his execution; in typical fashion, the murder takes place in 'the back way, where the men won't see' and the rebel/

Figure 6.9 Hecuba speaking to the women of Troy after its sack. *Trojan Incident*. New York, 1938.

agitator is killed.[55] Odysseus's more noble representation in Homer's works is completely reversed when, after ordering the murder, he readies Menelaus and Agamemnon to draw lots for the women in anticipation of the fall of Troy as the lights slowly fade.

When the lights come back on, the audience is confronted with a tableau scene of the Trojan women after Troy's destruction. Hecuba, their leader, is seen lying on the ground outside the wall but she slowly begins to rise up, mourning the loss that she and the other women have experienced (Figure 6.9). Davis's script has cut down on Hecuba's lamentations in order to build her up as a powerful matriarchal persona, around which the women can come together. She starts calming the women's fears of slavery and exile, the loss of their men and children, and shares their anger for Helen. When Talthybius arrives, he brings news of the group's separation and, as Hecuba bitterly puts it, the 'happy fate' that awaits them.[56] The first name that is mentioned is that of Cassandra; she is to be Agamemnon's concubine. He reveals the rest of the women's fate before Cassandra finally appears on stage.

In Davis's adaptation, Cassandra becomes the main heroine, outshining Hecuba at times, as she carries the antiwar message. Her entrance on to the stage is both dramatic and arresting of the audience's imagination. As shown in Figures 6.10 and 6.11, Cassandra entered the stage holding torches. While

Figures 6.10 and 6.11 Cassandra's dance. Tamiris as Cassandra. *Trojan Incident.* New York, 1938.

the other women initially think of her as mad, they slowly begin to see the symbolism of her dance; they give up on trying to understand why she acts the way she does and instead begin really to listen to her words, as 'she has spoken the truth before this'.[57] Simultaneously with her dance, the singing chorus begins the women's wedding song. To Hecuba's cry that this is no wedding, Cassandra continues to dance in a frenzied manner while repeating the prophecy of her and Agamemnon's death and the destruction of his house.

Once the music stops and she has calmed down, Cassandra delivers her antiwar message. She can see the further losses and disasters that the Greeks will suffer but she now concentrates on the everyday Greek citizen, and not the generals or kings. She tells the women and the audience that 'those Greeks that our men killed had no quarrel with us. / They murdered because they were told to murder.'[58] Like the Trojans, Greek women would have lost their husbands and sons, and Cassandra continues to profess,

> In Greece today women wonder why they brought us sons.
> In Greece, Mother, and in Troy, and in towns and
> villages far over the sea.
> Women will long be wondering.
> Must they always think of these things too late?
> A day will come when women will be stronger, and
> their voices heard.
> When men and women will know their world far better
> than now.
> When this time comes they must know themselves better too.
> Or these things will happen again forever.[59]

In this powerful speech, Cassandra – who had previously prophesised war and destruction – now presents a vision of peace and harmony. All parties involved in a war suffer, and experience loss, destruction and trauma, but war is not inevitable if people are willing to learn from past experiences. Cassandra's speech emphasises the need for women's voices to become stronger and more participatory, as they can counterbalance the dominant male ones. Once women and men are seen as equal in their experience of life, war, loss and reality, and develop a better understanding of themselves, then together – nationally and transnationally – they can promote peace and prevent future destruction.

Cassandra's speech emboldens the rest of the women; the ones from the dance chorus join her in a choral dance, and the ones from the singing chorus erupt into song, accompanied by the orchestra. What follows that empowering song is a dramatic scene. Andromache enters the stage, where, having learned her fate, she laments on her life with Hector. But more tragedy awaits her, as Talthybius brings her the news that her son is to be killed. A tragic exchange takes place between Talthybius and Andromache, with the later relinquishing her son and accepting his imminent death. As she faints and her body is carried off stage by Greek soldiers, Cassandra (who is still present) leaps to the front, inviting the rest of the dance chorus to a dance 'of women lost in a great void', while the singing chorus and the orchestra perform an ode of loss, betrayal and love to accompany their dance.[60] As the play nears its climax, Menelaus enters the stage and the audience is finally confronted with Helen. Hecuba and the rest of the women are in unison against her, sensing that she is about to charm Menelaus into taking her back unharmed and reinstating her as queen. When Helen invokes Aphrodite, the chorus encourages Hecuba to help them, to 'speak for your people / Speak for your country'.[61] Hecuba makes an impassionate speech to Menelaus and Helen, notifying him and reminding her that she begged Helen to go back to her husband to avert the war. But Hecuba, sensing that Menelaus is spell-bound with Helen, claims that

> Helen carries the seeds of war in her . . .
> Wherever Helen goes there will be men to want her,
> And to clothe her, and beautify her at the expense
> of nations –
> . . . But she will never be satisfied.[62]

In Hecuba's speech, Helen becomes a representative of war, a symbol of lust, power and riches. But despite Hecuba's warnings, Menelaus, as in Euripides' text, falls for Helen's charms once again. The women of Troy are not afforded any sense of justice; their fate is to remain slaves and be wronged. But unlike those in Euripides' tragedy, the women in this play gather their courage, move past their passive state as mourners and – directly addressing the audience – turn into didactic teachers. Following Hecuba's call to

> 'Sing, women. (*Then, as she indicates the audience*)
> They may hear you.
> Sing, women, (*Then, as she indicates the audience*)
> They may hear you,

the singing chorus confronts the audience with the atrocities, injustice and destruction brought by war, asking their ghost to 'let it sing'.[63] The audience can no longer afford to avoid war's realities and can no longer claim ignorance. What they have witnessed through this play has given them direct access to knowledge and to ways actively to disengage with the mythologies of war ideology.

If Hecuba and the chorus's song was not enough to mobilise the audience, the play ends in powerfully emotional and defiant manner. Talthybius returns on stage, bringing along with him Astyanax's dead body. Hecuba and the rest of the women are entrusted with burying him, along with Hector's shield. As Hecuba, half talking to herself and half talking to the child's body, prepares the body and places it on Hector's shield, one by one the Greek soldiers fling their torches towards Troy. As the flames rise to mark Troy's total destruction, Hecuba, Cassandra and the women of Troy scatter ornaments on the dead child's corpse. With the sky reddened, Hecuba's call is answered by

Cassandra's demand of the audience that 'those things *must* be remembered', while lifting the shield with the body before her.⁶⁴ Rather than admit defeat, Hecuba counsels the audience – 'if ever men learn to know war when they meet it, we shall not have died in vain' – making it aware of its responsibility to detect similar future events and to work actively to avert them. While Talthybius grows impatient and asks them if they are ready to proceed, all the women perform their last act of defiance.

> TALTHYBIUS: (From the wall)
>   Are you ready, women?
> HECUBA: (Straight to the audience)
>   Are <u>YOU</u> ready?
> SINGING CHORUS: (Echoing her words to the audience)
>   Are you ready?
>   Are you ready?
>   Are you ready?
>   Are you ready to understand?
> (HECUBA follows the last of the women. TALTHYBIUS follows her. The scene dissolves, with the music, in darkness.)⁶⁵

The play ends with a direct address to the audience. After everything they have witnessed, was the audience ready to recognise war, its destructive force, its repetitive patterns, the loss and pain it inflicts on all humans? Although not yet involved, the American audience was aware of the war raging in Europe, of the rise of Fascist ideology and of the persecution of people, countries and races that did not fit that ideology. With its newly found knowledge, how would the audience react in the face of contemporary reality? Similar to previous performances, the play did not offer answers. With its almost militaristic end, it aimed at promoting the need for the audience to become involved, to be aware of its reality and complexities, and to dissolve any apathy.

Trojan Incident received mixed reactions from the critics; the main arguments centred on whether it was an 'authentic' tragedy and how successfully an adaptation of a canonical text can portray contemporary issues. On the first issue, the main problem that critics had was that the play placed equal importance on both the speaking and the singing/dancing aspects. Unlike previous reconfigurations of Euripides' text, Davis produced a blueprint text for a production that would amalgamate speaking, singing and dancing. His text, with his choice to have Cassandra always on stage, made it abundantly clear that he was deviating in choice and spirit, but not in essence, from Euripides' text. The main theme of antiwar sentiment is present in both texts, the destruction of Troy and the fate of its women similarly portrayed and the heart-breaking image of a child's dead body equally powerful in evoking strong feelings and reactions. Promoted and publicised as a dance drama, the

Trojan Incident never hid its intentions to feature dance for almost half of the production time. As Davis commented, 'the singing chorus was the voice of people and the dancing chorus, the people's body'.[66] And this combination made for captivating viewing.

Riegger's musical composition was seen as an excellent example of a modern dramatic score and Bay's set design and costumes also received praise. Atkinson described the latter as 'dynamic' and 'one of the best pieces of dramatic designing of the season'.[67] Bay's design exemplified the sense of captivity that Trojan women were subjected to, as well as providing space for the dance movement. Influenced by Flanagan's belief that the stage should emphasise 'three-dimensional movement of three-dimensional bodies; voice, individual and choric', Bay's design adhered to her suggestion.[68] Using high walls at each end, the space conveyed a sense of entrapment and defeat; this sense was accentuated by the presence of a fallen and broken Liberty Bell, an iconic symbol of independence that would have definitely captured the attention of the American audience. Furthermore, boxes were added on stage in which the singing chorus was positioned.[69] This semi-realistic setting did indeed allow the space for two choruses to be present on it simultaneously, for the voice and the body of actors and dancers to explore it, and for the audience to connect with the themes and realities of loss, captivity, mourning and war.

Unlike the afore-mentioned praise, reactions to Tamiris's dance and choreography were mixed, with the drama critics looking at the play from different angles to the dance ones. The review of the play in *Variety* applauded the courage of the FTP in taking on an ancient tragedy and praised the acting (although dissatisfied with the New York accent of some actors), particularly that of Isabel Bonner as Hecuba. However, the review was not so kind to Tamiris; it found her voice too monotonous and at times thought that her choreography and dances 'assume[d] a barbarism not at all in keeping with the beaten, resigned miens of the Trojan women'.[70] The review revealed the inability of the drama critics and theatre professionals to acknowledge this production's departure from Euripides' original text, especially regarding the more powerful and defiant presentation of the Trojan women.

Brook Atkinson was also scathing. In his review, the day after the premiere, he described it as 'experimental ... which signifies work that is incompletely resolved'.[71] He argued that, although Euripides' play is well respected, especially among antiwar circles, it is rarely performed because it is not actable in the modern theatre; his question 'is every gesture supposed to have dramatic significance?', coupled with his comment on the experimental aspects of the production, revealed his exasperation with Davis, Flanagan and Tamiris's vision of uniting dance, theatre and chorus with social and contemporary political realities.[72] He further described Tamiris as an ideological dancer, who – as Cassandra – 'comes in with a macabre nuptial dance and a sheaf of group abstractions like mad notes of music spinning across the page'.[73] He further found her dance interpolations unintelligible, detracting rather than adding value and meaning to the production. He was also dismissive of the group dances, as he found the dancers behaved more as if they were illustrating a 'workers of the world – unite' theme, as opposed to displaying their anger with the pillaging Greeks.[74] Atkinson ended his review with a caution of probable avoidance for any future plans the FTP might have had to revive classical Greek tragedies. The production was, for him, plagued by ineptitude, but made for interesting viewing compared to the duller plays on offer.

The dance critics' reviews were different. Grant Code was enthusiastic about Tamiris's performance and, in a lengthy review, claimed that

> Tamiris put into this work the finest group and solo choreography she ever did and both she and her company gave their most magnificent performances in it. I am extremely impatient with the critics who could not see this because it was not Euripides ... it is a compliment to Tamiris's integration of the dances into the play, that the dances are stronger when supported by the entire action of the play ... the group dances were about the relation of women to life and to destruction. This is an extremely vital and contemporary theme for us as it was for Euripides ... Those who lack passion, pity, poetry, faith in life, hatred of destruction would miss *Trojan Incident*. The smart so-what, ashamed of feeling anything real would miss it.[75]

Code's passionate review not only highlighted the play's rightful place within contemporary reality and modern dance, but it also directly responded to Atkinson's comments regarding its unsuitability for modern theatre, the organic synthesis of dance with speech and choral singing, and the necessity to evoke strong feelings, images and movements. As Tish, who participated in the dance chorus, recalled, the chorus performed stag leaps, jumps and running, and the gestural parts of all the dancers moving together were very important to the play and its messages.[76]

John Martin's review argued that the script was too condensed, the casting weak and the relation between the two choruses and the action ineffectual. He reserved all his praise for Riegger's music and Tamiris's dances, which kept the production 'from transforming one of the world's greatest dramas into advertent farce'.[77] He went on to suggest that Tamiris, for all the obstacles she faced during the rehearsals,

> has done yeoman service with the dance, for only in choral odes does the production strike fire and touch at all upon emotional excitement ... For the present it is perhaps enough to vote a laurel to Tamiris for a creative and imaginative piece of work against the most formidable of odds.[78]

Similarly to Code, Martin found the choral dances powerful and indispensable to the production, in promoting to the audience excitement and engagement with the issues presented. The dance synchronicity, intensity and camaraderie that Code and Martin applauded and admired was what Atkinson deeply distrusted. His description of the dancers as 'cogs in a machine ... They are captives who have lost all power to think for themselves or have human emotions ... they behave more like workers of the world – unite' presented a view of the choral dance and the overall production as strictly political.[79] His suggestion (shared by the commercial theatre sector) that the production aimed to accomplish a Socialist agenda reinforced a prescribed opinion of the FTP and its productions as politically biased that further fuelled the mistrust towards the WPA and was used extensively by HUAC during its investigations and hearings.

With such controversies surrounding the production, the *Trojan Incident* – which opened on 21 April 1938 at the St James Theatre in New York and ran for twenty-six performances – gave its last performance on 21 May 1938. The production's closure marked a turning point for the whole FTP. The arguments no longer centred on productions, their 'authenticity' or respect for the original classical texts; rather, the debate became a matter of politics. Tamiris stayed on, facing the storm, attending meetings to keep the Project going and trying to organise another production. *Adelante*, her fourth and last production for the FTP, opened in April 1939 and closed in May of the same year. It was not long after that the FTP was terminated.

Tamiris and the End of the Federal Dance Unit

Red-baiting, political scapegoating and Communist paranoia were rife within American politics. HUAC, led by Martin Dies and J. Parnell Thomas, had been hard at work ever since the WPA was established. In Dies's words, the 'WPA was the greatest financial boon which ever came to the Communists in the United States. Stalin could not have done better by his American friends and agents.'[80] The committee was actively collecting any material from the project's productions that could be construed as anti-American and Communist. Anything that spoke of social realities, of poverty, of people cooperating and working together against war and racism, of demanding better living conditions and equal treatment, was deemed to be carrying an antiliberal identity and aiming at destroying the pillars of American politics, life and culture.

Even before the committee met, the people involved, and particularly J. Parnell Thomas, had already started his targeted attack on the FTP (along with the Writers' Project), claiming that 'practically every play presented under the auspices of the Project is sheer propaganda for Communism or the New Deal'.[81] The people on the committee did not differentiate between Communism or the New Deal; they saw both as threats to the way that

American politics worked and related to American society, to the way that American people viewed their representatives. And the fact that a federally funded project dared to call into question issues of politics, economics, race, ideologies and different ways of seeing, understanding and criticising the world, as well as demanding change, was not acceptable. It was as if the WPA and the FTP posed an existential threat to those politicians, to their way of working and living, or simply to their way of being American.

Although the Living Newspapers bore the brunt of most of the accusations leading up to disbandment, the works of the Dance project were also mentioned prominently in the HUAC hearings. The committee's star witness, Hazel Huffman, singled out *How Long Brethren?* in particular. The performance's ending and its use of the colour red, combined with its Socialist call to action and change, formed the basis of Huffman's accusation of it as 'communistic propaganda' when she testified.[82] Her accusation was based primarily on the fact that the *Negro Songs of Protest* book first appeared in print in 1931 in the *New Masses*, the American Marxist magazine that was closely associated with the Communist Party.

Fast forward a few months and Hallie Flanagan herself is testifying in front of the committee. While being questioned by Congressman Starnes, and following the infamous exchange regarding Marlowe (see Chapter 7), it was Euripides' turn to be described and accused as a Communist:

> Mr. Starnes: Of course, we had what some people call Communists back in the days of the Greek theater.
> Mrs. Flanagan: Quite true.
> Mr. Starnes: And I believe Mr. Euripides was guilty of teaching class consciousness also, wasn't he?
> Mrs. Flanagan: I believe that was alleged against all of the Greek dramatists.
> Mr. Starnes: So we cannot say when it began.[83]

This exchange highlights Starnes's ignorance but at the same time it served the purpose of seeding further doubts about the FTP, and its productions and aims. As Flanagan herself reflected a few years after its closure, whether the project had stayed away from its controversial Living Newspapers or not, it would still have faced closure. But at least, by not shunning controversy, the project exposed its audiences to new theatre, gave voice and representation to their social and economic realities, and educated it in both classical and modern plays and performances.

Tamiris was never invited to testify in front of the committee, as Flanagan was, and was never able to voice her frustration and disappointment. The demise of the FTP was a blow both to her and to the group of modern dancers she had worked so hard to organise and for whom she had sought to obtain a decent living wage. The importance of the FDP as a vehicle for permanent economic security in the midst of depression cannot be under-estimated. It was difficult for any dancer to concentrate on crafting a dance style or choreography when not receiving a sustainable income. Tamiris believed that dancers, similar to artists, writers, actors and musicians, equally deserved an opportunity to make a liveable wage without having to beg or resort to other work that could harm their physicality and reduce their dancing abilities. With the loss of the FTP came the loss of economic security, but also the loss of the dancers' community.

Similar to Flanagan's aspirations for the FTP, Tamiris hoped that the FDP would ultimately lead to the creation of a permanent national dance theatre that would support the works of dancers from all types of technical background, nurture new talent and continue to experiment with classical and new productions in educating and exposing American audiences to the magic of dance. The dynamic group of dancers that she worked with, described by Flanagan as 'a volcanic group, frequently in eruption', applied themselves fully to her choreographies, her vision for the productions and her ideas of how the body of the modern dancer can be further trained in movement, expression and physicality.[84] Her strong belief that dancers should, as much as possible, draw on native sources to create an essential American style of modern dance, while displaying social consciousness and acknowledging contemporary economic realities, was embraced, although not fully comprehended or appreciated, by her contemporaries.

Tamiris had devoted so much of her time, effort, energy and creative genius to the project; it was her home and with its demise she had nowhere to go. Her frustration was clear when she described how

> Participation in the Federal Theatre, with all its difficulties, was still in a sense the most rewarding period of my work ... [T]he knowledge of being wanted by the nation along with the other artists and arts of our country, meant a true coming of age and that is why the cruel, abrupt slaughtering of the Federal theatre by Congress was such a terrible blow.[85]

Having given up on her group and dance studio a few years back, Tamiris found herself with no job. Because of all the red-baiting and the political prosecution of the FTP, many of her contemporaries believed that 'she was foolish to work so hard for so shoddy an organization'.[86] This widely held view not only was an indictment of the totality of the FTP, it also trivialised her individual accomplishments within it. It seemed that any association with the FTP was no longer fashionable or something one wanted on a résumé.

Being out of step with the political realities of her country, Tamiris had to start all over again. Although emotionally and spiritually shocked by the project's termination and fully experiencing a sense of rejection of her previous efforts, she gathered enough energy to establish her new studio–theatre at a large basement on Lafayette Street. It was there that her followers came and where she slowly started producing new work such as *Liberty Song* (1941) and *Bayou Ballads* (1942) – both based on songs of native America – by returning to the material that felt more innate in her. The simplicity, sincerity and accessibility of these works made them popular with audiences and critics, and ultimately attracted club managers. It was through these works that Tamiris achieved her goal of producing shows for Broadway.

Her courtship of popular concert dance from the very beginning of her career and her later embrace of Broadway may have impacted on how Tamiris was viewed by her contemporaries. Although Graham and Humphrey were applauded for their renunciation of dance as entertainment and revered for their continual efforts to achieve for modern dance the status of an art (equal to music, literature, theatre and painting), Tamiris's efforts were discounted. But as Schlundt very convincingly argues, Tamiris's work on Broadway not only enriched dance, but it modernised the concert dance championed in the early 1930s, affirmed her strong belief in group collaboration and confirmed the appeal that her choreographies had for diverse and mass audiences.[87] Tamiris's long list of successful Broadway productions included *Up in Central Park* (1945), *Annie Get Your Gun* (1946), *Touch and Go* (1950), *Plain and Fancy* (1955) and *Fanny* (1955). Some of the brilliant dancers who performed for Tamiris in these shows were Daniel Nagrin (her future husband and co-director), Talley Beatty, Valerie Bettis, Dorothy Bird and Pearl Primus.

Tamiris's contribution to modern dance is immeasurable, from her choreography, to the importance of social consciousness, to her teaching new dancers at various colleges. And it is no exaggeration to claim that the FDP – with all its successes and shortcomings – could ever have been possible or have flourished without her at its helm. Tamiris and the FDP provided the opportunity for female dancers to produce engaging performances that dealt with contemporary issues and captivated their audiences. Through these works the female body was no longer a semi-naked object to be ogled by men but became a means through which gender, economic and social subjects were performed and realised. Tamiris's choreographies provided her dancers with a corporeal rationale of expression; her choice not to enforce and establish a systematic 'Tamiris' style of dancing meant that her dancers were enabled to explore their dance, feelings and ideas within a supportive environment, one that encouraged group action and collaboration. Her choices enabled the dancers to grow as individuals but also as a collective group that could reach more audiences, instead of remaining 'a cult' within themselves.[88]

Tamiris was aware of what she was asking of her dancers. In training their bodies, she instilled in them the responsibility for cultivating and serving an active social consciousness: 'the individual performing must see his part in the whole for the whole can succeed only when the parts succeed, for all parts have a responsibility to each other'.[89] And she made sure that the same responsibility was cultivated within the FDP, as, through it, modern dance could reach larger audiences. Reflecting in 1948, Tamiris wrote,

> when Charles Weidman's *Candide* and my *How Long Brethren?* and *Adelante* were presented to cheering audiences that had never seen a dance recital, I knew that the modern dance was not an esoteric passing phase of dance to be enjoyed only by the cognoscenti, but one that could reach large audiences.[90]

Tamiris's creative energy, vision for modern dance, social consciousness, activism and genuine interest in protesting against universal social injustices, regardless of political ideologies, were briefly realised within the FDP. The remarkable choreographies and performances, with all their simplicity, intensity, ambivalences, ambitions and dynamic incorporation of different dance and theatrical elements, are as relevant and exciting today as they were all those years ago. Perhaps contemporary dance and theatre have reached a point from which they can now examine Tamiris's legacy with fresh eyes, appreciate and emulate her passion and idealism, and re-examine her efforts to make modern dance an essential expressive form of American life.

7

THE LEGACIES OF THE FEDERAL THEATRE PROJECT

> The project was not ended as an economy move, though this was the ostensible reason given: the entire arts program, of which Federal Theatre was one of five projects, used less than three fourths of one per cent of the total WPA appropriation; and that appropriation was not cut one per cent by the end of Federal Theatre; the money was simply distributed among other WPA projects. It was ended because Congress, in spite of protests from many of its own members, treated the Federal Theatre not as a human issue or a cultural issue, but as a political issue.[1]
>
> Hallie Flanagan, *Arena*.

A Theatre Dies: The Political Prosecution of the FTP

From the very beginning, the FTP was attacked on several sides. Firstly, it was the only WPA division that was headed by a woman; secondly, Broadway reacted negatively to Flanagan's appointment, as she did not represent the commercial theatre and it was feared that the FTP productions would be of poor quality; and lastly, many Congressmen believed that the investment of money in theatre was a waste of valuable funds and that artists should not be a matter of government concern. Flanagan attempted to diffuse all these arguments by stating that the Federal Theatre would not compete with Broadway, as it would 'supplement our already existing splendid New York stage' by offering a repertoire of different subject matters and techniques.[2] To those Congressmen who criticised the idea of a government-subsidised American theatre, she replied:

> Art in a democracy cannot be regarded as a luxury. It is a necessity because in order to make democracy work, the people must increasingly participate [. . .] Art is of little value in a democracy as long as it remains an esoteric cult appreciated only by the few. It must increasingly be appreciated by many, and thus eventually become the strong rhythmic and natural expression of the free life of a free people.[3]

Flanagan's comment expressed a desire for art to become accessible to all people, increase the people's participation and represent their conditioning. Art could accomplish this function only through democracy, thus indicating the liberal cultural democracy of the New Deal as the sole legitimately apposite *topos* for an effective artistic appropriation.

At the same time, many artists and intellectuals expressed reservations that the productions of the Federal Theatre would be constantly censored, since it was subsidised completely by the American government. In response to this remark, Harry Hopkins commented, 'yes, it [theatre] is going to be kept free from censorship. What we want is a free, adult, uncensored theatre.'[4] Flanagan's emphasis on the democratic right of the people to participate actively in the artistic developments and Hopkins's firm belief that the American government would not censor any productions silenced, for at least the first six months of the project, both the political opposition and those sceptical artists.

However, by 1938, the political climate in the United States was changing. The early 1930s had witnessed the rising popularity of the American Communist Party, the extensive circulation of proletariat literature and the intellectual affiliation with Marxism that seemed to threaten the hegemonic power of liberalism. Both Republicans and Democrats were suspicious of the increasing influence of Marxism and Communism, and felt that they had to prevent their threatening propaganda from expanding any further. To their aid came the Moscow Trials, which reaffirmed their suspicions of Stalin's totalitarian regime and dissolved the intellectuals' and public's faith in the Communist system as a valid alternative to capitalism. At the same time, Europe was experiencing a growing expansion of Nazism that seemed to have reached America. Nazism and Communism became the two major threats to American democracy, especially after the 1939 Nazi–Soviet non-aggression pact. America reacted by establishing a special committee for the investigation of un-American propaganda activities on its soil, chaired by Senator Martin Dies. The Dies Committee, from which the House Un-American Activities Committee (HUAC) was developed, was appointed

> to investigate (1) the extent, character, and objects of Un-American propaganda activities in the United States (2) the fusion within the United States of subversive and Un-American propaganda that is instigated by foreign countries or of a domestic origin and attacks the principle of the

form of government as guaranteed by our constitution, and (3) all other questions in relation thereto that would aid congress in any necessary remedial legislation.[5]

The committee's work was supposed to concentrate mostly on Nazi and Ku Klux Klan (KKK) activities within the United States. It soon abandoned its investigation of the KKK and instead extended it to the American Communist Party. The committee believed, judging from the Living Newspaper productions, that the party had infiltrated the WPA, and particularly the FTP.

Before the committee actually met in 1938, Senator Parnell Thomas announced that 'it is apparent from the startling evidence received so far that the FTP not only is serving as a branch of the Communist organization but is also one more link in the vast and unparalleled New Deal propaganda machine'.[6] Although most plays produced by the FTP were non-political in content and outnumbered the overtly political Living Newspapers, it was the latter that caused so much controversy and drew a strong reaction from the more conservative politicians in both parties. The reasons for the political prosecution of the project, then, were some of the plays' social and political agendas and their overt support for the New Deal policies to which many senators were opposed. The individuals invited to testify against the project criticised the productions not for their aesthetic experimentations as such (form) but for their propagandistic nature (content), which they saw as greatly influenced by Flanagan's trip to Russia and the political affiliations of some members with Communism and liberalism.

The project had become accustomed to rebuffing charges of Communism from different veteran groups of actors and from conservatives on both sides of the political spectrum since its beginning. However, the charges brought by the committee deeply shocked Flanagan, who remarked in response to Thomas's comments that 'some of the statements reported to have been made by him are obviously absurd'.[7] At the same time, however, she realised that such accusations, coming from a member of HUAC, could not be easily discarded and she expected to be subpoenaed. Her offer to testify, on 11 August 1938, was initially rejected; although Thomas had claimed that 'we shall be fair and impartial at all times and treat every witness with fairness and courtesy', his initial refusal to allow Flanagan to be heard demonstrated that the committee did not intend to maintain an impartial stance.[8] This attitude was further underlined by the committee's refusal to take into consideration the credentials and generalisations of most witnesses, such as Hazel Huffman, Francis M. Verdi or Seymour Revzin (Huffman's husband), so long as they produced 'proof' of un-American, Communist activities within the Federal Theatre.

Flanagan was dissuaded by WPA officials from replying, either directly or indirectly, to the red-baiting accusations, and by the time she was finally subpoenaed on 8 December 1938 most New York newspapers had turned against the project. During her testimony, Flanagan was questioned about her trip to Russia, her book *Shifting Scenes*, why she returned to Russia in 1931, and her articles in *Theatre Arts Monthly* on Russian theatre and the American workers' theatre; she was also asked about supposed dissemination of Communist propaganda through such plays as *The Revolt of the Beavers*, *Injunction Granted* and the appearance of Earl Browder in *Triple-A Plowed Under*. Throughout the session, she responded to all questions and accusations with facts, reports and records. It was during her examination by Senator Starnes that this now infamous episode took place.

> Mr. Starnes: [reading from her *Theatre Arts Monthly* article]: Unlike any art form existing in America today, the workers' theatres intend to shape the life of this country, socially, politically, and industrially. They intend to remake a social structure without the help of money – and this ambition alone invests their undertaking with a certain Marlowesque madness. You are quoting from this Marlowe. Is he a Communist?
>
> Mrs. Flanagan: I am very sorry. I was quoting from Christopher Marlowe.
>
> Mr. Starnes: Tell us who Marlowe is, so we can get the proper reference, because that is all we want to do.
>
> Mrs. Flanagan: Put in the record that he was the greatest dramatist in the period of Shakespeare, immediately preceding Shakespeare.[9]

However, it was during her examination by Dies that the opposition to the project on political rather than aesthetic grounds was unambiguously revealed. This opposition exposed the desire to define clearly certain modes of artistic expression as 'American' and others as 'un-American'.

> Chm. Dies: Do you think that the Federal Theatre should be used for the one purpose of conveying ideas along social, economic, or political lines?
>
> Mrs. Flanagan: I would hesitate on the political.
>
> Chm. Dies: Eliminate political. Upon social and economic lines.
>
> Mrs. Flanagan: I think it is one logical, reasonable, and I might say imperative thing for our theater to do.
>
> Chm. Dies: And for educational purposes, is that right?
>
> Mrs. Flanagan: Yes. [. . .]
>
> Chm. Dies: You think it is entirely proper that the Federal Theater produces plays for the purpose of bringing out some social idea that is a heated issue at a particular time?
>
> Mrs. Flanagan: It is one of the things that the theater can do. [. . .]

Chm. Dies: Do you not also think that since the Federal Theater Project is an agency of the Government and that all of our people support it through their tax money, people of different classes, different races, different religions, some who are workers, some who are businessmen, don't you think that no play should ever be produced which undertakes to portray the interests of one class to the disadvantage of another class, even though that might be accurate, even though factually there may be justification normally for that, yet because of the very fact that we are using taxpayers' money to produce plays, do you not think it is questionable whether it is right to produce plays that are biased in favour of one class against another?

Mrs. Flanagan: I think we strive for objectivity, but I think the whole history of the theater would indicate that any dramatist holds a passionate brief for the things he is saying.[10]

Flanagan's testimony was never completed, as she was dismissed just after 1.15 pm and not allowed to make a final statement. However, her answers in front of the committee pronounced the need for a theatre that would embody a social function and comment on all aspects of the political and economic life that affected most people. But for Dies and the committee, such a theatre represented a threat, not simply to its established political power, but to the symbolic significance of public and governmental patronage and to the democratic cultural standards that produced art embodying a purely American perspective. The new aesthetic values that the Federal Theatre appropriated from its European and American predecessors challenged traditional views on what American art should present, and at the same time redressed the balance between theatrical formal experimentation and a politically and socially affiliated ideological discourse. However, this new aesthetic world view was deemed un-American, as both the political arena and the Broadway theatrical world reacted against any political theatrical creation. Because of the Dies Committee, the American artistic and intellectual world was faced with a scheme that opposed social commentary on representational art. At the same time, it was also un-American because, although it was making use of the taxpayers' money, the Federal Theatre rejected the norms of performance established by Broadway by combining high and popular genres, mixing audiences, abolishing expensive sets and refusing to use star actors. By not using propaganda to put forward the already recognised 'American values', the project was deemed unprofessional and dangerous.

Many intellectuals, artists and officials connected with the project attempted to diffuse the image of the Federal Theatre as a 'hotbed' of Communism. It was in these circumstances that Arent raised the Living Newspaper as an example of an all-American experiment. Rebuffing any connection with the Soviet Living Newspaper, he claimed,

> I don't know where the Living Newspaper began [...] As a matter of fact, it was only about a year ago that I learned there had been anything like a Living Newspaper before ours [...] And so, while admitting the possibility of a whole avalanche of predecessors, I deny their influence and, for the balance of this article at least, that will be that.[11]

Even such bold declarations could not undo the infamy of and hostility to the project that the Dies Committee had instigated. The Federal Theatre was killed by an Act of Congress on 30 June 1939, almost four years since it began. Although it can be argued that the FTP failed in its attempt to reconcile its commitment to its relief status with its commitment to an autonomous and socially viable theatre, one also needs to reflect on the politically artistic void it ventured to fill. The FTP never attempted to create a revolutionary theatre like Meyerhold's, but rather aimed at a more democratised version that could be applied within American society. It wished to break the monopoly of the socially detached commercial theatre and present a different theatrical alternative with a social and political agenda. However, such aspirations aimed at forming a new perception of the theatre as an autonomous sphere willing to conduct cultural critique and social representation, and as such, it presented a threat to the liberal and conservative political establishment. It is no wonder, then, that of all five divisions comprising the WPA, it was only the FTP that was disbanded.

The political prosecution of the Federal Theatre, the advent of McCarthyism and the growing intellectual distrust of Marxism and the American Communist Party resulted in a decline of intellectual vitality and the reclamation of a more conservative, though still liberal, ideological discourse. Newton Arvin claimed in 1936 that

> we maintain that the real meaning of the American social and cultural adventure has been its democratic meaning, and that one of the truest things to be said of American literature is that it has reflected over a period of three centuries, the gradual maturing, rationalization, and deepening of the democratic idea.[12]

What Arvin suggested was an intrinsic link between American culture and liberal democracy. Determining this relationship's lifespan as covering at least three centuries, he underlined the interdependency of the two and the need for a discourse that would include both. Democracy was (and still is) relevant within American culture and, as Fishman asserted, 'so far as literature participates in the life of society, American literature cannot have failed to be marked by democracy'.[13] In the two decades that followed the cessation of the

FTP, American society experienced the intellectual world's effort to reaffirm this strong relationship between art and liberal democracy as a way of rectifying their previous brief ideological association with Marxism. The discourse of liberal democracy infiltrated all aspects of social, economic and political life and the artistic world had to abide by it, as nobody wished to be labelled as un-American in the midst of the ideological Cold War. The Federal Theatre's prosecution was still vivid in the artistic world's mind, but whatever his/her previous or current political commitments were, the artist felt compelled to commit to liberalism. The autonomous and socially active national theatre that Flanagan aspired to create would not have been allowed to proceed with its work within such an environment. The government continued to subsidise art and the film industry that echoed its liberal policies; however, the main thematic interest was no longer social equality and justice, but an embrace of 'Americanism' and the creation of a united front against the new ideological enemy. As a result, the intellectual and artistic world soon abandoned its commitment to a socially enthused agenda and embraced the political fortification of art in the name of liberalism.

Moving Forward: Flanagan's $E=MC^2$

The end of the FTP was not easy for Flanagan to accept but, once again exhibiting the resilience and pragmatism that carried her through life, she decided to move on and try to maintain the spirit of theatrical experimentation instilled in the project. Having received a grant from the Rockefeller Foundation to conduct some research on the theatrical works of the FTP, Flanagan returned to Vassar College, where her husband was still teaching. Her research resulted in the 1940 publication of her book *Arena*, a collection and recollection of the entire history of the FTP. During her time at Vassar, she also resumed her theatrical work. Her most famous project was a production of T. S. Eliot's *Murder in the Cathedral*. Unlike the FTP's interpretation a few years back, which highlighted the church's call for religious submission, Flanagan's production emphasised the fall of the female chorus 'into a "pattern of fate" against their will and the struggle of the Archbishop against inner temptations and outer forces over which he has little control'.[14]

Tragedy struck once again and in 1940 her husband, Philip Davis, died. She decided to take a three-year leave of absence from Vassar and accepted the position of acting Dean at Smith College, as well as teaching drama. By 1945, Flanagan had been diagnosed with Parkinson's disease; the diagnosis drove her decision to remain at Smith permanently, resigning her post as Dean and instead becoming a Professor of Drama. It was amid all these changes that Flanagan took up writing once again. In the summer of 1947, she began working on a Living Newspaper entitled $E=mc^2$: *A Living Newspaper about the Atomic Age*. The Hiroshima and Nagasaki bombings and the devastation they caused were still freshly imprinted on people's minds; the events also generated growing concerns regarding the future of humanity if atomic energy remained unregulated or unchallenged in the hands of governments, the military and politicians. A desire to educate people on such matters became pertinent among theatre practitioners and the responses were not contained solely to the USA but were universal. Interestingly, there was an almost synchronised response to events by Flanagan, Ewan MacColl and Bertolt Brecht. These three individuals, writing and producing their plays almost simultaneously in the USA and Europe, and using similar theatrical techniques immersed in the traditions of the Living Newspaper, agit-prop, didactic and the epic theatre, continued (perhaps unbeknown to them) the close connection and dialogue between the FTP and continental modernism/avant-garde. In her play, Flanagan – drawing on her own past theatrical experiments, the FTP's approaches to Living Newspapers and the traditions of the European modernist political theatre – voiced her reaction to the new socio-political realities of an atomic age.

$E=mc^2$ was first produced in 1947; the play was written by Flanagan (it is the only play she signed as Hallie Flanagan Davis – using her late husband's last name), assisted by Sylvia Gassel and Day Tuttle. The play employs many of the techniques used in the FTP's productions, as well as some agit-prop elements. But before these are discussed, it is important to note how the script, unlike the other examples mentioned, incorporated material from two earlier performed plays. The first was Robert Nichols and Maurice Browne's 1928 *Wings over Europe*, in which Francis Lightfoot, a brilliant young physicist, has discovered how to create an atomic bomb. He informs the British government of his discovery and gives it a one-week ultimatum to achieve world peace. Lightfoot is assassinated, thus revealing the greediness of the British cabinet, but the latter's plans for world dominance are foiled when it discovers that other scientists have also produced atomic bombs, which are carried by planes over the world's capital cities. The play, although written by British playwrights, was first produced by the Theatre Guild and was performed in New York before touring the USA. It was not until 1932 that it was produced in the UK. The script proved to be prophecy rather than science fiction, and its importance is highlighted by its inclusion as condensed two-page scene in $E=mc^2$. The second was Louis Ridenour's one-act playlet entitled *Pilot Lights of the Apocalypse*. Ridenour was a physicist who was instrumental in developing the use of radar in the USA. His play, published in 1946 a few months after the dropping of the atomic bombs in Japan, depicted the hysteria, fear and panic of a post-atomic bomb world. In his imagined scenario, San Francisco is struck by an earthquake, which triggers a false alarm in the operation room buried beneath the city. In a moment of hysteria and panic, a colonel launches a counterattack targeting and annihilating Copenhagen, which then launches a strike against Sweden and subsequently initiates a series of atomic explosions around the world. In the end, the world is destroyed, triggered by the combination of atomic science and human fear, paranoia and recklessness. Ridenour's play revealed his and others' fear of what would happen if a nuclear arms race developed. Flanagan, sharing Ridenour's vison, incorporated an edited version of his play as the penultimate scene of $E=mc^2$, thus ending her own piece with an apocalyptic vision of the world in an age of atomic misinformation and madness.

The play is comprised of two acts, containing scenes with a large cast. Flanagan insisted in her stage directions that the acts should be played continuously, with no curtain or any other formal or informal interruption.[15] There are five main characters: the Stage Manager, the Professor, the Atom, Clio and Henry. Twenty further actors are required to play the remaining characters, each one taking several parts. The structure of the play reflects the aims of its authors: act one concentrates on the history and nature of atomic energy, whereas act two considers ethical and political questions regarding its usage and control. The aim of the structure is to have the audience firstly educated on what atomic energy entails, and how it has affected and will continue to affect their daily lives, both directly or indirectly, and then, by engaging the audience in critical listening, to participate in the debate regarding the future of atomic energy and to ponder the social, economic and political outcomes of its usage and existence. These considerations are encouraged to include a universal viewpoint, not a narrow one concentrating only on American life. In doing so, Flanagan's Living Newspaper continues from where the FTP's projects left off, coming full circle: whereas the first few Living Newspapers, such as the censored *Ethiopia*, concentrated on international events, later ones had a more local and topical focus. With $E=mc^2$ Flanagan combines both attitudes and clearly illustrates how one affects the other, how there is a close connection and continuity between local and international events, and how everyone is part of this one humanity. What one nation or one person does affects another, whether in proximity or not. And although the responsibility for a decision or action might appear to be individual, Flanagan points to the universality of the consequences; after all, as the Atom points out, we are all 'citizen[s] of the world'.[16]

In terms of formal elements, $E=mc^2$ followed many of the techniques used in the FTP's productions. The Loudspeaker is replaced by the Stage Manager, and the little or common man by Henry. The Stage Manager makes the audience aware that they are in a theatrical space by calling for technical effects and scene changes, as well as addressing it directly. The play uses film projections, music, dance and graphs. Reminiscent of *Triple-A Plowed Under*, it begins with a symbolic scene. A man, not to be identified as Japanese, arrives on stage and reaches the centre just as the music climaxes and finishes with a crash. The man flings his arms in the air, adopting a grotesque and terrifying position; his shadow is then elongated and projected on the wall. Although he falls to the ground, his shadow remains on the wall for the audience to keep in view. It is then that the Stage Manager enters, relating to the audience the symbolism of the shadow as 'man's terrible power to destroy himself' after the dropping of the bomb in Hiroshima.[17] As the Stage Manager steps aside, the audience is confronted with differing attitudes to and views on the event. An old lady laments the dropping of the bomb but considers how the Japanese could have done the same to the Americans instead, and a policeman reacts to her remarks by suggesting she diverts her mind to the baseball game, whereas a marine proclaims that 'we've got the bomb and it's going to end the war damn quick'.[18] The military thinking of other countries is also revealed, either as being in denial or lamenting that it was the Americans who developed the bomb first. The scene ends with the audience seeing a young Henry, infatuated with a radio programme on atomic energy, arguing with his father about whether there is a curving space or if two parallel lines can meet.

The next scene introduces *Wings Over Europe* and quotes Lightfoot's line, 'Yesterday man was a slave; today, he's free! – Matter – obeys him.'[19] The Stage Manager reappears and involves himself in a conversation with scientists to understand atomic energy. The urgent need for educating the public is highlighted by E. U. Condon, an adviser to the Senate Atomic Commission, who proclaims

> atomic energy is *not* just the discovery of another weapon, but of a whole way of life. Or of death. You know, I wish that everyone in the world today could learn all about atomic energy – what it is – where it came from – in some very simple way.[20]

It is at this stage that the Atom appears. Flanagan's instructions are for the character to be a woman and for her voice to be docile and meek with a hint of hysteria and comedy. The instructions make sense because, as soon as she speaks, the Atom portrays her dual personality, underlining, in a very theatrical manner, the instability and unpredictability of atomic energy. She plainly states, 'I'm a dual personality. Hyde and Jekyll, you know. I can't control myself. Other people have to do it for me – But *will* they? That's the question.'[21]

The play, from early on, portrays a contemporary nuclear world where 'there is no defense' as 'any nation can make an atom bomb as soon as it has mastered purely technical problems'.[22] While a ballet performance creatively illustrates an atomic chain reaction, Clio, the Muse of History, enters the stage on roller skates (reminiscent of *Revolt of the Beavers*), and along with the Atom and a grown-up Henry, gives the audience a history lesson.[23] Throughout the trip, the audience is informed about the impact of the Atom and the unmeasurable power that atomic energy can release. Near the end of the lesson, with Clio, the Atom and Henry off stage, the Stage Manager directly addresses the audience, bringing into play the ethical considerations around energy and the dropping of the bombs on Japan: 'Well, we've seen the impact of the Atom – but the moral question remains, doesn't it? Should – we – have used atomic energy for destruction of civilians in the first place?'[24] In a highly energetic sequence, civilians, writers, the press, the Army, the Marines, the Navy and politicians occupy the stage to debate the issue. The Secretary of War, Stimson, clearly states that the bomb should be used against Japan, on both military and civilian targets, and without prior warning. With his views endorsed by the administration, Stimson's later comment that the dropping of the bombs 'make[s] it wholly clear that we must never have another war' appears duplicitous; emitting the Atom's duality, those in charge of the atomic energy have fallen prey to her powers.[25]

Act two elaborates further on the moral considerations around atomic energy. The Atom, confident and truculent, navigates her way among the audience, sitting on different men's laps while addressing all those present directly. In her rumbling speech, it becomes clear that she does not know who she is, what her use is or how she should be handled. Her rumbling is followed by some fantastical examples of the energy's potentialities, ranging from a super-fast commute, instantaneous atomic laundry services and expedited seed growth. This image of limitless potentialities and bright future is juxtaposed with the cautious voice of the Professor. Although he acknowledges atomic energy's prospects, he highlights its destructive aspects too.[26] Keeping this balance in check is 'going to be up to you and me ... It's going to take education – a lot more than we've got for the situation at present'.[27] Like the previous Living Newspapers, $E=mc^2$ calls for both individual and collective responsibility. The audience and people all over the world need to become educated, informed and realistic about what the usage of atomic energy entails, both for themselves and for the world in general. Like the ballet's chain reaction at the end of act one, the usage of atomic energy by one country has a direct effect on its neighbour.

What follows the Professor's call for collective responsibility and education are excerpts from hearings in front of the Senate. As the script notes indicate, the dialogues are verbatim, but the testimonies have been cut due to their length. However, as with past FTP productions, Flanagan made sure that the intent was not altered. As the actual hearings are quoted, the audience can listen to the views promoted by the advocates of the government and the military. Their views are then discussed further by Clio, the Atom and Henry, interchanged with quotations in the March of Time's voice. In the end, the audience is informed that the control of atomic energy no longer rests with civilian organisations; in a highly stylised scene, we see the Atom courted by the Army, the Navy, the Businessman and the Politician in succession, highlighting in this way which groups are invested in the power game over atomic energy, which is reframed as war versus peace. But all these debates leave the Atom even more confused and unstable. In her last speech, in a wild voice, she calls on people to

> get together with people all over the world and take control! . . . I showed you Hiroshima! – I showed you Nagasaki! – I *showed* you Bikini! . . . You won't control me? – Then here goes – here *goes!* – If you *don't* control me, *this* is the way it's going to be![28]

The Atom disappears from the stage and the play ends with an adapted version of Ridenour's play, mentioned earlier. As the explosion takes place and the room becomes filled with smoke, the Stage Manager emerges with the play's epilogue. In it, he reminds people that the shadow of the man on a wall in Hiroshima that the play started with remains a 'mute symbol of man's terrible power to destroy himself'; he reiterates that the responsibility for atomic energy rests not only with the scientists but with all humanity, 'with you and with me'.[29] The play's didactic message is clear, and as the Stage Manager mentioned, the subject was treated 'the *theatre* way'.[30]

Flanagan's stage directions reveal an indebtedness to Brechtian aesthetics. She offers the potential director the option of producing the play as simply or as elaborately as desired:

> it could use all projected scenery; or a revolving stage; or simply cut-outs which could be put on jacks and pushed on stage. We produced it with no front curtain, a small stage with several movable units and two small side stages with gauze front curtains which made possible instantaneous revelation, such as *Marines, Nightclub* and *Alphabet* scenes. The simple units on the center stage were changed in darkness, usually to music and often as part of the action.[31]

She also pays attention to the music used – thus highlighting its impact both as a formal element of the play and as part of its content – and makes alternative suggestions if the original music score is not used (similar to Brecht's use of songs to comment on unfolding events). Lastly, she remarks on the stage's simplicity and the clever use of lighting in order to correspond, successfully and organically, to the fast-pacing changes of the play's thirty-six scenes. The stage, being a singular unit set, can show the various aspects of the show without the need for complete visual change. Such changes can be achieved by using lighting (highlighting various levels and ramps), by breaking the set into rolling units which could be revealed in different combinations, and by employing projected backdrops.

The play engaged directly with the social, political and ethical questions around the use of atomic energy and its further scientific developments. It looked at the arrival of the atomic bomb, its impact on humanity, its destructiveness and the power games between politicians and the military. Although the play did not serve or derive from a Marxist perspective (like Brecht or MacColl), it still served the liberal agenda inhibited within American culture of the 1940s and 1950s. This agenda was no longer set to examine a social, political and economic issue as part of the class struggle; instead, it focused on the individual's responsibility towards him/herself and then as part of a common humanity. Flanagan wanted to unite all classes under the threat of the atomic bomb and show that there was no class distinction when it came to world destruction. Although written from different ideological perspectives, the three plays endorsed the idea of a socially motivated science and of a socially, economically and politically conscious audience. Highlighting the relinquishing of science, knowledge and thinking in the hands of the authorities and the catastrophic results of this action, Flanagan's play calls for a universally strong consciousness on the audience's part to regulate and keep in check scientists, politicians and businesses.

Flanagan's play presents an excellent example of the transatlantic dialogue between European and American theatrical modernism and the intrinsically interwoven relationship between these two traditions. By bringing together the experimentations of the FTP (with its inherited practices from the American workers' theatre, Meyerhold and the Blue Blouses) with Brecht's contemporary theatrical practices, $E=mc^2$ exemplifies their closeness and their similar aesthetic approaches, but also their congruently different ideological backgrounds. Bridging similarity with difference and accepting their co-existence is a valuable dialectical path of approaching these traditions. Rather than seeing them as opposites, by reading them in tandem our understanding and knowledge of modernist theatrical experimentations can only be enriched. Whether knowingly or unknowingly, Flanagan's early work, her commitment to the project of the FTP and her later play paved the way for such considerations.

EPILOGUE: WAS IT ALL WORTH IT? THE LEGACY OF THE FTP IN CONTEMPORARY PERFORMANCE

The FTP occupies a special place and space within American culture, and more archival material relating to its productions, performances, oral histories, anecdotes and administrative records is increasingly being discovered and uncovered. As part of the WPA relief project, it offered employment to an array of out-of-work theatre professionals. As a professional platform, it created many career opportunities to established and up-and-coming actors. Apart from the ones discussed in this book, others included Arthur Miller, Harry Belafonte, Sidney Poitier and Rudy Dee. As a cultural movement it diverted its audiences' minds away from the politics of Depression while at the same time capturing and nurturing their imagination in terms of their social, political and economic conditioning. The FTP achieved an incredibly broad reach into a variety of communities by using multiple theatrical forms to address and attract different audiences. It was not afraid to stage performances in a multiplicity of languages, or to perform classical or experimental drama, vaudeville, circus, comedy and children's plays. Its performances were not restricted to the traditional theatrical space; instead, it ventured out to parks, schools, hospitals, factories and universities. By doing all of the above, it offered unparalleled access to theatre to a variety of audiences that had a lot of, or little or no, experience of it.

The FTP, recognising the limitations of Broadway, attempted to renegotiate the European theatrical experimentations, the interrelation between politics and aesthetics, the legitimate representation of a new audience and the persistent tension between an audience, its social conditioning and the pertinence of actual change. Its radical revision of the theatre's role and function in response to the specific historical moment represented a conscious attempt to create a theatre for the American people. None the less, the continued uncomfortable dialectic between its aesthetic and social agenda, its theatrical enactment and its governmental patron, firstly, precluded a continuation of this attempt; secondly, solicited certain dramaturgical modifications that directed the audience towards a subjectively empathetic response to the issues exposed; and thirdly, led to the project's problematic political identification as both 'red' and 'New Deal' propaganda.

In its attempt to create an identity of its own, the FTP became uncomfortable with the inherited theatrical traditions of the European and American left theatre of the 1920s, as well as with the influence of contemporary European modernist aesthetics. Although it initially acknowledged said influences, these were very soon disclaimed as incompatible with the new, more democratically representative theatrical aesthetics of the New Deal. As a result, although the FTP still advocated social motivation and action, this was to be realised through a liberal discourse that was in tune with the political agenda of their funding source, the US government. One could, therefore, argue that the project had undergone a narrative, political and social change and refused to engage with its European contemporaries in the debate concerning the development of theatrical aesthetics. The failure of the FTP to negotiate the European aesthetics of commitment within the historical context of the New Deal resulted in its political prosecution by the Dies Committee and foreshadowed the mostly hostile reception of similar dramaturgy (whether American or European) within the realm of American culture.

The disbandment of the FTP in 1939 left a void within American political theatre for almost the next twenty years; it was not until 1958 that the Off-Off Broadway movement in New York reignited a renewed experimentation with avant-garde and modernist techniques. But the FTP's history was disavowed for much longer; boxed away in crates and put in storage, the history of the FTP remained there, forgotten, till 1974. Ever since its discovery at a Library of Congress storage depot, a sustained effort has been instigated to uncover the material, archive it properly and make it readily available to the public, theatre scholars and practitioners both in the USA and internationally.

The excitement surrounding these findings is shared by many scholars and practitioners, who can study them and incorporate them into their university teachings or publications. But how can we situate these findings in contemporary performance theory? Are these experimentations still relevant and can they be adapted? Can they inspire a new generation of performers, set designers, directors and playwrights? And lastly, is there space for their critical consideration in an age of fake news and expediated exchange of information?

The answers to these questions, in a way, can be found within the FTP material discussed in this book and that in archives still waiting to be read, enjoyed and considered in depth.

Theatre has always been the medium that responded to life's changing socio-political circumstances quickest. The Living Newspapers in the Soviet Union responded to the need for the quick, informative, engaging and simple representation of the current news; in America, they responded to a similar need to educate, expose, inform and voice the concerns of a silenced audience. And in both cases, the news was thoroughly researched and checked. In doing that, the Living Newspapers brought the members of the audience together in a shared safe space that negotiated their concerns and promoted a dialectically engaged interaction. Never claiming to be anything other than theatre, the productions did not hypnotise their audiences with tales of wealth and conformity, and counted on them actively participating by commenting, shouting or laughing. Their aim of informing and bringing together an audience could have been achieved only in that shared space.

Producing a Living Newspaper type of drama would present a challenge for any director, performer and playwright, as it would need constant revisions throughout its run (for example, that is exactly what MacColl was doing for *Uranium 235*). Through this challenge, though, the performance would bring the audience back into that shared space, where collectively – rather than individually, in front of a screen – it would engage with the issues presented, with the modes of presentation and the different reactions. The challenges of performing a contemporary Living Newspaper would involve a theatrical company committed to constant script reviews, to critically interacting with the audience, to improvising if necessary, and to being mindfully engaged with contemporary realities. Flanagan and Tamiris's vision of the artist and actor as a socially conscious being, whose societal maturity would be reflected in their performance, can inform contemporary performances and creative works.

At the same time, the issues regarding race, gender, misrepresentation or non-representation of socially excluded groups that the FTP productions presented are still relevant, active and demanding our attention. By studying and observing these past productions, we can critically assess how they approached their subject matters, what techniques they used to attract and interact with the audience's awareness, and how they opened the theatrical space to experimentation. Acting as guidance, *Lysistrata*, *How Long Brethren?*, *The Trojan Incident* and the 'voodoo' *Macbeth* – for all their shortcomings – demonstrate alternative ways of approaching canonical texts and their prescribed narrative, ways of rewriting and re-engaging with racial and gender themes, and processes of reimagining those themes' theatrical representation. Similarly, plays such as *The Revolt of the Beavers* can inspire new playwrights to experiment with the world of children's theatre in an attempt to reignite children's imagination, and connect with their contemporary realities, anxieties, dreams and aspirations. In this way, children claim a place in the theatrical space that is rightfully theirs.

One last observation regards the transatlantic relationship between the FTP and European avant-garde/modernism. Although influenced by each other, both trends refused to voice this underlying reciprocal relationship. In this otherwise disengaged stand-off, there are a few elements that point towards an acknowledgement of the 'other' side. What this acknowledgement reveals is a complicated relationship of simultaneous development, borrowing and constant (re)interpretation. By looking critically at this complicated relationship, we can reach a new way of engaging with modernist theatre; the concurrent productions of $E=mc^2$, *Uranium 235* and 'Galileo', the plays' parallel reading of the scientist's social responsibility and their use of similar techniques for formal expression uncover, in a dialectical manner, the transatlantic relationship between European and American modernist theatre and simultaneously propose a critical enactment of both theatrical traditions.

The FTP is a treasured example of a fearless theatre; all the obstacles, rejections, censorship, cuts, discrimination and scepticism it faced were counteracted by experimentation, inclusion, creativity, community, energy, activism and a deep yearning to form a theatre relevant to all people. Not without its shortcomings, it was none the less the only attempt to create a national federation of theatres that would engage in socially relevant drama with a local and national perspective. A breeding ground for new artists, it nurtured the American theatre's next generation of actors from all walks of life. And it was instrumental in making the theatre a space of belonging for a previously unrepresented audience. The FTP both succeeded and failed in changing American theatre (as its short existence indicates) but it remains a most innovative, explosive, engaging and influential movement within the history of American drama.

NOTES

INTRODUCTION

1. This is Flanagan's dedication on the opening page of her book, *Arena*.
2. Hooverville is a term used to describe a crudely built town for the homeless during the Great Depression. These settlements were named after President Hoover, who was widely blamed for the Depression, to reflect on the direct effect of his opposition to direct federal relief efforts on the American people.
3. Quoted in Rauch, *The History of the New Deal*, pp. 146–7.
4. Flanagan, 'Federal Theatre Project', p. 865.
5. Flanagan, *Arena*, p. 34. Italics my emphasis.
6. Ibid. pp. 42–3.
7. Ibid. p. 372.
8. Flanagan, *What was Federal Theatre?*, p. 4.

CHAPTER 1

1. The play was produced by Stanislavsky. Interestingly, Stanislavsky acted the role of Satine in the 1902 production of the same play.
2. For the purposes of this chapter, I will mirror Flanagan's use of 'Russia' and 'Russian theatre' as it appears in her book, *Shifting Scenes of the Modern European Theatre*.
3. Flanagan, *Shifting Scenes of the Modern European Theatre*, p. 7.

4. Ibid. p. 13.
5. Ibid. p. 34.
6. Ibid. p. 48.
7. Ibid. p. 59.
8. Ibid. pp. 60–1.
9. Ibid. p. 70.
10. Ibid. pp. 72–3.
11. Cosgrove, *The Living Newspaper: History, Production and Form*, p. iv.
12. Flanagan, *Shifting Scenes*, p. 98.
13. Ibid. pp. 86–7.
14. Ibid. p. 97.
15. Ibid. pp. 109–10.
16. Ibid. p. 100.
17. Ibid. pp. 115–16.
18. Ibid. p. 134.
19. Ibid. p. 135.
20. Ibid. p. 143.
21. Ibid. pp. 146–7.
22. Ibid. p. 148.
23. Ibid. p. 149.
24. Flanagan, 'Russia Reviewed in Symposium', 9 February.
25. Flanagan, *Shifting Scenes*, p. 189. Reinhardt was well known in the States and Oliver Sayler's book, *Max Reinhardt and his Theatre*, published in 1924, had introduced him to the American public and critics.
26. Kruger, *The National Stage: Theatre and Cultural Legitimation in England, France and America*, p. 3.
27. Flanagan, *Shifting Scenes*, p. 99.
28. Ibid. p. 112.
29. As quoted in Gorelik, *New Theatres for Old*, p. 358.
30. Slonim, *The Russian Theater: From the Empire to the Soviets*, p. 247.
31. Ibid.
32. Flanagan, *Shifting Scenes*, pp. 115–16.
33. Slonim, *The Russian Theater*, p. 258.
34. Bigsby, *A Critical Introduction to Twentieth-century American Drama*, p. 215.
35. Deák, 'Blue Blouse', p. 40.
36. Leach, *Revolutionary Theatre*, p. 169.
37. Blue Blouse, 'Simple Advice to Participants (1925)', p. 182.
38. Flanagan, 'The Soviet Theatrical Olympiad', p. 10.
39. Leach, *Revolutionary Theatre*, p. 168.
40. Deák, 'Blue Blouse', p. 36.
41. Brecht, 'On the Use of Music in the Epic Theatre', p. 86.

42. Brecht, 'Emphasis on Sport', p. 7.
43. Reinelt, *After Brecht: British Epic Theatre*, p. 39.
44. Kuhn and Giles, 'Introduction to Part Two', p. 59.
45. Brecht, 'A Short Organum for the Theatre', p. 196.
46. Brecht, 'Masterful Treatment of a Model', p. 212.
47. Brecht, 'The German Drama: Pre-Hitler', p. 78.
48. Ibid. p. 80.
49. Ciment, *Conversations with Losey*, p. 48.
50. Losey, 'The Individual Eye', p. 12.
51. Samuel, *Theatres of the Left 1880–1935*, p. 19.
52. Ibid. pp. 22–3.
53. MacColl, 'The Workshop Story Part 1: Grass Roots of Theatre Workshop', p. 59.
54. Füllöp-Miller, *The Russian Theatre: Its Character and History, with Especial Reference to the Revolutionary Period*, p. 127.
55. Samuel, *Theatres of the Left 1880–1935*, p. 47.
56. For more detailed discussion of the history of the fracture within the WTM and the different directions the theatrical groups and troupes took see Stourac and McCreery, *Theatre as a Weapon: Workers' Theatre in the Soviet Union, Germany and Britain, 1917–1934*, pp. 244–63 and 'Documents and Texts from the Workers' Theatre Movement (1928–1936)', pp. 102–42.
57. For an in-depth discussion and analysis of the plays and history of the Unity Theatre see Chambers, *The Story of the Unity Theatre*.
58. MacColl, 'Theatre of Action, Manchester', p. 242.
59. MacColl, 'The Workshop Story Part 1', p. 62.
60. The play was based on Max Brod and humourist Hans Reimann's translation of Hašek's novel. For a detailed discussion of the production and the differing accounts by Piscator and Brecht see Malina, *The Piscator Notebook*.
61. MacColl, 'The Workshop Story Part 1', p. 66.
62. MacColl, 'Theatre of Action, Manchester', p. 228.
63. MacColl, 'The Workshop Story Part 1', p. 66.
64. Auden, 'Spain 1937', p. 182.
65. Ben Blake, as quoted in Bernard, 'A Theatre for Lefty: USA in the 1930's', p. 54. Bernard also mentions how the groups mentioned and many more joined, in 1932, to form the League of Workers' Theatre.
66. Quoted in Kruger, *The National Stage*, p. 145.
67. For a more detailed study of these groups' objectives, see Bohn, 'Dramburo Report', p. 1.
68. Goldstein, *The Political Stage: American Drama and Theater of the Great Depression*, p. 34. Hallie Flanagan also mentions this play in her article 'A

Theatre is Born', when discussing the workers' theatre and the importance of the political content of their plays.
69. Flanagan, 'A Theatre is Born', p. 908.
70. Ibid. p. 915.
71. Ibid. pp. 908–9.
72. One could argue that Odets's play did not have the vigour of the workers' theatre performances, as it appealed to those already converted to social ideals. It is also very interesting that during Joseph Losey's trip to Moscow in 1935, he staged an English version of Odets's play for a Russian audience.
73. Kruger, *The National Stage*, p. 150.
74. *The New Theatre* counted among its contributors Hallie Flanagan (italics my emphasis).
75. Rabkin, *Drama and Commitment: Politics in the American Theatre of the Thirties*, p. 48.

Chapter 2

1. Flanagan, 'Introduction', in *Federal Theatre Plays: Prologue to Glory, One-third of a Nation, Haiti*, p. ix.
2. Flanagan, 'Opening Statement Containing Detailed Answers to Charges Made by Witnesses who Appeared Before the SPECIAL COMMITTEE to Investigate UN-AMERICAN ACTIVITIES, House of Representatives', p. 24.
3. Flanagan, 'Federal Theatre: Tomorrow', p. 6.
4. Flanagan, 'Theatre and Geography', p. 468; 'Federal Theatre: Tomorrow', p. 6.
5. Flanagan, 'Federal Theatre Project', p. 865.
6. Flanagan, *Arena*, p. 65.
7. Flanagan, 'Federal Theatre Project', p. 868.
8. Cosgrove, *The Living Newspaper*, p. 15.
9. Quoted in Flanagan, 'A Theatre is Born', p. 910.
10. 'Techniques Available to the Living Newspaper Dramatist'.
11. Arent, 'The Techniques of the Living Newspaper', p. 57.
12. Rice, *The Living Theatre*, p. 57.
13. Flanagan, *Arena*, p. 65.
14. Arent, '*Ethiopia*: The First "Living Newspaper"', p. 19.
15. Ibid. p. 31.
16. Flanagan, *Arena*, p. 66.
17. Ibid.
18. Ibid.; Bentley, *Hallie Flanagan*, p. 214.
19. Ibid. p. 69.
20. Flanagan, *Arena*, p. 184.

21. It needs to be pointed out here that, according to Rice, it was the intended production of the *South* and not *Ethiopia* (although the controversy surrounding the latter did influence his decision) that resulted in his resignation.
22. Flanagan, condemning the script for *Money*, claimed that 'it is just an adolescent, anti-capitalist scream of hate, and I will not have such nonsense done on our stage' (as quoted in Mathews, *Federal Theatre, 1935–1939*, p.117). *Russia* was abandoned before its completion 'on orders from above' (Arent, as quoted in Goldman, 'Life and Death of the Living Newspaper Unit', p. 81).
23. Rice, 'Statement of Resignations', p. 2.
24. Watson, 'The Living Newspaper', p. 7.
25. *Triple-A Plowed Under*, i, 2.
26. Ibid. i, 2–3.
27. Ibid. ii, 5.
28. Ciment, *Conversations with Losey*, p. 47.
29. *Triple-A Plowed Under*, iii, 9.
30. The final lines of *The Threepenny Opera* read: 'For the ones they are in darkness / And the others are in lights. / And you see the ones in brightness / Those in darkness drop from sight.' In Gardner, 'The Losey-Moscow Connection: Experimental Soviet Theatre and the Living Newspaper', pp. 258, 267. Gardner's articles make some very interesting comments regarding Losey, Soviet theatre and the Living Newspaper, which were also mentioned in my PhD dissertation: Ourania Karoula (2009), *A Thorn in the Body Politic: A Transatlantic Dialogue on the Aesthetics of Commitment Within Modernist Political Theatre*, Unpublished PhD dissertation, University of Edinburgh, pp. 116, 122–9.
31. *Triple-A Plowed Under*, xvii, 43.
32. Ibid. xxv, 73.
33. Quoted in Goldman, 'Life and Death of the Living Newspaper Unit', p. 73.
34. Bentley, *Hallie Flanagan*, p. 220.
35. Lockbridge, 'The Stage in Review: Terrors of Impartiality', p. 9.
36. B. G, 'The Living Newspaper Finally Gets Under Way with "Triple-A Plowed Under" – Two One-Act War Plays', p. 21.
37. Quoted in Mathews, *Federal Theatre, 1935–1939*, pp. 72–3. Those critics disapproving of *Triple-A* would not have been happy by the fact that, according to Losey, Brecht saw the performance and 'was impressed by it' (Ciment, *Conversations with Losey*, p. 48).
38. Goldman, 'Life and Death of the Living Newspaper Unit', p. 74.
39. As quoted in Bentley, *Hallie Flanagan*, p. 234.
40. *Injunction Granted*, xii, 103–4.
41. Ibid. xiii, 106.

42. Goldman, 'Life and Death of the Living Newspaper Unit', p. 75.
43. Ibid. Kruger also commented that this treatment of serious matters 'echoed similar agitprop plays like the Proletbühne's lampoon of the AFL in *I Need You and You Need Me* (1932)', *The National Stage*, p. 164.
44. *Injunction Granted*, xxviii, 136–7.
45. Ibid. pp. 139–40.
46. Ibid. p. 136.
47. Losey, 'Prefatory Notes to *Injunction Granted!*', p. 51.
48. Ciment, *Conversations with Losey*, pp. 37, 47.
49. Ibid. p. 47; Goldman, 'Life and Death of the Living Newspaper Unit', pp. 74–5.
50. Goldman, 'Life and Death of the Living Newspaper Unit', p. 76.
51. Quoted in Mathews, *Federal Theatre, 1935–1939*, pp. 110–11.
52. Flanagan, 'Federal Theatre: Tomorrow', p. 26.
53. Goldman, 'Life and Death of the Living Newspaper Unit', p. 81 [endnote 21].
54. Vernon, '*Injunction Granted*: Latest Edition of the Living Newspaper is Out and Out Propaganda of the Left', p. 407.
55. Quoted in Mathews, *Federal Theatre, 1935–1939*, p. 78.
56. Flanagan, *Arena*, p. 73.
57. Losey, as quoted in Goldman, 'Life and Death of the Living Newspaper Unit', p. 76.
58. Flanagan, 'Federal Theatre: Tomorrow', p. 6.
59. Mathews, *Federal Theatre, 1935–1939*, p. 122.
60. Blitzstein wrote 'Few Little English' for Lotte Lenya (Weill's wife) and also assisted in her securing an American reputation to enable her to work in the USA. During the summer of 1936, Blitzstein attended Weill's lecture 'Music in the Theatre' and had the opportunity to have further discussion with him.
61. Pollack, *Marc Blitzstein: His Life, His Work, His World*, p. 158.
62. Flanagan, *Arena*, p. 201.
63. Blitzstein, 'Author of "The Cradle" Discusses Broadway Hit', p. 7.
64. Weill, '*Gestus* in Music', pp. 28–32.
65. Blitzstein, 'Author of "The Cradle" Discusses Broadway Hit', p. 7. For a detailed and in-depth discussion of the play and its history see Pollack, *Marc Blitzstein*, pp. 151–71, 172–94.
66. Blitzstein, *The Cradle Will Rock*, iv, 18.
67. Ibid. iv, 20.
68. Ibid. iv, 22.
69. Ibid. iv, 22–4.
70. Blitzstein, 'Author of "The Cradle" Discusses Broadway Hit', p. 7.
71. Houseman, *Run-through: A Memoir*, p. 247.

72. Ibid. p. 248.
73. Flanagan, *Arena*, pp. 202–3.
74. Kaufman, 'Actors and Audiences All Mixed Up as WPA Goes Commercial', p. 62; Houseman, *Entertainers and Entertained*, p. 25.
75. Houseman, *Run-through*, pp. 268–9.
76. Atkinson, 'Marc Blitzstein's "The Cradle Will Rock" Officially Opens at the Mercury Theatre', p. 19.
77. Ibid.
78. Thomson, 'In the Theater', pp. 112–14.
79. Isaacs, 'An Industry Without a Product – Broadway in Review', p. 99; Nathan, 'Theater', p. 71.
80. As quoted in Bentley, *Hallie Flanagan*, p. 264.
81. Cosgrove, *The Living Newspaper*, p. 86.

CHAPTER 3

1. Orson Welles, as quoted in O'Connor, 'The Federal Theatre Project's Search for an Audience', p.182.
2. Atkinson, 'National Theater; Congressman Javits Proposes that the Stage, Opera and Ballet Draws Plans', p. 1.
3. Flanagan, 'A Brief Delivered', p. 5. It is also interesting to note that Flanagan repeated the exact same phrase in her HUAC hearing when questioned by both Chairman Dies and Congressman Thomas.
4. As quoted in Zimmerman, *The Federal Theatre: An evaluation and comparison with foreign national theatres*, p. 114.
5. Burke, 'Revolutionary Symbolism in America', p. 269.
6. Ibid. pp. 269–270.
7. Ibid. p. 270.
8. Ibid. p. 272.
9. Ibid. pp. 272–273.
10. Gold, 'Discussion of Burke's Speech at the Congress', p. 275.
11. Ibid. p. 276.
12. Wolf, 'Discussion of Burke's Speech at the Congress', p. 277.
13. Ibid. p. 277.
14. Burke, 'Revolutionary Symbolism in America', p. 279.
15. Arent, 'The Techniques of the Living Newspaper', p. 59.
16. Ibid. p. 59
17. Kruger, *The National Stage*, p. 167.
18. Flanagan, 'Introduction', in *Federal Theatre Plays: Triple A Plowed Under, Power, Spirochete*, p. 4.
19. *Power*, I, i, 1.
20. Ibid.
21. *Power*, I, ii, 3.

22. Goldman, 'Life and Death of the Living Newspaper Unit', p. 77.
23. Kruger, *The National Stage*, p. 167.
24. *Power*, I, xv, 8.
25. Highshaw, *A theatre of action: The Living Newspapers of the Federal Theatre Project*, p. 232.
26. Mathews, *Federal Theatre, 1935–1939*, p. 115. Italics my emphasis.
27. As quoted in Mathews, ibid. p. 114.
28. It should be noted here that *Power* received negative criticism, especially from Republican Congressmen and representatives of corporations that capitalised on electricity.
29. According to Flanagan it was Pierre de Rohan, the editor of the *Federal Theatre* magazine, who suggested the title (*Arena*, p. 211), but Cosgrove has suggested that it was a collective decision ('Introduction', p. 16).
30. Roosevelt, 'Second Inaugural Address January 20, 1937', p. 243.
31. Bolton, 'Production Plan', p. 18.
32. Ibid. He further commented on the same page that 'there is no place in this production for any department or individual to attract attention by unrelated novelty, or experimentation for experimentation's sake'.
33. Ibid. p. 19.
34. Ibid.
35. As quoted in de Rohan, *First Federal Summer Theatre . . . A Report*, p. 29.
36. As quoted in Highsaw, *A theatre of action*, p. 361.
37. As quoted in de Rohan, *First Federal Summer Theatre . . . A Report*, p. 36.
38. Cosgrove, *The Living Newspaper*, p. xvi.
39. *One-third of a Nation*, I, iv, 6.
40. Ibid. I, i, 2.
41. Ibid. II, ii, 3–4. Italics my emphasis.
42. Goldman, 'Life and Death of the Living Newspaper Unit', p. 76.
43. *The Living Newspaper*, p. xvi.
44. *One-third of a Nation*, II, iii, 10.
45. Flanagan, 'Introduction', in *Federal Theatre Plays: Prologue to Glory, One-third of a Nation, Haiti*, p. 4; Atkinson as quoted in Mathews, *Federal Theatre, 1935–1939*, p. 169; Richard Watts and John Mason Brown as quoted in Kruger, *The National Stage*, p. 233 [footnote 100].
46. Lockridge, Anderson, Krutch as quoted in Highsaw, *A theatre of action*, pp. 367–8 [footnotes 60, 62, 63].
47. As quoted in Kruger, *The National Stage*, p. 232 [footnote 97].
48. 'The Federal Theatre Settles Down', p. 43.
49. Ibid. p. 47.
50. Kruger, *The National Stage*, p. 168.
51. 'The Techniques of the Living Newspaper', pp. 57–58. Italics my emphasis.
52. 'Second Inaugural Address January 20, 1937', p. 240. Italics my emphasis.

53. As quoted by Flanagan, in de Rohan, *First Federal Summer Theatre . . . A Report*, p. 35.
54. Kruger, *The National Stage*, p. 171.
55. *One-third of a Nation*, II, x, 9.
56. As quoted in de Rohan, *First Federal Summer Theatre . . . A Report*, p. 36.
57. McCarthy, *Sights and Spectacles*, p. 28.
58. Atkinson as quoted in Kruger, *The National Stage*, p. 182.
59. 'Dudley Murphy's Film of *One-third of a Nation* Opens at the Rivoli', p. 18.
60. Mathews, *Federal Theatre, 1935–1939*, p. 173.
61. 'Theatre and Geography', p. 464.

CHAPTER 4

1. Harry Hopkins, as quoted in Witham, *The Federal Theatre Project: A Case Study*, p. 62.
2. Gates, *Figures in Black: Words, Signs and the 'Racial' Self*, pp. 45–6.
3. Du Bois, 'Krigwa Players Little Negro Theatre', p. 124.
4. Theodore Ward, as quoted in Brown, 'The Federal Theatre', p. 107.
5. Flanagan, *Arena*, p. 36.
6. As one of the play's reviews reported, a 'half-white, half-Negro cast' took their first bows holding hands before a wildly enthusiastic 'half-white, half-Negro audience'. 'Review of *Haiti*', p. 34.
7. For an in-depth analysis of the *Big White Fog* production, and the controversies it provoked and reception it met, see Fraden, *Blueprints for a Black Federal Theatre*, pp. 115–35.
8. Ibid. pp. 4–5.
9. Cooke, 'Third Moscow Theatre Festival', p. 59. Also see O'Neil, 'The Negro in Dramatic Art', pp. 155–7; Brown, 'A Literary Parallel', p. 153; Du Bois, 'Criteria of Negro Art', p. 290–7.
10. McClendon, 'As to a New Negro Stage', p. 1.
11. Flanagan, *Arena*, p. 54.
12. Ibid. p. 63; Houseman, *Run-through: A Memoir*, p. 175.
13. Carlton Moss, as quoted in Fraden, *Blueprints*, p. 97.
14. Houseman, *Run-through*, p. 184.
15. Ibid. p. 185.
16. Hammond, 'Review of the "Voodoo" *Macbeth*', p. 35; Burns Mantle, as quoted in Callow, *Orson Welles: The Road to Xanadu*, p. 238; Atkinson, '"Macbeth" or Harlem Boy Goes Wrong, Under Auspices of Federal Theatre Project', p. 25.
17. Houseman, *Run-through*, p. 201.
18. Flanagan, *Arena*, p. 74.
19. *Macbeth*, I, i, 1.

20. Ibid. I, i, 5.
21. Ibid. II, i, 8.
22. Ibid. II, i, 13.
23. Atkinson, '"Macbeth"', p. 25.
24. *Macbeth*, II, ii, 2; II, ii, 5.
25. Fraden, *Blueprints*, p. 98.
26. Zorn, as quoted in Fraden, *Blueprints*, p. 105.
27. Ibid. p. 108.
28. Hilb, 'Afro-American Ritual Power: *Vodou* in Welles-FTP *Voodoo Macbeth*', pp. 649–81; Batiste, *Darkening Mirrors: Imperial Representation in Depression-Era African American Performance*, p. 76; Rippy, *Orson Welles and the Unfinished RKO Projects: A Postmodern Perspective*, p. 75.
29. Burton James accused Glenn Hughes of being directly involved with the building's acquisition because of professional jealousy. Hughes always denied it, and the University of Washington claimed that Hughes had protested against the appropriation, but the rumours regarding Hughes's involvement have persisted to this day. For a more detailed discussion of the relationship see Witham, *The Federal Theatre Project*.
30. As quoted in Witham, *The Federal Theatre Project*, p. 68.
31. Kotzamani, 'Lysistrata Joins the Soviet Revolution: Aristophanes as Engaged Theatre', p. 83.
32. Nemirovich-Danchenko, as quoted in Kotzamani, 'Lysistrata Joins the Soviet Revolution', p. 84.
33. Ibid. p. 85.
34. Smolin, '*Lysistrata*', p. 74.
35. Ibid. p. 23.
36. Sayler, *Inside the Moscow Art Theatre*. The photographs are positioned between pages 92 and 93.
37. The play was produced by the Philadelphia Theatre Association and designed and directed by Geddes. Music was composed by Leo Ornstein, with dance choreography by Doris Humphrey and Charles Weidman. It opened at the Walnut Street Theatre in Philadelphia on 12 May 1930, and on 9 June 1930 moved to New York at the 44th Street Theatre. It eventually transferred to Chicago at the Majestic Theatre on 4 November 1930.
38. Seldes, 'Preface', p. x.
39. For a more in-depth discussion of the changes that Seldes made in his adaptation see Kotzamani, '*Lysistrata* on Broadway', pp. 810–12, and Robson, 'Aristophanes, Gender and Sexuality', pp. 44–66.
40. Kotzamani, '*Lysistrata* on Broadway', p. 813.
41. Savery, 'Dancing in the Depression', p. 285.
42. Houseman, *Run-through*, p. 205.

43. Ibid.
44. Theodore Browne (1975), Transcript of interview with Lorraine Brown. 22 October. Box 2, Folder 11. George Mason University Libraries Special Collections. Federal Theatre Collection, 1885–1986, Fairfax, VA, 6–7.
45. Browne, *Lysistrata of Aristophanes, an African Version*, I, 3.
46. Ibid. I, 4.
47. Ibid. I, 12 & I, 6.
48. Ibid. I, 7–8 & I, 12.
49. Hill, 'A New Stage of Laughter for Zora Neale Hurston and Theodore Browne: Lysistrata and the Negro Units of the Federal Theatre Project', p. 296.
50. Browne, *Lysistrata*, I, 8.
51. Ibid. II, 24.
52. Ibid. II, 14–15.
53. Ibid. II, 20–1.
54. Flanagan, *Arena*, p. 304.
55. Witham, *The Federal Theatre Project*, p. 73.
56. Ibid. pp. 72–4; Klein, *Sex and War on the American Stage: Lysistrata in Performance, 1930–2012*, pp. 43–7; and Wetmore 'She (Don't) Gotta Have It: African-American Reception of *Lysistrata*', pp. 787–91.
57. Flanagan, *Arena*, p. 304.
58. Hill and Hatch, *A History of African American Theatre*, p. 328.
59. Witham, *The Federal Theatre Project*, p. 74.
60. Fraden, *Blueprints*, p. 199.
61. Hazel Huffman was a former employee of the mail division of the New York City WPA branch, who was dismissed because of her dubious activity of reading Federal Theatre mail. Sallie Saunders, originally from Vienna, Austria, but an American citizen since 1920, was employed as an actress.
62. Hazel Huffman testimony, in *Investigation of Un-American Propaganda Activities in the United States*, 1:784–5.
63. Sallie Saunders testimony, in *Investigation of Un-American Propaganda Activities in the United States*, 1:857.
64. Ibid. 1:859.
65. Ibid. 1:860.
66. Du Bois and Provenzo, *The Illustrated Souls of Black Folk*, p. 29.
67. Mumford, *Seven Stars and Orion: Reflections Of The Past*, p. 75.

Chapter 5

1. Flanagan, *Arena*, p. 372.
2. Saul and Lantz, 'The Revolt of the Beavers', I, i, 129.

3. Bennett, 'A History and Perspective', p. 12.
4. For an informed overview of the Karamu House productions see Abookire and McNair, 'Children's Theatre Activities at Karamu House, 1915–1975', pp. 69–84.
5. Rosenberg, *Creative Drama and Imagination: Transforming Ideas into Action*, p. 27.
6. Flanagan, *Arena*, p. 152; Webb, 'Betty Kessler Lyman and the Indiana Federal Children's Theatre', p. 69.
7. Flanagan, *Arena*, p. 153.
8. Flanagan, 'Instructions for Federal Theatre Projects', p. 2.
9. Rennick, 'Report on "The Children's Theatre"'.
10. Rennick, 'Children's Theatre – New York', p. 27.
11. Flanagan, *Arena*, p. 197.
12. Saul and Lantz, 'The Revolt of the Beavers', I, i, 127.
13. Ibid. I, i, 128.
14. Ibid.
15. Ibid. I, i, 129.
16. Ibid. I, ii, 135.
17. Ibid. I, ii, 136.
18. Ibid. I, ii, 135.
19. Ibid. I, ii, 137.
20. Ibid. I, ii, 140.
21. Ibid. I, ii, 141.
22. Ibid. I, ii, 140.
23. Ibid. I, iii, 142–3.
24. Ibid. I, iii, 147.
25. Ibid. I, iii, 148.
26. Ibid. II, i, 150.
27. Ibid. II, i, 156.
28. Ibid. II, iii, 162.
29. Ibid. II, iii, 167.
30. Ibid. II, iii, 169.
31. Ibid. II, iii, 172–3.
32. Harkins, '"Beaver's Revolt" Pleasing Fantasy for the Children', p. 11.
33. Gilbert, 'Four Weekly Matinees of "Beaver's Revolt" Play Presented at the Children's Theatre by the Federal WPA Drama'; 'Mother Goose Joins the Union – WPA Theatre Stages a Leftist Fantasy Called "the Revolt of the Beavers"', p. 78.
34. Atkinson, 'The Play: "The Revolt of the Beavers," or Mother Goose Marx Under WPA Auspices', p. 19.
35. Ibid.
36. Ibid.

37. Bentley, *Thirty Years of Treason*, p. 26.
38. Ibid. p. 27.
39. Flanagan, 'Brief delivered by Hallie Flanagan before the Committee on Patents, House of Representatives, February 8, 1938'.
40. Ibid.
41. Flanagan, *Arena*, pp. 200–1.
42. Ibid. pp. 298–300.
43. Frank, 'Pinocchio', I, i, 212.
44. Ibid. I, i, 214–15.
45. Ibid. II, i, 220.
46. Ibid. II, i, 221.
47. Ibid. II, i, 223.
48. Atkinson, 'The Play: Uncle Sam Produces "Pinocchio" Primarily for the Citizens of Future Generations', p. 19.
49. 'Pinocchio', II, iii, 228.
50. Ibid. III, iii, 234–5.
51. Atkinson, 'The Play: Uncle Sam Produces "Pinocchio" Primarily for the Citizens of Future Generations', p. 19.
52. Ibid.
53. Ibid.
54. Cobb, 'Click' Review of *Pinocchio*, p. 59.
55. Flanagan, *Arena*, p. 352.
56. Ibid. p. 365.
57. Ibid. p. 346.

Chapter 6

1. Tamiris, 'Tamiris in Her Own Voice: Draft of an Autobiography', p. 52.
2. Meyerhold, as quoted in Braun, *Meyerhold on Theatre*, p. 198.
3. Seltzer, *Bodies and Machines*, p. 64.
4. Martin, 'The Dance: WPA Project: Three Units to Function Under Federal Theatre Plan – Week's Programs'.
5. Tamiris, 'Tamiris in Her Own Voice', pp. 51–2.
6. As quoted in Lloyd, *The Borzoi Book of Modern Dance*, p. 133.
7. Ibid. pp. 141–2.
8. Schlundt, *Tamiris: A Chronicle of Her Dance Career, 1927–1955*, p. 100. Also see O'Connor and Brown, *Free, Adult, Uncensored: The Living History of the Federal Theatre Project*, pp. 214–15.
9. Code, 'Dance Theatre of the WPA: A Record of National Accomplishment, Pt 1', p. 265. For a detailed and in-depth discussion of the events leading to Becque's resignation see Graff, *Stepping Left: Dance and Politics in New York City, 1928–1942*, pp. 84–91.

10. Nadya Chilkovsky, as quoted in Gilfond, 'Public Hearing: Federal Dance Theatre', p. 97.
11. Ibid.
12. Flanagan, *Arena*, pp. 199–200; Schlundt, *Tamiris*, p. 98.
13. Tish, 'Remembering Helen Tamiris', p. 338.
14. Ibid. p. 337.
15. Ibid. p. 340.
16. Whitman, *Leaves of Grass*, p. 119.
17. Tish, 'Remembering Helen Tamiris', p. 341.
18. Ibid. pp. 341–2.
19. Flanagan, *Arena*, p. 76.
20. Lloyd, *The Borzoi Book of Modern Dance*, p. 144.
21. For a detailed account regarding the retrieval and publication of the songs, along with some biographical details regarding Lawrence Gellert, see Garabedian, 'Reds, Whites, and the Blues: Lawrence Gellert, "Negro Songs of Protest," and the Left-Wing Folk-Song Revival of the 1930s and 1940s', pp. 179–206.
22. Manning, 'Black Voices, White Bodies: The Performance of Race and Gender in "How Long Brethren"', p. 28
23. Tish, 'Remembering Helen Tamiris', pp. 347, 349.
24. As quoted in Graff, *Stepping Left*, p. 94.
25. Ibid. p. 197.
26. Tish, 'Remembering Helen Tamiris', p. 347.
27. Graff, *Stepping Left*, pp. 197–8.
28. Ibid. p. 198.
29. Tish, 'Remembering Helen Tamiris', p. 347.
30. Ibid. p. 348.
31. Graff, *Stepping Left*, p. 198.
32. Ibid. p. 199.
33. Tish, 'Remembering Helen Tamiris', pp. 348–9.
34. Graff, *Stepping Left*, p. 197.
35. Production note, as quoted in Manning, 'Black Voices, White Bodies', p. 33.
36. As quoted in Flanagan, *Arena*, p. 199.
37. As quoted in Manning, 'Black Voices, White Bodies', p. 33.
38. Gilfond, 'Tamiris – Charles Weidman', p. 68.
39. As quoted in Tish, 'Remembering Helen Tamiris', p. 352.
40. Graff, *Stepping Left*, p. 95.
41. See Perpener, *African-American Concert Dance: The Harlem Renaissance and Beyond*, and Foulkes, *Modern Bodies: Dance and American Modernism from Martha Graham to Alvin Ailey*.
42. Martin, *John Martin's Book of the Dance*, pp. 178–9.

43. Manning, 'Black Voices, White Bodies', pp. 37–8.
44. Franko, *The Work of Dance: Labor, Movement and Identity in the 1930s*, pp. 91–9.
45. Graff, *Stepping Left*, p. 96.
46. For example, Hemsley Winfield's Negro Art Theatre in Harlem (which included such dancers as Edna Guy and Ollie Burgoyne) gave its first concert in April 1931. It was advertised as the 'First Negro Concert in America' and one of the suites included was based on Negro spirituals. John Martin considered the concert a success and praised its novelty. See Emery, *Black Dance in the United States from 1619 to 1970*, pp. 242–3.
47. Flanagan, *Arena*, p. 201. For more details of the actual events and people involved see Graff, *Stepping Left*, pp. 99–101.
48. Ironically, Dies's book on uncovering the Communist cells within the USA was entitled *The Trojan Horse in America*.
49. Browne, as quoted in Hartigan, *Greek Tragedy on the American Stage: Ancient Drama in the Commercial Theatre, 1882–1994*, p. 18. For more information on both performances see Hartigan and also Foley, *Reimagining Greek Tragedy on the American Stage*.
50. As quoted in Davis, 'Is Mr. Euripides a Communist? The Federal Theatre Project's 1938 *Trojan Incident*', pp. 462–3.
51. Davis, *Trojan Incident – Based on Trojan Women of Euripides*. Box 265, Folder 1. George Mason University Libraries Special Collections. Federal Theatre Collection, 1885–1986, Fairfax, Virginia, USA, p. 4.
52. As quoted in Davis, 'Is Mr. Euripides a Communist?', p. 462.
53. Tish, 'Remembering Helen Tamiris', p. 353.
54. Davis, *Trojan Incident*, p. 8.
55. Ibid. p. 17.
56. Ibid. p. 22.
57. Ibid. p. 28.
58. Ibid. p. 32.
59. Ibid. p. 33.
60. Ibid. pp. 42–3.
61. Ibid. p. 49.
62. Ibid. p. 51.
63. Ibid. p. 54, p. 58.
64. Ibid. p. 61. Italics my emphasis.
65. Ibid. pp. 61–2.
66. Davis, 'Is Mr. Euripides a Communist?', p. 464.
67. Atkinson, 'THE PLAY: Women of Troy According to a Federal Theatre Pattern in Dance, Song and Drama', p. 15.
68. Flanagan, *Arena*, p. 321.
69. Tish, 'Remembering Helen Tamiris', p. 354; Schlundt, *Tamiris*, p. 47.

70. 'WPA Play: *Trojan Incident*', p. 58.
71. Atkinson, 'THE PLAY: Women of Troy According to a Federal Theatre Pattern in Dance, Song and Drama', p. 15.
72. Ibid.
73. Ibid.
74. Ibid.
75. Code, 'Dance Theatre of the WPA: A Record of National Accomplishment, Pt 2', p. 281.
76. Tish, 'Remembering Helen Tamiris', pp. 354–5.
77. Martin, 'The Dance: Greek Chorus', p. 8.
78. Ibid.
79. Atkinson, 'THE PLAY: Women of Troy According to a Federal Theatre Pattern in Dance, Song and Drama', p. 15.
80. Dies, *The Trojan Horse in America*, p. 298.
81. As quoted in Bentley, *Thirty Years of Treason*, p. 3.
82. Huffman, Hazel (1938), 'Testimony', in *Investigation of Un-American propaganda Activities in the United States*, 1:785. Available at <https://archive.org/details/investigationofu193801unit> (last accessed 27 May 2020).
83. Bentley, *Thirty Years of Treason*, p. 25.
84. Flanagan, *Arena*, p. 76.
85. As quoted in Cooper, 'Tamiris and the Federal Dance Theatre 1936–1939', p. 43.
86. Schlundt, *Tamiris*, p. 61.
87. Ibid. p. 68.
88. Flanagan, *Arena*, p. 76.
89. Tamiris, as quoted in Schlundt, *Tamiris*, pp. 69–70.
90. Ibid. pp. 75–6.

Chapter 7

1. Flanagan, *Arena*, pp. 334–5.
2. Flanagan, 'Federal Theatre Project', p. 865.
3. As quoted in Kreizenbeck, *The Theatre Nobody Knows: Forgotten Productions of the Federal Theatre Project 1935–1939*, p. 59.
4. As quoted in Flanagan, *Arena*, p. 28.
5. United States Congress House Special Committee on Un-American Activities (1938–1944) (1938), *Investigation of Un-American Propaganda Activities in the United States*, Washington, DC: Government Printing Office, p. 8.
6. Mathews, *Federal Theatre 1935–1939*, p. 199.
7. Ibid.
8. As quoted in Bentley, *Thirty Years of Treason*, p. xvii.

9. Ibid. p. 25.
10. Ibid. pp. 34–6.
11. Arent, 'The Techniques of the Living Newspaper', p. 57.
12. As quoted in Fishman, *The Disinherited of Art*, p. 148.
13. Ibid.
14. Bentley, *Hallie Flanagan*, p. 363.
15. Flanagan's choice of devices was similar to the ones MacColl used in *Uranium 235*; they included rapid scene and costume changes, the use of dancing and chorus, sound effects and lighting, and absence of a curtain. She also adopted techniques employed by Brecht in the *Life of Galileo* (and his previous productions), such as direct address to the audience, projections and the use of historical and allegorical figures.
16. Flanagan, $E=mc^2$: *A Living Newspaper about the Atomic Age*, I, 34.
17. Ibid. I, 12.
18. Ibid. I, 14.
19. Ibid. I, 21.
20. Ibid. I, 24.
21. Ibid. I, 25.
22. Ibid. I, 24, 30.
23. In MacColl's play the process of atomic fission is also presented through an atomic ballet scene. The members of the ballet include Mass (female), Energy (muscular male figure), the Alpha particle, Neutrons and Protons. While their routine is being performed, the audience participates in a visually frenzied spectacle that theatrically recreates the formation of atomic energy. The dance ends in a loud and sustained explosion with a blackout signalling in dramatic fashion the creation of this new form of energy. *Uranium 235*, p. 124.
24. Flanagan, $E=mc^2$, I, 38.
25. Ibid. I, 43.
26. The Professor's comments were similarly echoed in Brecht's 'Galileo', which also voiced concerns over the relationship between science and knowledge, and the ways this knowledge was used. Brecht's play put more emphasis on the role and responsibility of the scientist, whom he saw as the main figure that needed to educate people and the audience. It is the figure of the scientist, through Galileo, that is in possession of the scientific knowledge that could influence the current social structure and world order, and effect change that would improve the living conditions and social relations of the lower classes.
27. Flanagan, $E=mc^2$, II, 50.
28. Ibid. II, 75.
29. Ibid. II, 83. MacColl's play's original ending offers a similar conclusion to Flanagan's. In it, the audience is reminded that they 'are the main pro-

tagonists in the play' and is asked, 'which is it to be? Which way are you going?' MacColl, in a direct manner, addresses the audience and forces it to think, recall everything watched on stage and critically decide both whether to act and the manner of acting. *Uranium 235*, pp. 121, 126.
30. Flanagan, *E=mc²*, I, 26. The Stage Manager's proclamation echoes and is echoed by both MacColl's and Brecht's plays, which equally assert their theatricality; all three plays make the audiences aware of the theatrical space they are in, reminding them that within this safe space they can question, argue, critique, act and consider everything that has been unfolded.
31. Ibid. II, 84.

ARCHIVAL MATERIAL

Arent, Arthur (1938), *One-third of a Nation*. Box 311, Folders 2–4. Special Collections Research Center, George Mason University Libraries. Federal Theatre Project Collection, Fairfax, VA, USA.

Blitzstein, Marc (1937), *The Cradle Will Rock*. Box 136, Folders 5–6. Special Collections Research Center, George Mason University Libraries. Federal Theatre Project Collection, Fairfax, VA, USA.

Browne, Theodore (1936), *Lysistrata of Aristophanes, an African Version*. Box 2, Folder 2. Special Collections Research Center, George Mason University Libraries. Federal Theatre Project Collection, Fairfax, VA, USA.

— (1975), Transcript of interview with Lorraine Brown. 22 October Box 2, Folder 11. Special Collections Research Center, George Mason University Libraries. Federal Theatre Project Collection, Fairfax, VA, USA.

Davis, Philip H. (1938), *Trojan Incident – Based on Trojan Women of Euripides*. Box 265, Folder 1. Special Collections Research Center, George Mason University Libraries. Federal Theatre Project Collection, Fairfax, VA, USA.

Flanagan, Hallie (1935), 'Instructions for Federal Theatre Projects', 24 October 1935 to May 1936. Box 3, Folder 9. Special Collections Research Center, George Mason University Libraries. Federal Theatre Project Collection, Fairfax, VA, USA.

— (1936), 'To All Directors, Actors, Designers, and Producers on the Federal

Theatre Project'. Instructions for Federal Theatre Projects by Hallie Flanagan, 24 October 1935 to May 1936. Box 3, Folder 9. Special Collections Research Center, George Mason University Libraries. Federal Theatre Project Collection, Fairfax, VA, USA.

— (1938), 'A Brief Delivered by Hallie Flanagan, Director, Federal Theatre Project, Works Progress Administration before the Committee on Patents, House of Representatives, February 8, 1938'. Box 1, Folder 4. Special Collections Research Center, George Mason University Libraries. Federal Theatre Project Collection, Fairfax, VA, USA.

— (1939), 'Opening Statement Containing Detailed Answers to Charges Made by Witnesses who Appeared Before the SPECIAL COMMITTEE to Investigate UN-AMERICAN ACTIVITIES, House of Representatives'. Box 368, Folders 2–4. Special Collections Research Center, George Mason University Libraries. Federal Theatre Project Collection, Fairfax, VA, USA.

Living Newspaper Unit (1936), *Triple-A Plowed Under*. Box 264, Folders 2–7. Special Collections Research Center, George Mason University Libraries. Federal Theatre Project Collection, Fairfax, VA, USA.

— (1937a), *Injunction Granted*. Box 178, Folders 7–8. Box 179, Folders 1–5. Special Collections Research Center, George Mason University Libraries. Federal Theatre Project Collection, Fairfax, VA, USA.

— (1937b), *Power*. Box 229, Folders 2–6. Special Collections Research Center, George Mason University Libraries. Federal Theatre Project Collection, Fairfax, VA, USA.

— (1938), *One-third of a Nation*. Box 220, Folders 2–6. Special Collections Research Center, George Mason University Libraries. Federal Theatre Project Collection, Fairfax, VA, USA.

— (1939), 'Techniques Available to the Living Newspaper Dramatist' by staff of the New York Living Newspaper Unit. Box 7, Folders 5–7. Special Collections Research Center, George Mason University Libraries. Federal Theatre Project Collection, Fairfax, VA, USA.

Rennick, Jack (1936), 'Report on "The Children's Theatre"', 28 August. Box 495. National Archives, Washington, DC.

Shakespeare, William (1936), *Macbeth*, adapted and staged by Orson Welles. Box 138, Folders 4–5. Special Collections Research Center, George Mason University Libraries. Federal Theatre Project Collection, Fairfax, VA, USA.

BIBLIOGRAPHY

Abookire, Noerena and Jennifer Scott McNair (1989), 'Children's Theatre Activities at Karamu House, 1915–1975', in R. L. Bedard and J. C. Tolch (eds), *Spotlight on the Child: Studies in the History of American Children's Theatre, Contributions in Drama and Theatre Studies*, New York: Greenwood Press, pp. 69–84.

Anderegg, Michael (1999), *Orson Welles, Shakespeare and Popular Culture*, New York: Columbia University Press.

Anonymous (1936), 'Editorial Statement', *Federal Theatre Magazine*, 1.6, 5.

Arent, Arthur (1968), '*Ethiopia*: The First "Living Newspaper"', *Educational Theatre Journal*, 20.1, 15–31.

— (1971), 'The Techniques of the Living Newspaper', *Theatre Quarterly*, 1.4, 57–9.

Atkinson, Brooks (1930a), 'Direct from Athens', *The New York Times*, 1 June, X1.

— (1930b), '"Lysistrata" Here With Broad Humor', *The New York Times*, 6 June, 26.

— (1936), '"Macbeth" or Harlem Boy Goes Wrong, Under Auspices of Federal Theatre Project', *The New York Times*, 15 April, 25.

— (1937a), '*Power* Produced by the Living Newspaper Under Federal Theatre Auspices', *The New York Times*, 24 February, 18.

— (1937b), 'The Play: "The Revolt of the Beavers," or Mother Goose Marx Under WPA Auspices', *The New York Times*, 21 May, 19.

— (1937c), 'Marc Blitzstein's "The Cradle Will Rock" Officially Opens at the Mercury Theatre', *New York Times*, 6 December, 19.
— (1938a), 'Living Newspaper of the Federal Theatre Reports the Housing Situation', *The New York Times*, 18 January, 27.
— (1938b), 'THE PLAY: Women of Troy According to a Federal Theatre Pattern in Dance, Song and Drama', *New York Times*, 22 April, 15.
— (1939), 'The Play: Uncle Sam Produces "Pinocchio" Primarily for the Citizens of Future Generations', *The New York Times*, 3 January, 19.
— (1949), 'National Theater; Congressman Javits Proposes that the Stage, Opera and Ballet Draws Plans', *New York Times*, 30 January, 1.
Auden, W. H. (1945), *Collected Poetry of W. H. Auden*, New York: Random House.
Batiste, Stephanie Leigh (2012), *Darkening Mirrors: Imperial Representation in Depression-Era African American Performance*, Durham, NC: Duke University Press.
Baxandall, Lee (1967), 'Brecht in America, 1935', *TDR*, 12.1, 69–87.
Bennett, Stuart (2005), 'A History and Perspective', in S. Bennett (ed.), *Theatre for Children and Young People: 50 Years of Professional Theatre in the UK*, London: Aurora Metro, pp. 11–28.
Bentley, Eric (1971), *Thirty Years of Treason: Excerpts from Hearings Before the House Committee on Un-American Activities, 1938–1968*, New York: Viking Press.
Bentley, Joanne (1988), *Hallie Flanagan: A Life in the American Theatre*, New York: Alfred A. Knopf.
Bernard, Heinz (1971), 'A Theatre for Lefty: USA in the 1930's', *Theatre Quarterly*, 1.4, 53–6.
B. G. (1936), 'The Living Newspaper Finally Gets Under Way with "Triple-A Plowed Under" – Two One-Act War Plays', *New York Times*, 16 March, 21.
Bigsby, C. W. E. (1982), *A Critical Introduction to Twentieth-century American Drama: 1, 1900–1940*, Cambridge: Cambridge University Press.
Blitzstein, Marc (1938), 'Author of "The Cradle" Discusses Broadway Hit', *Daily Worker*, 3 January, 7.
Blue Blouse (1995), 'Simple Advice to Participants (1925)', in R. Drain (ed.), *Twentieth-century Theatre: A Sourcebook*, London and New York: Routledge, pp. 181–3.
Bohn, John (1931), 'Dramburo Report', *Workers Theatre*, 1, 1.
Bolton, Harold (1937), 'Production Plan', in P. de Rohan (ed.), *First Federal Summer Theatre . . . A Report*, New York: Federal Theatre National Publications, pp. 16–19.
Braun, Edward (1969), *Meyerhold on Theatre*, London: Methuen.

Brecht, Bertolt (1980a), *Life of Galileo*, in John Willett and Ralph Manheim (eds), London: Eyre Methuen.
— (1980b), 'Foreword', in J. Willett and R. Manheim (eds), *Life of Galileo*, London: Eyre Methuen, 1980, pp. 115–17.
— (1980c), 'Preamble to the American Version', in J. Willett and R. Manheim (eds), *Life of Galileo*, London: Eyre Methuen, 1980, p. 125.
— (1980d), 'Galileo', trans. Charles Laugthon, in J. Willett and R. Manheim (eds), *Life of Galileo*, London: Eyre Methuen, 1980, pp. 201–65.
— (1990a), *Letters 1913–1956*, in J. Willett and R. Manheim (eds), London: Methuen.
— (1990b), 'Emphasis on Sport', in J. Willett (ed. and trans.), *Brecht on Theatre: The Development of an Aesthetic*, London: Methuen, pp. 6–9.
— (1990c), 'The Modern Theatre is the Epic Theatre', in J. Willett (ed. and trans.), *Brecht on Theatre: The Development of an Aesthetic*, London: Methuen, pp. 33–42.
— (1990d), 'The German Drama: Pre-Hitler', in J. Willett (ed. and trans.), *Brecht on Theatre: The Development of an Aesthetic*, London: Methuen, pp. 77–81.
— (1990e), 'On the Use of Music in the Epic Theatre', in J. Willett (ed. and trans.), *Brecht on Theatre: The Development of an Aesthetic*, London: Methuen, pp. 84–90.
— (1990f), 'On Gestic Music', in J. Willett (ed. and trans.), *Brecht on Theatre: The Development of an Aesthetic*, London: Methuen, pp. 104–6.
— (1990g), 'Building up a Part: Laughton's Galileo', in J. Willett (ed. and trans.), *Brecht on Theatre: The Development of an Aesthetic*, London: Methuen, pp. 163–8.
— (1990h), 'A Short Organum for the Theatre', in J. Willett (ed. and trans.), *Brecht on Theatre: The Development of an Aesthetic*, London: Methuen, pp. 179–205.
— (1990i), 'Masterful Treatment of a Model', in J. Willett (ed. and trans.), *Brecht on Theatre: The Development of an Aesthetic*, London: Methuen, pp. 209–15.
— (2003), 'On Art and Socialism', in T. Kuhn and S. Giles (eds), *Brecht on Art and Politics*, London: Methuen, pp. 34–9.
Brown, Hilda Meldrum (1991), *Leitmotiv and Drama: Wagner, Brecht, and the Limits of 'Epic' Theatre*, Oxford: Clarendon Press.
Brown, Sterling (1932), 'A Literary Parallel', *Opportunity*, 10.5, 153.
— (1967), 'The Federal Theatre', in L. Patterson (ed.), *The Anthology of the American Negro in the Theater*, New York: The Publishers Co., pp. 101–10.
Burke, Kenneth (1989), 'Revolutionary Symbolism in America', in H. W.

Simons and T. Melia (eds), *The Legacy of Kenneth Burke*, Madison: University of Wisconsin Press, pp. 267–73.
Callow, Simon (1996), *Orson Welles: The Road to Xanadu*. London: Vintage.
Carpenter, Charles A. (1999), *Dramatists and the Bomb: American and British Playwrights Confront the Nuclear Age, 1945–1964*, Westport, CT: Greenwood Press.
Chambers, Colin (1989), *The Story of the Unity Theatre*, London: Lawrence and Wishart.
Ciment, Michel (1985), *Conversations with Losey*, London and New York: Methuen.
Cobb, William T. (1939), 'Click' Review of *Pinocchio*, *Wall Street Journal*, 3 January, p. 59.
Code, Grant (1939a), 'Dance Theatre of the WPA: A Record of National Accomplishment, Pt 1', *Dance Observer*, 6.8, 264–5, 274.
— (1939b), 'Dance Theatre of the WPA: A Record of National Accomplishment, Pt 2', *Dance Observer*, 6.9, 280–1, 290.
— (1939c), 'Dance Theatre of the WPA: A Record of National Accomplishment, Pt 2 Conclusion', *Dance Observer*, 6.10, 302.
— (1940a), 'Dance Theatre of the WPA: A Record of National Accomplishment, Pt 3', *Dance Observer*, 7.3, 34–5.
— (1940b), 'Dance Theatre of the WPA', *Dance Observer*, 7.6, 86.
Cooke, Anne (1936), 'Third Moscow Theatre Festival', *Opportunity*, 14.2, 59.
Cooper, Elizabeth (1997), 'Tamiris and the Federal Dance Theatre 1936–1939: Socially Relevant Dance Amidst the Policies and Politics of the New Deal Era', *Dance Research Journal*, 29.2, 23–48.
Cosgrove, Stuart (1982), *The Living Newspaper: History, Production and Form*, Unpublished PhD Dissertation, University of Hull.
— (1989), 'Introduction', in L. Brown (ed.), *Liberty Deferred and Other Living Newspapers of the 1930's*, Fairfax, VA: George Mason University Press, pp. ix–xxv.
Davis, Robert (2010), 'Is Mr. Euripides a Communist? The Federal Theatre Project's 1938 *Trojan Incident*', *Comparative Drama*, 45.1, 457–76.
de Rohan, Pierre (1937), *First Federal Summer Theatre ... A Report*, New York: Federal Theatre National Publications.
Deák, František (1973), 'Blue Blouse', *The Drama Review*, 17, 35–46.
Dies, Martin (1940), *The Trojan Horse in America*, New York: Dodd.
'Documents and Texts from the Workers' Theatre Movement (1928–1936)' (1977), *History Workshop*, no. 4 (Autumn), pp. 102–42.
Du Bois, W. E. B. (1926a), 'Krigwa Players Little Negro Theatre', *Crisis*, 32, 124.
— (1926b), 'Criteria of Negro Art', *Crisis*, 32.6, 290–7.

Du Bois, W. E. B. and E. F. Provenzo (2016), *The Illustrated Souls of Black Folk*, London and New York: Routledge.
Emery, Lynne Fauley (1972), *Black Dance in the United States from 1619 to 1970*, Palo Alto, CA: National Press Books.
Fineman, Frances (1925), 'The Moscow Theatre', *New York Times*, 11 January, X2.
Fishman, Solomon (1953), *The Disinherited of Art*, Berkeley and Los Angeles: University of California Press.
Flanagan, Hallie (1928a), *Shifting Scenes of the Modern European Theatre*, New York: Coward–McCann.
— (1928b), 'Experiment At Vassar', *Theatre Arts Monthly*, 12.1, 70–1.
— (1929a), 'Theatre Experiment', *Theatre Arts Monthly*, 13.7, 543–6.
— (1929b), 'Russia Reviewed in Symposium', *Vassar Miscellany News*, 9 February.
— (1930), 'The Soviet Theatrical Olympiad', *Theatre Guild Magazine*, September, 10.
— (1931), 'A Theatre Is Born', *Theatre Arts Monthly*, 15.11, 908–15.
— (1935), 'Federal Theatre Project', *Theatre Arts Monthly*, 19.11, 865–8.
— (1936a), 'Federal Theatre: Tomorrow', *Federal Theatre*, 2.1, 5–6.
— (1936b), 'What Are We Doing With Our Chance?', *Federal Theatre*, 2.3, 5–6.
— (1938a), 'Introduction', in P. de Rohan (ed.), *Federal Theatre Plays: Triple-A Plowed Under, Power, Spirochete*, New York: Random House, pp. 1–6.
— (1938b), 'Introduction', in P. de Rohan (ed.), *Federal Theatre Plays: Prologue to Glory, One-third of a Nation, Haiti*, New York: Random House, pp. 1–6.
— (1938c), 'Theatre and Geography', *American Magazine of Art*, 40, 464–8.
— (1939a), 'Open Letter to Congressman Woodrum', *Sunday Worker*, 18 June.
— (1939b), *What was Federal Theatre?*, Washington: American Council on Public Affairs.
— (1940), *Arena*, New York: Duell, Sloan and Pearce.
— (1948), $E=mc^2$: *A Living Newspaper about the Atomic Age*, New York City: Samuel French.
Foley, Helene P. (2012), *Reimagining Greek Tragedy on the American Stage*, Berkeley: University of California Press.
Foulkes, Julia L. (2002), *Modern Bodies: Dance and American Modernism from Martha Graham to Alvin Ailey*, Chapel Hill: University of North Carolina Press.
Fraden, Rena (1996), *Blueprints for a Black Federal Theatre, 1935–1939*, Cambridge: Cambridge University Press.
Frank, Yasha (1986), 'Pinocchio', in Lowell Swortzell (ed.), *Six Plays for*

Young People from the Federal Theatre Project (1936–1939), Westport, CT: Greenwood Press, pp. 208–35.
Franko, Mark (2002), *The Work of Dance: Labor, Movement and Identity in the 1930s*, Middletown, CT: Wesleyan University Press.
Füllöp-Miller, René and Joseph Gregor (1930), *The Russian Theatre: Its Character and History, with Especial Reference to the Revolutionary Period* (trans. Paul England), London: Harrap.
Garabedian, Steven (2005), 'Reds, Whites, and the Blues: Lawrence Gellert, "Negro Songs of Protest," and the Left-Wing Folk-Song Revival of the 1930s and 1940s', *American Quarterly*, 57.1, 179–206.
Gardner, Colin (2014), 'The Losey-Moscow Connection: Experimental Soviet Theatre and the Living Newspaper', *New Theatre Quarterly*, 30, 249–68.
Gates, Henry Louis, Jr (1987), *Figures in Black: Words, Signs and the 'Racial' Self*, New York: Oxford University Press.
G. B. (1936), 'The Living Newspaper Finally Gets Under Way With "Triple-A Plowed Under" – Two One-Act War Plays', *New York Times*, 16 March, 21.
Geddes, Norman Bel (1926), 'A Word on the Russians', *New York Times*, 31 January, X2.
Gemünden, Gerd (1999), 'Brecht in Hollywood: *Hangmen also Die* and the Anti-Nazi Film', *TDR*, 43.4, 65–76.
Gilbert, Douglas (1937), 'Four Weekly Matinees of "Beaver's Revolt" Play Presented at the Children's Theatre by the Federal WPA Drama', *The World Telegram*, 21 May.
Gilfond, Henry (1936), 'Public Hearing: Federal Dance Theatre', *Dance Observer*, 3.9, 97.
— (1937), 'Tamiris – Charles Weidman', *Dance Observer*, 4.6, 67–8.
Given, John (2015), 'Aristophanic Comedy in American Musical Theater, 1925–1969', in K. Bosher, F. Macintosh, J. McConnell and P. Rankine (eds), *The Oxford Handbook of Greek Drama in the Americas*, Oxford: Oxford University Press, pp. 301–32.
Gold, Michael, (1989), 'Discussion of Burke's Speech at the Congress', in H. W. Simons and T. Melia (eds), *The Legacy of Kenneth Burke*, Madison: University of Wisconsin Press, pp. 274–80.
Goldberg, Moses (1974), *Children's Theatre: A Philosophy and a Method*, Englewood Cliffs, NJ: Prentice-Hall.
Goldman, Arnold (1973), 'Life and Death of the Living Newspaper Unit', *Theatre Quarterly*, 3.9, 69–83.
Goldstein, Malcolm (1974), *The Political Stage: American Drama and Theater of the Great Depression*, New York: Oxford University Press.
Goorney, Howard and Ewan MacColl (eds) (1986), *Agit-prop to Theatre Workshop*, Manchester: Manchester University Press.

Gorelik, Mordecai (1940), *New Theatres for Old*, London: Dennis Hobson.
Graff, Ellen (1997), *Stepping Left: Dance and Politics in New York City, 1928–1942*, Durham, NC: Duke University Press.
Gray, John (1995), *Liberalism*, Buckingham: Open University Press.
Greenberg, Clement (1939), 'Avant-Garde and Kitsch', *Partisan Review*, 6.5, 34–49.
Hammond, Percy (1936), 'Review of the "Voodoo" Macbeth', *New York Herald Tribune*, 16 April, 35.
Harkins, John (1937), '"Beaver's Revolt" Pleasing Fantasy for the Children', *The New York American*, 21 May, sec. 1, 11.
Hartigan, Karelisa (1995), *Greek Tragedy on the American Stage: Ancient Drama in the Commercial Theatre, 1882–1994*, Westport, CT: Greenwood Press.
Heard, Doreen B. (1989), 'Children's Theatre in the Federal Theatre Project', in R. L. Bedard and J. C. Tolch (eds), *Spotlight on the Child: Studies in the History of American Children's Theatre, Contributions in Drama and Theatre Studies*, New York: Greenwood Press, pp. 99–118.
Hecht, Werner (1961), 'The Development of Brecht's Theory of the Epic Theatre, 1918–1933', *The Tulane Drama Review*, 6.1, 40–97.
Highsaw, Caroline Anne (1988), *A Theatre of Action: The Living Newspapers of the Federal Theatre Project*, Unpublished PhD Dissertation, Princeton University.
Hilb, Benjamin (2014), 'Afro-American Ritual Power: *Vodou* in Welles-FTP *Voodoo Macbeth*', *Shakespeare Bulletin*, 32.4, 649–81.
Hill, Anthony Duane (ed.) (2008), *A Historical Dictionary of African American Theater*, Prevessin: Scarecrow Press.
Hill, Errol and James Vernon Hatch (2005), *A History of African American Theatre*, Cambridge: Cambridge University Press.
Hill, Lena (2015), 'A New Stage of Laughter for Zora Neale Hurston and Theodore Browne: Lysistrata and the Negro Units of the Federal Theatre Project', in K. Bosher, F. Macintosh, J. McConnell and P. Rankine (eds), *The Oxford Handbook of Greek Drama in the Americas*, Oxford: Oxford University Press, pp. 286–300.
Houseman, John (1972), *Run-through: A Memoir*, New York: Simon & Schuster.
— (1986), *Entertainers and Entertained*, New York: Simon & Schuster.
Huffman, Hazel (1938), 'Testimony', *Investigation of Un-American Propaganda Activities in the United States*, 1:775–829, <https://archive.org/details/investigationofu193801unit> (last accessed 27 May 2020).
Isaacs, Edith (1938), 'An Industry Without a Product – Broadway in Review', *Theatre Arts Monthly*, 22, 99.
Jackson, Naomi M. (2000) *Converging Movements: Modern Dance and*

Jewish Culture at the 92nd Street Y, Hanover, NH: Wesleyan University Press.

Karoula, Ourania (2009), *A Thorn in the Body Politic: A Transatlantic Dialogue on the Aesthetics of Commitment Within Modernist Political Theatre*. Unpublished PhD dissertation, University of Edinburgh, pp. 116, 122–129.

Kaufman, Wolfe (1937), 'Actors and Audiences All Mixed Up as WPA Goes Commercial', *Variety*, 23 June, 62.

Klein, Emily B. (2014), *Sex and War on the American Stage: Lysistrata in Performance, 1930–2012*, London: Routledge.

Kotzamani, Marina (2005), 'Lysistrata Joins the Soviet Revolution: Aristophanes as Engaged Theatre', in J. Dillon and S. E. Wilmer (eds), *Rebel Women: Staging Ancient Greek Drama Today*, London: Methuen, pp. 78–111.

— (2014), '*Lysistrata* on Broadway', in S. Douglas Olson (ed.), *Ancient Comedy and Reception: Essays in Honor of Jeffrey Henderson*, Berlin: De Gruyter, pp. 807–23.

Kramer, Lawrence (2002), *Musical Meaning: Toward a Critical History*, Berkeley and London: University of California Press.

Kreizenbeck, Alan (1979), *The Theatre Nobody Knows: Forgotten Productions of the Federal Theatre Project 1935–1939*, Unpublished PhD dissertation, NYU, Graduate School of Arts and Science.

Krieg, Joann P. (2007), 'Whitman and Modern Dance', *Walt Whitman Quarterly Review*, 24.4, 208–15.

Kruger, Loren (1992), *The National Stage: Theatre and Cultural Legitimation in England, France and America*, Chicago and London: University of Chicago Press.

Kuhn, Tom and Steve Giles (2003), 'Introduction to Part Two', in T. Kuhn and S. Giles (eds), *Brecht on Art and Politics*, London: Methuen, pp. 57–63.

Leach, Robert (1994), *Revolutionary Theatre*, London and New York: Routledge.

— (2004), *Makers of Modern Theatre: An Introduction*, London and New York: Routledge.

— (2006), *Theatre Workshop: Joan Littlewood and the Making of Modern British Theatre*, Exeter: Exeter University Press.

Lloyd, Margaret (1949), *The Borzoi Book of Modern Dance*, New York: Alfred Knopf.

Lockbridge, Richard (1936), 'The Stage in Review: Terrors of Impartiality', *New York Sun*, 21 March, 9.

Losey, Joseph, (1961), The Individual Eye', *Encore*, 8.2, 5–15.

— (1973), 'Prefatory Notes to *Injunction Granted!*', *Minnesota Review*, New Series 1, 51–3.

Lyon, James K. (1980), *Bertolt Brecht in America*, Princeton, NJ: Princeton University Press.
McCarthy, Mary (1938), 'The Federal Theatre Settles Down', *Partisan Review*, 4.6, 43–7.
— (1956), *Sights and Spectacles*, New York: Farrar, Straus & Cudahy.
McCaslin, Nellie (1987), *Historical Guide to Children's Theatre in America*, Westport, CT: Greenwood Press.
McClendon, Rose (1935), 'As to a New Negro Stage', *New York Times*, 30 June, 1.
MacColl, Ewan (1973), 'The Workshop Story Part 1: Grass Roots of Theatre Workshop', *Theatre Quarterly*, 3.9, 58–68.
— (1985), 'Theatre of Action, Manchester', in *Theatres of the Left 1880–1935*, London: Routledge & Kegan Paul, pp. 205–55.
— (1986), *Uranium 235*, in H. Goorney and E. MacColl (eds), *Agit-prop to Theatre Workshop*, Manchester: Manchester University Press, pp. 73–130.
— (2009), *Journeyman: An Autobiography*. Manchester and New York: Manchester University Press.
Malina, Judith (2012), *The Piscator Notebook*, London and New York: Routledge.
Manning, Susan (1998), 'Black Voices, White Bodies: The Performance of Race and Gender in "How Long Brethren"', *American Quarterly*, 50.1, 24–46.
— (2004), *Modern Dance, Negro Dance: Race in Motion*, Minneapolis: University of Minnesota Press.
Martin, John (1936), 'The Dance: WPA Project: Three Units to Function Under Federal Theatre Plan – Week's Programs', *New York Times*, 12 January.
— (1938), 'The Dance: Greek Chorus', *New York Times*, 1 May, 8.
— (1963), *John Martin's Book of the Dance*, New York: Tudor.
Mathews, Jane de Hart (1967), *Federal Theatre, 1935–1939: Plays, Relief and Politics*, Princeton, NJ: Princeton University Press.
— (1975), 'Art and the People: The New Deal for a Cultural Democracy', *The Journal of American History*, 62.2, 316–39.
— (1976), 'Art and Politics in Cold War America', *The American Historical Review*, 81.4, 762–87.
Metzer, David (1995), 'Reclaiming Walt: Marc Blitzstein's Whitman Settings', *Journal of the American Musicological Society*, 48.2, 240–71.
'Mother Goose Joins the Union – WPA Theatre Stages a Leftist Fantasy Called "The Revolt of the Beavers"' (1937), *Life*, 21 June, 78.
Mumford, Esther Hall (1986), *Seven Stars and Orion: Reflections of the Past*, Seattle: Ananse Press.
Nathan, George Jane (1938), 'Theater', *Scribner's Magazine*, 103, 71.

New York Times (1925), 'The Play: The Synthetic Russians', 15 December, 28b.
Nugent, Frank (1939), 'Dudley Murphy's Film of *One-third of a Nation* Opens at the Rivoli', *New York Times*, 11 February, 18.
O'Connor, J. and L. Brown (eds) (1980), *Free, Adult, Uncensored: The Living History of the Federal Theatre Project*, London: Eyre Methuen.
O'Connor, John (1985), 'The Federal Theatre Project's Search for an Audience', in B. A. McConachie and D. Friedman (eds), *Theatre for Working-class Audiences in the United States, 1830–1980*, Westport, CT: Greenwood Press, pp. 171–83.
O'Neil, Raymond (1924), 'The Negro in Dramatic Art', *Crisis*, 27.4, 155–7.
Perpener, John O. (2001), *African-American Concert Dance: The Harlem Renaissance and Beyond*, Urbana and Chicago: University of Illinois Press.
Perry, Edward (1943), 'Actor Lauds Orson Welles for Working in Negro Theatre', *Los Angeles Tribune*, 25 October, 18.
Pilcher, Verona (1927), 'The Theatre of the Revolution', *Theatre Arts Monthly*, 11.4, 258–72.
Plum, Jay (1992), 'Rose McClendon and the Black Units of the Federal Theatre Project: A Lost Contribution', *Theatre Survey*, 33.2, 144–53.
Pollack, Howard (2013), *Marc Blitzstein: His Life, His Work, His World*, Oxford: Oxford University Press.
Rabkin, Gerald (1964), *Drama and Commitment: Politics in the American Theatre of the Thirties*, Bloomington: Indiana University Press.
Rauch, Basil (1944), *The History of the New Deal*, New York: Creative Age Press.
Reinelt, Janelle G. (1994), *After Brecht: British Epic Theatre*, Ann Arbor: University of Michigan Press.
Rennick, Jack (1936), 'Children's Theatre – New York', *The Federal Theatre Magazine*, 2.3, 27.
'Review of *Haiti*' (1938), *Time*, 31 October, 34.
Rice, Elmer (1936), 'Statement of Resignations', *New Theatre*, February, 2.
— (1960), *The Living Theatre*, London: William Heinemann.
Rippy, Marguerite (2009), *Orson Welles and the Unfinished RKO Projects: A Postmodern Perspective*, Carbondale: Southern Illinois University Press.
— (2018), 'The Death of the *Auteur*: Orson Welles, Asadata Dafora, and the 1936 *Macbeth*', in J. N. Gilmore and S. Gottlieb (eds), *Orson Welles in Focus: Texts and Contexts*, Bloomington: Indiana University Press, pp. 11–33.
Robson, James (2016), 'Aristophanes, Gender and Sexuality', in P. Walsh (ed.), *Brill's Companion to the Reception of Aristophanes*, Leiden and Boston: Brill, pp. 44–66.
Roosevelt, Franklin D. (1961), 'Second Inaugural Address January 20, 1937',

in *Inaugural Addresses of the Presidents of the United States from George Washington 1789 to John F. Kennedy 1961*, Washington, DC: United States Government Printing Office, pp. 240–43.

Rosenberg, Helane S. (1987), *Creative Drama and Imagination: Transforming Ideas into Action*, New York: Holt, Rinehart, and Winston.

Ross, Ronald (1974), 'The Role of Blacks in the Federal Theatre, 1935–1939', *The Journal of Negro History*, 59.1, 38–50.

Rossen, Rebecca (2014), *Dancing Folk*, Oxford: Oxford University Press.

Samuel, Raphael, Ewan MacColl and Stuart Cosgrove (1985), *Theatres of the Left, 1880–1935: Workers' Theatre Movements in Britain and America*, London: Routledge & Kegan Paul.

Saul, Oscar and Louis Lantz (1986), 'The Revolt of the Beavers', in L. Swortzell (ed.), *Six Plays for Young People from the Federal Theatre Project (1936–1939)*, Westport, CT: Greenwood Press, pp. 128–74.

Saunders, Sallie (1938), 'Testimony', *Investigation of Un-American Propaganda Activities in the United States*, 1:857–860, <https://archive.org/details/investigationofu193801unit> (last accessed 27 May 2020).

Savery, Helen (1984–5), 'Dancing in the Depression', *Dance Chronicle*, 7.3, 279–93.

Sayler, Oliver Martin (1925), *Inside the Moscow Art Theatre*, New York: Brentano's.

Schlundt, Christena L. (1972), *Tamiris: A Chronicle of Her Dance Career, 1927–1955*, New York: New York Public Library.

Seldes, G. S. and G. Seldes, *Plays of the Moscow Art Theatre Musical Studio* (trans. 1925), New York: Brentano's.

Seldes, Gilbert (1930), 'Preface', in *Aristophanes' Lysistrata: A New Version*, New York: Farrar and Rinehart, p. x.

Sellers, Marion (1936), 'The Dance Project – W. P. A. Stepchild', *New Theatre*, 8 August.

Seltzer, Mark (1992), *Bodies and Machines*, London: Routledge.

Sklaroff, Lauren Rebecca (2009), *Black Culture and the New Deal: The Quest for Civil Rights in the Roosevelt Era*, Chapel Hill: University of North Carolina Press.

Slonim, Marc (1963), *The Russian Theater: From the Empire to the Soviets*, London: Methuen.

Smolin, Dmitry (1925), '*Lysistrata*' (trans. George S. and Gilbert Seldes), in *Plays of the Moscow Art Theatre Musical Theatre*, New York: Brentano's, pp. 1–78.

Stourac, Richard and Kathleen McCreery (1986), *Theatre as a Weapon: Workers' Theatre in the Soviet Union, Germany and Britain, 1917–1934*, London and New York: Routledge & Kegan Paul.

Tamiris, Helen (1936), 'Dance Groups', *Dance Observer*, 3.5, 56.

— (1989), 'Tamiris in Her Own Voice: Draft of an Autobiography', *Studies in Dance History* I.I, 1–64.
Taxidou, Olga (1995), 'Crude Thinking: John Fuegi and Recent Brecht Criticism', *New Theatre Quarterly*, 11.44, 381–4.
'The Theatre: New Plays: Dec. 28, 1925' (1925), *Time*, 28 December.
Thomson, Virgil (1938), 'In the Theater', *Modern Music*, 15, 112–14.
Tish, Pauline (1994), 'Remembering Helen Tamiris', *Dance Chronicle*, 17.3, 327–60.
United States Congress House Special Committee on Un-American Activities (1938–1944) (1938), *Investigation of Un-American Propaganda Activities in the United States*, Washington: Government Printing Office.
Urell, Maude Babcock (1928), 'The Dancer Who Stages Herself', *Dance Magazine*, July, 61.
Vernon, Granville (1936), '*Injunction Granted*: Latest Edition of the Living Newspaper is Out and Out Propaganda of the Left', *The Commonweal*, 24, 407.
Watson, Morris (1936), 'The Living Newspaper', *New Theatre*, June, 7.
Webb, Dorothy (1995), 'Betty Kessler Lyman and the Indiana Federal Children's Theatre', *Youth Theatre Journal*, 9.1, 68–78.
Weill, Kurt (1961), '*Gestus* in Music', *The Tulane Drama Review*, 6.1, 28–32.
Weisstein, Ulrich (1963), 'Brecht in America: A Preliminary Survey', *MLN*, 78.4, 373–96.
West, Ron (1996), 'Others, Adults, Censored: The Federal Theatre Project's Black *Lysistrata* Cancellation', *Theatre Survey*, 37.2, 93–113.
Wetmore, Kevin J. (2014), 'She (Don't) Gotta Have It: African-American Reception of *Lysistrata*', in S. Douglas Olson (ed.), *Ancient Comedy and Reception: Essays in Honor of Jeffrey Henderson*, Berlin: De Gruyter, pp. 786–96.
Whitman, Walt (1891–2), *Leaves of Grass*, Philadelphia: David McKay.
Willett, John (1984), *Brecht in Context: Comparative Approaches*, London and New York: Methuen.
— (1990), *Brecht on Theatre: The Development of an Aesthetic*, London: Methuen.
Witham, Barry B. (2003), *The Federal Theatre Project: A Case Study*, Cambridge: Cambridge University Press.
Wolf, Friedrich (1989), 'Discussion of Burke's Speech at the Congress', in H. W. Simons and T. Melia (eds), *The Legacy of Kenneth Burke*, Madison: University of Wisconsin Press, pp. 274–80.
'WPA Play: *Trojan Incident*' (1938), *Variety*, 27 April, 58.
Zimmerman, Leland Lemke (1955), *The Federal Theatre: An Evaluation and Comparison with Foreign National Theatres*, Unpublished PhD Dissertation, University of Wisconsin.

INDEX

Page numbers in italics refer to illustrations and those followed by n are notes

Abbey Theatre, 12–13, 92, 168
Abel, Don, 106, 115–16
Adelante, 178, 182
Adelphi Theatre, 80–1, 102, 125
Æ (George William Russell), 12
African Americans, 42–3, 89–119, 154–67; *see also* race
African drummers, 43–4, 53, 90, 93–101, 111
African witches, 97, 99–101
agit-prop theatre, 23–4, 29–30, 33–5, 63, 65, 190, 205n
Agricultural Adjustment Act (AAA), 47–50
Allan Tower (Electric Company Manager), 75
'America', 26–7
American Communist Party, 154, 184–5, 188–9
American Constitution, 52–3
American dream, 68–9, 90–1
American Music League, 154
American workers' theatre, 34–7, 40, 186
American Writers' Congress, 69–71
'Americana', 26–7
Ancient Greek theatre, 5, 14, 32, 167–8, 170
Andrews, Senator Charles O., 87
anticapitalism *see* capitalism
Appia, Adolphe, 36, 169
Arent, Arthur
 Ethiopia, 42
 Injunction Granted, 46, 50–1, 55–6
 Living Newspaper, 41, 69, 187–8
 One-third of a Nation, 72, 77–85
 Power, 72
 Triple-A Plowed Under, 46

Aristophanes, 104–19
 Acharnians, 106
 Lysistrata, 32
Aristotle, 83
Artef (Yiddish Workers Theatre), 34
Arvin, Newton, 188
Asimov, Nikolai, 20–1
Assen, Abdul, 97
Atkinson, Brooks
 The Cradle Will Rock, 65–6
 democracy, 68
 Ethiopia, 45
 Injunction Granted, 59
 Macbeth, 96, 101
 One-third of a Nation, 83
 Pinocchio, 143–4
 Power, 77
 The Revolt of the Beavers, 134–5
 The Trojan Incident, 176–8
Auden, W. H., 34
Austria, Flanagan in, 19
authorship, sole, 71–87
avant-garde, 21–2, 24, 57–8, 69
 European, 6, 33, 199

Babes in the Wood, 30
Baker, George Pierce, 11–12
Baker, Jacob, 45
Barber, Philip, 46, 47, 58, 69, 94, 102, 149
Barker, Harley Granville, 168–9
Barrie, J. M., *Peter Pan*, 121
Bassa Moona, 90
Batiste, Stephanie, 103
Bay, Howard, 78–9, 80–1, 169, 176
Bayou Ballads, 181
Becque, Don Oscar, 149–50
Bennett, Stuart, 121

Bentley, Eric, 27
Bernard, Heinz, 202n
Bernard Shaw, George, 13
Bertha Waddell's Children's Theatre, 121
Bigsby, C. W. E., 22
Bill of Rights, 52–3
Biltmore Theatre, 42–3, 50
biomechanics, 16–17, 21, 29, 31, 34
Birmain, Serafima, 17
Bjørson, Bjørn, 13
Blitzstein, Marc, 27–8, 61–7
  The Cradle Will Rock, 28
  'Few Little English', 205n
  'The Nickel Under Your Foot', 28
Bloch, Ernst, 21
Bloxa, The Flea, 17
Blue Blouse movement
  The Cradle Will Rock, 63, 65
  influence on FTP, 20–4
  Injunction Granted, 50–1
  Living Newspaper, 40
  MacColl, 32
  Russian theatre, 15, 17
  'Simple Advice to Participants', 22–3
  tour to Germany, 24
  workers' theatre, 34
The Blue Blouse, 22
Bohm, Jerome, 164
Bolton, Harold, 77–80, 169
Bonn, John, 34, 37
Bonner, Isabel, 176
Bontemps, Arna, 90
Bosse, Harriet, 13–14
Bovingdon, John, 151
Bowder, Earl, 59
Bowhill Players, 29
Bragaglia, Anton, 19
Braun, Edward, Meyerhold on Theatre, 147
Brecht, Bertolt
  Blitzstein, 61
  The Cradle Will Rock, 63
  'crude thinking', 26
  $E=mc^2$, 190, 194–5, 217n
  epic theatre, 20
  'Galileo', 46, 199
  influence on FTP, 6, 24–8, 34
  Injunction Granted, 27, 50–1
  In the Jungle of Cities, 27
  Lehrstücke plays, 124
  Life of Galileo, 216n
  Losey, 55–6

Meyerhold, 21
The Mother, 27
Mother Courage and Her Children, 30
One-third of a Nation, 79
Saint Joan of the Stockyards, 27
Theatre Union, 32
The Threepenny Opera, 48, 61, 204n
Triple-A Plowed Under, 204n
Vakhtangov, 31
Bridge, William, 11
British Workers' Theatre Movement, 12, 20, 28–33
Broadway
  capitalism and, 35–6
  children's theatre, 124
  different audience to FTP, 2–5, 39, 196
  Flanagan and, 183
  FTP as 'un-American,' 187
  Living Newspaper and, 66, 72
  Lysistrata, 106
  Tamiris, 181
Brod, Max, 202n
Browder, Earl, 186
Brown, John Mason, 83
Brown, Sterling, 92
Browne, Maurice, 168
  Wings over Europe, 190, 192
Browne, Theodore
  A Black Woman Called Moses, 91
  Lysistrata, 91, 93, 105–6, 110–19
  Natural Man, 91
  Seattle Negro Repertory Unit, 91
  Swing, Gates, Swing, 91
Buckland, Robert, Where's That Bomb? 30
Burke, Kenneth, 69–71, 72, 74
Burroughs, Eric, 97
Buttonkooper, Mr (character), 74, 81–2, 151
Byrd, Senator Harry, 87

Campbell, Dick, 94
Candide, 149, 154, 167, 182
Canwell Committee, 105
capitalism
  anticapitalism, 35–6, 70–1, 134
  Brecht, 26
  Communism and, 184
  The Cradle Will Rock, 61–3
  Great Depression, 1–2
  Injunction Granted, 76
  Meyerhold, 16–17

capitalism (*continued*)
  One-third of a Nation, 82, 84–5
  The Revolt of the Beavers, 134
  workers' theatre, 34–6
Carson, Nat, 97–9, *98*
Carter, Jack, *96*
censorship, 45, 50, 60, 65, 116, 184, 191
Chekhov, Michael, 17
Chicago, Brecht in, 27
Chicago Little Theatre, 168
Chicago Negro Theatre unit, 90–1
Children's Educational Theatre, 121
children's theatre, 120–46, 198–9
Children's Theatre of Evanston, 121–2
Children's Theatre unit, 120–46
Chorpenning, Charlotte, *The Emperor's New Clothes*, 125
The Christian Science Monitor, 23–4
Civic Repertory Theatre, Seattle, 91, 105
class struggle
  Brecht and Piscator, 24
  Burke, Kenneth, 70–1
  The Cradle Will Rock, 65
  $E=mc^2$, 195
  Injunction Granted, 55
  The Revolt of the Beavers, 134
  Tamiris, 166
  Triple-A Plowed Under, 47
  workers' theatre, 34–5
  see also working-class
Clown (character), 51, 53, *57*
Cobb, William, 144
Code, Grant, 149, 177–8
Cold War paranoia, 5–6, 189
Colonial Theatre, 11
Commedia dell'Arte, 16–17, 19, 74
Communism
  African Americans and, 117–18
  Federal Dance Unit, 178–9
  FTP accused of, 184–9
  Injunction Granted, 59
  Lysistrata, 113–14
  paranoia, 5–6
  Power, 76
  The Revolt of the Beavers, 120, 125, 134–6
  Triple-A Plowed Under, 47
  workers' theatre, 34–5
Communist Party, United States, 59
Congress, 119, 146, 183–4

Congress of Industrial Organizations (CIO), 51, 54–5, 58, 59
constructivism, 20–1, 22, 106–9
Cooke, Anne, 92
Copeau, Jacques, 19
Cornish College of the Arts, 105
Cosgrove, Stuart, 66, 83, 207n
costumes, 81, *98*, 109–10, *111*, 155
Coward, Noël, 12
Cowley, Malcolm, 36
The Cradle Will Rock, 61–7, *62*, 116, 125
  Project 891, 103
Craig, Gordon
  The Art of the Theatre, *The Theatre Advancing*, 14
  Flanagan meeting with, 12, 14
  in Italy, 19
  The Mask, 14
  Trojan Women, 169
  workers' theatre, 36
Crommelynck, Fernand, *The Magnificent Cuckold*, 21
Cullen, Countee, 90
Czech Republic, Flanagan in, 19

Dafora, Asadata, 97, 166
dance, 18, 31, 90, 97, 147–82
Dance, 154
Daniel, Jimmie, 102
Davis, Philip H., 167–8, 169–78, 189
Davis, Senator James, 59
Dean, Alexander, 11
democracy
  Ethiopia, 45
  FTP and, 5, 184, 188
  Lysistrata, 106
  One-third of a Nation, 85
  'people's theatre', 68–70
  Power, 74, 76
  Triple-A Plowed Under, 49
  Trojan Women, 168–9
Democratic government, 45, 85
Democratic Party, 45–6
Denmark, Flanagan in, 14
Dies, Senator Martin
  Federal Dance Unit, 178–9
  FTP and, 186–7
  Negro unit, 118
  New York unit, 6
  The Revolt of the Beavers, 120
  Trojan Incident, 167

Dies Committee
  FTP and, 87, 184–9, 197
  Negro unit, 117–19
  Pinocchio, 146
  The Revolt of the Beavers, 125, 135
Disney, Walt, 122
documentary themes, 22, 26, 34, 47
Dr Faustus, 64
The Drama magazine, 11
Drama League of America, 11
Du Bois, W. E. B., 92, 118
  'Krigwa Players Little Negro Theatre', 88
DuBois, William, *Haiti*, 90

$E=mc^2$: *A Living Newspaper about the Atomic Age*, 189–95, 199, 216n, 216–17n
Educational Alliance, 121
Edward, H. F. V., 90
Edward, Harry, 103
Eisenstein, Sergei, 29, 46
Eisler, Hans, 46
Eliot, T. S., *Murder in the Cathedral*, 189
Elks Lodge band, 101–2
Emergency Relief Appropriation Act, 89
epic theatre, 20, 24–8, 79, 190
episodic structure, 32, 48, 72, 78
Ethiopia, 42–6
  and Communism, 59
  The Cradle Will Rock, 66
  $E=mc^2$, 191
  Lysistrata, 93, 106, 113, 116
  Rice, Elmer, 204n
Euripides
  Hippolytus, 168
  House Un-American Activities Committee (HUAC), 179
  Trojan Incident, 167–78
  Trojan Women, 167–9
An Evening with Dunbar, 119
Experimental Theatre, New York, 151
expressionism, 17, 18, 21–2, 23, 24

Farnsworth, Bill, 46, 58
Fay, Frank, 12–13
Feder, Abe, 98–9, 154
Federal Art Project, 2–3
Federal Dance Project, 147–82
Federal Music Project, 2–3
Federal Project Number One, 2–3
Federal Theatre Negro Chorus, 156

Federal Theatre Plays: Prologue to Glory, One-third of a Nation, Haiti, 'Introduction' to, 38
Federal Theatre Project
  establishment of, 1–9
  legacies of, 183–95
  legacy in contemporary performance, 196–9
  political prosecution of, 183–9
Federal Theatre Veteran League, 47
Federal Theatre's Summer Theatre School at Vassar Experimental Theatre, 77–9, 78
Federal Writers Committee, 86–7
Federal Writers Project, 2–3
59th Street Theatre, 108
Fisher, Rudolph, *The Conjure Man Dies*, 90, 95
Fishman, Solomon, 188
Flanagan, Frederic, 10–11
Flanagan, Hallie
  Arena, 1, 60, 116, 120, 137, 183, 189
  Austria, 19
  on Blue Blouse group, 23
  Browne, Theodore, 105
  Chicago Negro Theatre unit, 90
  children's theatre, 122–5, 136–7, 145–6
  The Cradle Will Rock, 62, 64–6
  The Curtain, 11
  Denmark, 14
  $E=mc^2$, 216–17n, 216n
  Federal Dance Unit, 147–50
  France, 19
  and FTP, 3–5, 10–20
  The Garden of Wishes, 11
  Germany, 18
  House Un-American Activities Committee (HUAC), 38, 179–80, 206n
  How Long, Brethren? 154–5
  Hungary, 19
  Incense, 11
  Injunction Granted, 58–60
  Ireland, 12–13
  Italy, 19
  Living Newspaper, 23, 38–40, 69, 198
  London, 12
  Lysistrata, 93, 116–18
  Macbeth, 98–9, 102
  McClendon, Rose, 94
  Money, 204n

Flanagan, Hallie (*continued*)
  Negro units, 89
  One-third of a Nation, 79, 83, 86–7
  Oslo, 13
  Paris, 19
  political prosecution of the FTP, 183–9
  Power, 73, 76–7
  The Revolt of the Beavers, 133, 135–6
  Rice, Elmer, 45–6
  Russia, 15–18, 20, 185–6
  Shifting Scenes of the Modern European Theatre, 12, 19, 186
  Sweden, 13–14
  theatre and capitalism, 35–6
  'A Theatre is Born,' 202–3n
  travels in Europe, 11–19
  Triple-A Plowed Under, 47
  Trojan Incident, 167–8, 176–7
Flanagan, Jack, 10–11
Flanagan, Murray, 10
Flight, 125
44th Street Theatre, New York, 209n
47 Workshop, 11
Four Saints in Three Acts, 94
Fraden, Rena, 91–2
France, Flanagan in, 19
Frank, Allan, 144
Frank, Yasha, *Pinocchio*, 136–44, 144–6
Franko, Mark, 166
Freeman, Joseph, 71
Füllöp-Miller, René, 29

Galsworthy, John, *Escape*, 12
Gary Theatre, Indiana, 122–3
Gassel, Sylvia, 190
Gates, Henry Louis Jr, *Figures in Black: Words, Signs and the 'Racial' Self*, 88
Geddes, Bel, 109–10, 209n
Gellert, Lawrence, 154
  Negro Songs of Protest, 154
gender themes, 108, 110–19, 160, 165–6, 181, 198
George Mason University Libraries Special Collections on the Federal Theatre Project, 6–7
Germany
  Blue Blouse tour, 24
  Flanagan in, 18
  Living Newspaper, 40
Gilbert, Douglas, 133
Gilfond, Henry, 164–5

Gluck-Sandor, 149
Gold, Mike, 41, 71
Goldbeck, Eva, 27
Goldman, Arnold, 53, 83
Goldstein, Malcolm, 34–35
Gorelik, Mordecai, 27
Gorky, Maxim
  The Lower Depths, 11
  The Mother, 27
government-sponsored theatre, 39, 42, 66, 87
Graff, Ellen, 165
Graham, Martha, 181
Graham, Shirley, 90, 92
Great Depression, 1–2
  African Americans, 89, 113
  children's theatre, 122, 145–6
  Federal Dance Unit, 147
  FTP and, 196
  Hooverville, 200n
  Living Newspaper, 40
  'people's theatre,' 69
  The Revolt of the Beavers, 126–7, 136
  Tamiris, 151
  workers' theatre, 36
Greek chorus
  Lysistrata, 107–8, 111
  Meyerhold, 16
  Murder in the Cathedral, 189
  One-third of a Nation, 79
  Triple-A Plowed Under, 49
  Trojan Women, 168–70, 173–7
Greek tragedy, 147–82
Greenberg, Clement, 22
Gregory, Lady Augusta, 13, 168
Grinnell College, 10–11
Group Theater, 36
Guggenheim Fellowship, 12
Gyseghem, André van, 30, 50

Hailparn, Dorothy, *Horse Play*, 125
Haiti, 95–6, 103–4
Hammond, Percy, 96
Harkins, John, 133
Harlem, 88–119
Harlem Experimental Theatre, 94
Harvard, 11–12
Hašek, Jaroslav, 202n
  The Good Soldier Schweik, 32
Hatch, James Vernon, 116
Herts, Alice Minnie, 121
Hilb, Benjamin, 103

Hill, Abram, *Liberty Deferred*, 103
Hill, Errol G., 113, 116
Hippolytus, 169
Historical Records Survey, 2–3
Hodge, Herbert
  Cannibal Carnival, 30
  Where's That Bomb? 30
Holborn Constituency Labour Party, 29
Hollywood, 1, 46, 86–7
'Hoovervilles,' 2, 200n
Hopkins, Harry
  Baker, Jacob, 45
  censorship, 60, 184
  democracy, 85
  Federal Dance Unit, 148, 149
  Flanagan, 10
  Living Newspaper, 69
  Lysistrata, 93, 116
  Negro theatre, 88
  Power, 76
  Rice, Elmer, 42
  WPA, 2–3
Horse Eats Hat, 103
House Un-American Activities Committee (HUAC), 6, 35, 38, 66, 178–9, 184–9, 206n
Houseman, John
  The Cradle Will Rock, 61–2, 64–5
  Lysistrata, 110
  Macbeth, 96–7, 101–3
  New York Negro Theatre unit, 89–90, 94–5
housing, 77–9
How Long, Brethren?, 157, 158, 160, 161, 164
  Dies Committee, 118
  House Un-American Activities Committee (HUAC), 179
  narrator, 151
  picketing, 167
  race and dance in, 154–67
  Tamiris, 155, 182
Huffman, Hazel, 117–18, 179, 185, 210n
Hughes, Glen, 104–5, 209n
Humphrey, Doris, 149, 181, 209n
Hungary, Flanagan in, 19
Hurston, Zora Neale, 110

Ibsen, Henrik, 13
  The Pretenders, 14
Independent Labour Party (ILP), 28–9

Injunction Granted, 46–60, 54, 55
  artistic experimentations, 84
  capitalism, 76
  Clown (character), 57
  Communism, 186
  Living Newspaper, 71–2, 83, 86
  set design, 56
  Variety, 79
Institute of Journalism, Moscow, 22
Iowa State Playwriting Contest, 11
Ireland, Flanagan in, 12–13
Isaacs, Edith, 66
Italian Futuristic theatre, 19
Italy
  Flanagan in, 19
  Meyerhold, 16

Jackson, Sarah Oliver, 118
James, Burton, 91, 104–5, 209n
James, Florence, 91, 104–5
jazz, 16, 17
Jewish ethnicity, 121, 148, 155, 165
John, Augustus, 12
Johnson, Momodu, 90

Kaiser, Georg, *Gas*, 29
Kamerny, 15, 17–18
Karamu House, Cleveland, Ohio, 121
Karnot, Stephen, 150
Kirstein, Lincoln, 150
Kotzamani, Marina, 107, 109
Kruger, Loren, 36, 73, 205n
Ku Klux Klan (KKK), 185
Kykunkor (The Witch Woman), 97, 166

Lafayette Theatre, Harlem, 90, 93, 94, 102, 165
Lantz, Louis, 125
League of Workers' Theatres, 36, 202n
Lederman, Minna, 61
The Left Front of the Arts, 22
Lenya, Lotte, 205n
Lesser Free Trade Hall, 32–3
Lewis, John L., 54–5
Lewis, Sinclair, *It Can't Happen Here*, 117
liberalism, 67, 185, 195
Liberty Song, 181
Life, 77, 133–4, 144
lighting, 16–17, 98–101, 154, 194
Lindsay, Jack, *On Guard for Spain*, 30

237

Little Black Sambo, 90
'little man' character, 72–3, 81–2, 151, 191–194
Littlewood, Joan, 28–33
Living Newspaper, 38–67, 68–87
  Blue Blouse movement, 22–4
  Brecht, 27–8
  Busmen, 30
  challenges of, 198
  children's theatre, 125
  Dies Committee, 185, 187–8
  $E=mc^2$, 189–95
  Ethiopia, 93
  Germany, 40
  Holborn Constituency Labour Party, 29
  House Un-American Activities Committee (HUAC), 179
  The Last Edition, 32–3
  Liberty Deferred, 103
  MacColl, 32–3
  'un-American' behaviour, 118
  Welles, Orson, 99
  workers' theatre, 36
Lloyd, Margaret, 154, 164
Lloyd, Norman, 50, 53, 57, 75
Lockbridge, Richard, 50
Locke, Alain, 92
London, Flanagan in, 12
Losey, Joseph, 27–8, 46–50, 55–60, 203n, 204n
Loudspeaker (character), 79, 80–2
Lukács, Georg, 21–2
Lyman, Betty Kessler, 122–3
Lysistrata, 104–19, 209n

Macbeth, 93–104, 96
  Bassa Moona, 90
  Carson, Nat, 98
  gender and race, 118–19
  Lysistrata, 110–11
  Tamiris, 166
  voodoo, 100, 102
McCarthy, Mary, 84
McCarthyism, 188
McClendon, Rose, 89, 94–5, 102, 118
MacColl, Ewan, 28–33, 190, 198, 216n, 216–17n
MacLeish, Archibald, 65
Majestic Theatre, Chicago, 209n
Manning, Susan, 156, 165–6
Mantle, Burns, 96

Marlowe, Christopher, 179
  Tragical History of Dr. Faustus, 103
Martin, John, 165, 177–8, 214n
Marx, Harpo, 53
Marxism, 25–6, 34–5, 55, 134, 184, 188–9
masks, 16, 31, 97, 98, 101, 123
Mathews, Jane de Hart, 60
Maxine Elliott Theatre, 61, 65
Mayakovsky, Vladimir, 22
Medicine, 61
Mercury Theatre, 103
Meyerhold, Vsevolod
  biomechanics, 29, 31, 34, 107
  Camille, 46
  dance, 147
  The Death and Destruction of Europe, 16
  Flanagan and experimentation, 40
  FTP and, 188
  Injunction Granted, 50
  The Inspector General, 16, 46
  Italy, 16
Karnot, Stephen, 150
Losey, 46, 55–6
Russian theatre, 15–17, 20–4
theatre and audience, 20
'Mickey Mouse Players', 122
Miller, J. Howard, 116
Moman, Bob, 156
Money, 45–46, 204n
montage, 29, 72
Moore Theatre, 115
Moscow Art Theatre (MAT), 11, 15, 16, 17, 20, 92, 106–9
Moscow State Central Theatre for Juvenile Audiences, 123
Moscow Theatre for Children, 121
Moscow Trials, 76, 184
Moss, Carlton, 90, 94, 95, 103
Municipal Housing Authority of New York, 79
Murray, Gilbert, 168–169
music, 61, 63, 81, 97, 99–100, 154, 194

Nagrin, Daniel, 166, 181
narrator, 125, 151
Nathan, George Jane, 66
The Nation, 77
National Theatre of Oslo, 13
Nazism, 184–5
Nazi-Soviet non-aggression pact, 184

Negro Art Theatre, Harlem, 214n
Negro Dramatists Laboratory, 103
Negro People's Theatre, 94
Negro Repertory Company (NCR), 105–6, 119
Negro Repertory Theatre (NRT), 118
Negro Songs of Protest, 179
Negro spirituals, 148, 154–67, 214n
Negro Theatre Project (NTP), 88–119
Negro Theatre unit, 88–119
Nemirovich-Danchenko, Vladimir, 31, 106–9
Nemirovich-Danchenko Musical Theatre, 106–9
New Deal
  cultural democracy, 68–9, 184
  Dies Committee, 178–9, 185, 197
  Injunction Granted, 55, 58, 60
  Living Newspaper, 66
  One-third of a Nation, 83, 85–7
  Power, 74–6
  Triple-A Plowed Under, 47–50
  WPA, 2–3
New Masses, 179
New Theatre, 36
New Theatre League, 36
New York City Children's unit, 123–4
New York Negro Theatre unit, 90, 93–104
The New York Times, 27, 45, 50
Newcastle People's Theatre, 33
Newsboy, 31
Newspaper Guild, 39
Nichols, Robert, *Wings over Europe*, 190, 192
Noah, 105, 116
Nora Bayes Theatre, New York, 154, 156
Northwestern University, 121–2
Nugent, Frank, 87

O'Casey, Sean, 12–13
O'Connor, John, 'The Federal Theatre Project's Search for an Audience', 68
Odets, Clifford, *Waiting for Lefty*, 28, 30, 36, 46, 94, 203n
Off-Off Broadway movement, 197
Okhlopkov, Nikolai, 46–7, 56
O'Neil, Raymond, 92
O'Neill, Eugene, 13
  The Emperor Jones, 95

One-third of a Nation, 32, 42, 58, 66, 71–87, 78, 81
Ornstein, Leo, 209n
Orpheum Theatre, Seattle, 93
Orrick, Mildred, 109–10
Oslo, Flanagan in, 13

Parable Players, 121
Paramount Pictures, 86–7
Paris, Flanagan in, 19
Parkhurst, Winthrop, 151
'people', 70–1
'people's theatre', 5, 68–71
Perry, Edward, 90, 95
Philadelphia Theatre Association, 209n
Pichel, Irving, 11
picketing, 167
Pinocchio, 120–46, *140*, *141*, *142*
Pirandello, Luigi, 19
Piscator, Erwin, 24, 31, 32, 34
Pitoëff, Georges, 19
Pitot, Genevieve, 149, 151, 154, 169
Plant in the Sun, 30
Pollitzer, Alice K., 135
Post, Langdon, 79
Poulsen, Johannes, 14
poverty
  children's theatre, 145
  Dies Committee, 178
  Great Depression, 1–2
  How Long, Brethren? 151, 156, 158, 166
  Macbeth, 104
Power, 42, 60, 66, 71–87, 75, 207n
The Prodigal Son, 149
Project 891, 61, 103
projections
  Brecht, 24, 27
  $E=mc^2$, 191, 216n
  Ethiopia, 44
  Living Newspaper, 40
  One-third of a Nation, 78, 81
  Power, 73
  Theatre Union, 32
  Triple-A Plowed Under, 48, 50
Prokofiev, Sergei, *Peter and the Wolf*, 121
Proletbühne, 34
Proletkult, 32
propaganda
  Burke, Kenneth, 70
  Dies Committee, 178–9, 184–9

propaganda (*continued*)
  FTP and, 197
  Injunction Granted, 59
  October Revolution, 15
  Power, 76–7
  The Revolt of the Beavers, 134–6
  Tairov, 18
  Triple-A Plowed Under, 50
  workers' theatre, 34, 36

Rabinovich, Isaac, 108, 109
race, 89–93, 147–82, 198; *see also* African Americans
Rammelkamp, Rhoda, 81
Rebel Players, London, 29–30
Reimann, Hans, 202n
Reinhardt, Max, 18–19, 169
Rennick, Jack, 124
The Revolt of the Beavers, 120–46, *128*, *129*, *132*, 186, 192, 198–9
Revolutionary Theatre, 15–16
Rice, Elmer
  The Adding Machine, 29
  Ethiopia, 42, 93
  Federal Dance Unit, 147
  Living Newspaper, 39–40
  Negro unit, 94
  resignation, 45–6, 204n
  theatre for the American people, 36
Ridenour, Louis, *Pilot Lights if the Apocalypse*, 190–1
Riegger, Wallingford, 169, 176, 177
Rippy, Marguerite, 103–4
Ritz Theatre, Manhattan, 136
Rockefeller Foundation, 189
Rohan, Pierre de, 207n
roller skates, 125–36, 192
Roosevelt, Franklin D.
  Democratic government, 85
  FTP and, 58
  gender and race, 118
  New Deal, 2–3
  One-third of a Nation, 77, 83
  Power, 76
  Triple-A Plowed Under, 50
  WPA, 147
Royal Theatre, Copenhagen, 14
Russia
  Flanagan in, 15–18, 20
  October Revolution, 15, 106–7, 121
  see also Soviet Union

Russia, 46, 204n
Russian theatre, 186

Salford 'Red Megaphones', 29
Salut au Monde, 149, 151–4, *153*
Samuel, Ralph, 28
Sats, Natalya, 121
Saul, Oscar, 125
Saunders, Sallie, 118, 210n
Sayler, Oliver, 108
scenery
  Bolton, Harold, 78–9
  The Cradle Will Rock, 64–5
  Craig, Gordon, 14
  $E=mc^2$, 194
  Flanagan, 19
  How Long, Brethren? 155
  Macbeth, 98
  Meyerhold, 16–17
  The Revolt of the Beavers, 144
Schlundt, Christena L., 150, 181
Schruers, Edwin, 64
Seattle, 104–19
Seattle Negro Repertory Unit, 91, 104–19
Seattle Repertory Company, 105
Seattle Repertory Playhouse, 105
Second Art Theatre, 15
Second Moscow Art Theatre (MAT2), 17–18
Seldes, George, 108
Seldes, Gilbert, 69, 108–10, 116
Seltzer, Mark, *Bodies and Machines*, 147
set design, 98
  African Americans, 89
  Bay, Howard, 176
  FTP and, 36
  Geddes, Bel, 109–10
  Injunction Granted, 56
  Rabinovich, 108
Shakespeare, William, 12, 93–104
Shock Troupe, 150
Shologa Oloba, 97
Silvera, John, *Liberty Deferred*, 103
Sinclair, Upton, *Singing Jailbirds*, 28–9
Sketch No. 1, 61
Slade, Peter, 121
Slonim, Marc, 21
Smith, Gus, 103
Smith College, 189
Smolin, Dmitry, 107–8
Smyser, William Lèon, 19

Socialism, 28–9, 76, 178, 179
Socialist Realism, 22
Sorel, Felicia, 149
South, 45–6, 204n
Soviet Living Newspaper, 188, 198
Soviet theatre, 106–9
Soviet Union
  African Americans, 92
  Living Newspaper, 40, 198
  Losey, 46, 59
  The Revolt of the Beavers, 134
  Rice, Elmer, 42
  see also Russia
Spanish Civil War, 31–2
Spencer, Arthur, 151
St James Theatre, New York, 178
Stage Manager (character), 191–4, 217n
staging
  Blue Blouse movement, 23
  Losey, 46–7, 56
  Macbeth, 93
  MacColl, 32–3
  One-third of a Nation, 79–80
  Triple-A Plowed Under, 47, 50
Stalinism, 76, 178, 184
Stanislavsky, Konstantin, 15–17, 20, 107, 200n
  method, 31, 33
  Tsar Fyodor Ivanovich, 17
Stanton, Olive, 65
Starnes, Senator Joe, 179, 186
Stevedore, 105, 116
Strindberg, August, 13–14
Suite in F, 149
Supreme Court, 47–50, 76
Sweden, Flanagan in, 13–14
The Swing Mikado, 90
Synge, J. M., 13

Tairov, Alexander Yakovlevich, 17–18, 107
Tamiris, Helen, 147–82, *153*, *155*, *172*, 178–82, 198
  'Tamiris in Her Own Voice: Draft of an Autobiography', 147
Teatro degli Indipendenti, 19
Teatro Goldoni, Venice, 19
The Tempest, 121
Theater Guild, 36
Theatre Action, Manchester, 29
Theatre Arts Monthly, 186
Theatre of Action, Manchester, 31

Theatre Union, 27, 28, 31–2, 36
Theatre Workshop, 33
Thomas, Edna, 96
Thomas, J. Parnell, 178–9, 185
Thompson, Virgil, 65, 66
Three Arts Club, 11
Till Eulenspiegel, 149
Tish, Pauline, 150–1, 152–4, 156, 162
Toller, Eric, *Masses and Man*, 28
Tretyakov, Sergei, *Roar, China!* 16–17
Triple-A Plowed Under, 46–60, *51*
  criticism of, 76, 204n
  Dies Committee, 186
  $E=mc^2$, 191
  'people', 72
  Power, 74
The Trojan Incident, 167–78, *171*, *172*
The Trojan Women, 168–9
Turpentine, 103
Tuttle, Day, 190
Tydings, Senator Millard, 87

'un-American' behaviour, 117–18, 124, 184–9
Unemployed, 34–5
unemployment, 1–3, 32, 38–9, 47–50, 54–5, 86, 154–7
Unity Theatre, 29–30
universities, 121–2
University of Washington, 209n
Uranium 235, 33, 198, 199, 216n, 216–17n

Vakhtangov, Yevgeny, 31
Vakhtangov Theatre, 46
Variety, 79, 176
Vassar College, 3, 5, 10, 11, 19, 167–8, 189
Vassar Experimental Theatre, 19, 77
Vega, Lope de, *Fuente Ovejuna (The Sheep-well)*, 32
Venice Theatre, 65
Vernon, Granville, 59
Voice of the Living Newspaper, 40, 47–9, 72–3, 74
Volkenburg, Ellen van, 168

Waddell, Bertha, 121
Wagner-Steagall Housing Bill, 87
Wainer, Lee, 81
Walk Together Chillum! 95
Wall Street Journal, 144

Walnut Street Theatre, Philadelphia, 209n
Walt Whitman Suite, 149
War and Taxes, 61
Ward, Theodore, *Big White Fog*, 90–1
Ward, Winifred, 121–2
　Creative Dramatics, 121–2
Watson, Morris, 39, 45, 46, 50, 58, 59–60
Watts, Richard, 83
Weidman, Charles, 149, 154, 182, 209n
Weill, Kurt, 61, 63
　'Music in the Theatre' lecture, 205n
Welles, Orson
　audience, 68
　The Cradle Will Rock, 61–2, 64–6
　Macbeth, 93–104, 111, 166
　New York Negro Theatre unit, 90
West Ham United Front, 29
Whitman, Walt, 151
Wigman, Mary, 18
Winfield, Hemsley, 214n
Witham, Barry, 117
　The Federal Theatre Project, 88
Workers' Laboratory Theatre, New York, 31, 34, 150
Workers' Theatre, 36
Workers Theatre Movement (WTM), 29
working-class
　Blue Blouse movement, 22
　Buttonkooper, Mr (character), 74
　Children's Theatre unit, 124–5, 136
　The Cradle Will Rock, 65
　How Long, Brethren? 166
　Injunction Granted, 59

　Living Newspaper, 69
　Lysistrata, 110
　'people', 70–1
　Theatre Workshop, 33
　Triple-A Plowed Under, 51–3
　workers' theatre, 20, 35, 37
　see also class struggle
Works Progress Administration (WPA), 2–5
　African Americans, 89, 117
　The Cradle Will Rock, 64–5
　Davis, Senator James J., 59
　Dies Committee, 185–6, 188
　Ethiopia, 45–6
　Federal Dance Unit, 147–8
　FTP and, 183
　Great Depression, 40
　House Un-American Activities Committee (HUAC), 178–9
　How Long, Brethren? 155
　Huffman, Hazel, 210n
　Injunction Granted, 58
　Living Newspaper, 60, 61, 69
　Lysistrata, 106
　Negro units, 119
　Power, 76–7
　unemployment, 196
World War I, 169
World War II, 6, 32–3

Yeats, W. B., 12–13
The Young Tramps, 149

Zalka, Máté, 15–16, 17
Zorn, George, 103

EU representative:
Easy Access System Europe
Mustamäe tee 50, 10621 Tallinn, Estonia
Gpsr.requests@easproject.com

www.ingramcontent.com/pod-product-compliance
Lightning Source LLC
Chambersburg PA
CBHW070340240426
43671CB00013BA/2378